Microsoft SharePoint 2010 Developer's Compendium: The Best of Packt for Extending SharePoint

Build an engaging SharePoint site with Visual Studio, Silverlight, PowerShell, and Windows Phone 7

Series Editor

Carl Jones

BIRMINGHAM - MUMBAI

Microsoft SharePoint 2010 Developer's Compendium: The Best of Packt for Extending SharePoint

First published: February 2012

Production Reference: 1150212

Published by Packt Publishing Ltd.
Livery Place
35 Livery Street
Birmingham B3 2PB, UK.

ISBN 978-1-84968-680-8

www.packtpub.com

Cover Image by Tina Negus (tina_manthorpe@sky.com)

Credits

Series Editor

Carl Jones

Contributors

Gastón C. Hillar

Balaji Kithiganahalli

Mike Oryszak

Yaroslav Pentsarskyy

Todd Spatafore

Technical Editor

Sonali Tharwani

Indexer

Hemangini Bari

Production Coordinator

Prachali Bhiwandkar

Cover Work

Prachali Bhiwandkar

About the Contributors

Gastón C. Hillar has been working with computers since he was eight. He began programming with the legendary Texas TI-99/4A and Commodore 64 home computers in the early 80s. He has a Bachelor's degree in Computer Science in which he graduated with honors and he also has an MBA (Master in Business Administration) in which he graduated with an outstanding thesis. He has worked as a Developer, an Architect, and Project Manager for many companies in Buenos Aires, Argentina. Now, he is an independent IT Consultant and a freelance author looking for new adventures around the world. He also works with electronics (he is an Electronics Technician). He is always researching about new technologies and writing about them. He owns an IT and electronics laboratory with many servers, monitors, and measuring instruments. He has written two additional books for Packt Publishing, *C# 2008 and 2005 Threaded Programming: Beginner's Guide* and *3D Game Development with Microsoft Silverlight 3: Beginner's Guide*. He contributes to Dr. Dobb's Go Parallel programming portal http://www.ddj.com/go-parallel/ and he is a guest blogger at Intel Software Network http://software.intel.com/. In 2009, he was awarded an Intel® Black Belt Software Developer award. He is the author of more than 40 books in Spanish about computer science, modern hardware, programming, systems development, software architecture, business applications, balanced scorecard applications, IT project management, the Internet, and electronics. He lives with his wife, Vanesa and his son, Kevin. When not tinkering with computers, he enjoys developing and playing with wireless virtual reality devices and electronics toys with his father, his son, and his nephew, Nico. You can reach him at gastonhillar@hotmail.com. You can follow him on Twitter at http://twitter.com/gastonhillar. Gastón's blog is at http://csharpmulticore.blogspot.com.

Balaji Kithiganahalli has been a computer nerd since 1995. He has a Master's degree in Systems Engineering and is currently serving as CEO and partner for Integrate, LLC. His company specializes in systems integration and custom software development. He has over 15 years of software development and architectural experience. He has consulted with several government and multi-national clients. He is a technology agnostic who used to mainly work on J2EE related technologies. Since 2003, he is mainly involved in implementing SharePoint and .NET technologies. He is currently architecting SharePoint 2010 implementation for a very large government organization in Atlanta, GA. When not working, he enjoys going for bike rides with his kids and reading books about other technologies. He currently lives in Atlanta, GA with his beautiful wife and two kids.

Mike Oryszak is a Consultant and Practice Manager with Intellinet, a Microsoft Gold-Certified Partner located in the South Eastern US. Mike works with customers to design and implement business solutions that leverage SharePoint as a platform. Mike is actively involved in the SharePoint community as a leader to Triangle SharePoint User Group in Raleigh, NC as well as a frequent speaker at SharePoint events and conferences. Mike has been recognized for his community involvement as a three time Microsoft Valuable Professional (MVP) for SharePoint Server. When not working, Mike can be found at home with his family or off hiking the many trails in the mountains of western North Carolina. Mike can be reached at nextconnect@ live.com or through his blog at http://www.mikeoryszak.com.

Yaroslav Pentsarskyy has been involved in SharePoint solution architecture and implementation since 2003. He is also a Microsoft MVP since 2009 and keeps a close touch with SharePoint product team. Yaroslav frequently presents technical events worldwide as well as online; you can always find a fresh bit of SharePoint information on his blog: http://www.sharemuch.com. To learn everything Yaroslav knows about SharePoint, check out his two new books *Top 60 Custom Solutions built on SharePoint 2010* and *SharePoint 2010 branding in practice*.

Todd Spatafore is a Professional Web Developer and Software Architect who enjoys living life on the sharp edge of technology. Todd is an expert in HTML, CSS, JavaScript, ASP. NET (WebForms and MVC), C#, and Silverlight. Todd is currently the Director of Technology at Draftfcb. Before starting at Draftfcb, Todd was a Senior Software Architect for MRM Worldwide. Todd was the Principal Software Architect for many of Microsoft's websites including Windows Server 2008, Microsoft Offce 2007 Real Life Tools, and SQL Server 2008. In addition to these defining pages, Todd worked closely with internal teams at Microsoft to introduce a new content management system for www.Microsoft.com, the fourth most visited website on the Internet. These content management systems were designed and built on top of SharePoint 2010. Prior to MRM, Todd was a Software Architect building websites such as the California Teachers Association, Novellus, and Technology Credit Union (TechCU). These sites utilized the Microsoft Content Management System, which has since been integrated into SharePoint. Beyond traditional websites and campaign landing sites, Todd has worked on unique applications such as a Windows Media Center application for ClickStar, a Santa Monica startup designed to showcase independent films from very well-known filmmakers. Todd maintains his own blog at http://www.spatacoli.com/, on which he muses about current programming topics such as Silverlight, JavaScript, HTML, CSS, and Hyper-V. Currently, Todd is working on a few independent Windows Phone 7 apps, and speaks at MSDN conferences on web application architecture, RIA development in Silverlight, Windows Phone 7, and SharePoint. Follow Todd on Twitter at http://twitter.com/Spatacoli. Todd graduated from Montana State University with a BS in Physics.

www.PacktPub.com

Support files, eBooks, discount offers and more

You might want to visit www.PacktPub.com for support files and downloads related to your book.

Did you know that Packt offers eBook versions of every book published, with PDF and ePub files available? You can upgrade to the eBook version at www.PacktPub.com and as a print book customer, you are entitled to a discount on the eBook copy. Get in touch with us at service@packtpub.com for more details.

At www.PacktPub.com, you can also read a collection of free technical articles, sign up for a range of free newsletters and receive exclusive discounts and offers on Packt books and eBooks.

http://PacktLib.PacktPub.com

Do you need instant solutions to your IT questions? PacktLib is Packt's online digital book library. Here, you can access, read and search across Packt's entire library of books.

Why Subscribe?

- ▶ Fully searchable across every book published by Packt
- ▶ Copy and paste, print and bookmark content
- ▶ On demand and accessible via web browser

Free Access for Packt account holders

If you have an account with Packt at www.PacktPub.com, you can use this to access PacktLib today and view nine entirely free books. Simply use your login credentials for immediate access.

Instant Updates on New Packt Books

Get notified! Find out when new books are published by following @PacktEnterprise on Twitter, or the *Packt Enterprise* Facebook page.

Table of Contents

Preface

A Packt Compendium is a book formed by drawing existing content from several related Packt titles. In other words, it is a mash-up of published Packt content – Professional Expertise Distilled in the true sense. Such a compendium of Packt's content allows you to learn from each of the chapters' unique styles and Packt does its best to compile the chapters without breaking the narrative flow for the reader.

Please note that the chapters in this compendium were originally written and intended as a part of various separate Packt titles, so you might find that the information included in this instance is more akin to that of a stand-alone chapter, rather than creating step-by-step, continuous flowing prose. We are sure that you will find this medley a useful resource with which you can benefit from the value and range of Packt books - and their authors' expertise!

Microsoft SharePoint 2010 Developer's Compendium: The Best of Packt for Extending SharePoint is a medley of five separate titles from Packt's existing collection of excellent SharePoint books:

- ▶ SharePoint 2010 Business Application Development Blueprints
- ▶ Microsoft SharePoint 2010 and Windows PowerShell 2.0: Expert Cookbook
- ▶ Microsoft Silverlight 4 and SharePoint 2010 Integration
- ▶ Microsoft SharePoint 2010 Development with Visual Studio 2010 Expert Cookbook
- ▶ Microsoft SharePoint 2010 Enterprise Applications on Windows Phone 7

What this book covers

Chapter 1, Understanding SharePoint Development Choices, provides some high level guidance over the different customization options that are available, tools that can be used to create different solutions, as well as some additional considerations when choosing a development path.

Chapter 2, Building an Engaging Community Site, takes the reader through the configuration and development of a community site that is meant to enhance collaboration and provide information sharing capabilities.

Chapter 3, PowerShell scripting methods and creating custom PowerShell commands, takes you further with PowerShell to create your own PowerShell commands (CMDLETs) and snap-ins and share them with your team.

Chapter 4, Integrating Silverlight 4 with SharePoint 2010, briefs you about the integration of Silverlight 4 applications with SharePoint 2010 sites and solutions. In this chapter, you will learn to prepare a development environment and look at the tools to work with Silverlight 4 RIAs. You will also configure the SharePoint 2010 server and add Silverlight Web Parts to a new page. Finally, you will create your first Silverlight RIA and then make it available in a SharePoint site.

Chapter 5, Interacting with Rich Media and Animations, will help you access asset libraries in a Silverlight RIA rendered in a SharePoint Visual Web Part. In this chapter, you will learn to take advantage of Silverlight 4 rich media features to add effects and interactive animations to images and videos.

Chapter 6, List Definitions and Content Types, will help you discover the world of content types. You will use object models to create content types, add new columns, document templates, and workflows to content types using Visual Studio 2010. This chapter also guides you through the process of creating external content types that are linked to an external data source such as the SQL Server database. At the end of the chapter, you will also learn how to create list definitions using Visual Studio.

Chapter 7, Workflows, will teach you about sequential workflows, site workflows and deploying custom initiation forms with workflows using ASPX pages and InfoPath forms. You will also learn to create custom InfoPath task forms with the workflows.

Chapter 8, Introduction to Programming Windows Phone 7 with the SharePoint Client Services, dives into building Windows Phone 7 applications that utilize SharePoint data. After a brief discussion of security in SharePoint, the chapter provides an example of building a simple RSS reader. The simple RSS reader gets data from an anonymous RSS feed from a SharePoint list, and discusses many of the basics of building a Windows Phone 7 application.

Chapter 9, Building SharePoint Pages for Windows Phone 7, begins with an examination of the difference between data stored as lists and libraries. Then it describes adding columns to a list and customizing the list item output. The chapter ends with an example of replacing the mobile home page.

Chapter 10, Building a Windows Phone 7 Dashboard Application with SharePoint Data, begins with a discussion of security in SharePoint and the example in this chapter utilizes forms based authentication in SharePoint. After a brief discussion of the tools available for building SharePoint applications on the desktop, the focus turns to building out the dashboard application for Windows Phone 7.

What you need for this book

As this Packt Compendium is a mash-up of published Packt content, the prerequisites may vary between each chapter. Everything you need for this book is detailed here respectively according to each original title.

Chapters taken from *SharePoint 2010 Business Application Development Blueprints* require only that you have SharePoint 2010 Server installed.

Chapters taken from *Microsoft SharePoint 2010 and Windows PowerShell 2.0: Expert Cookbook* require that you have a system with SharePoint 2010 Server Standard installed. You may also need to have installed and configured FAST Search. We recommend downloading and installing 2010 Information Worker Demonstration and Evaluation Virtual Machine (RTM) Virtual Machine environment if you do not have a compatible system set up. The most current link to download the virtual environment can be retrieved by searching for the 2010 Information Worker Demonstration and Evaluation Virtual Machine (RTM). By downloading the preceding environment, you will ensure all of the configurations and setups have been performed and your system is ready for using PowerShell with SharePoint.

Chapter taken from *Microsoft Silverlight 4 and SharePoint 2010 Integration* require that you have:

- ❑ Visual Studio 2010 Professional, Premium, or Ultimate
- ❑ SharePoint 2010 Server or SharePoint 2010 Foundation, installed on the same computer that runs Visual Studio 2010
- ❑ SharePoint Designer 2010

Chapters taken from *Microsoft SharePoint 2010 Enterprise Applications on Windows Phone 7* require that you have a Windows Phone 7 device, as well as:

- ❑ Windows 7 with Visual Studio 2010 and the Windows Phone 7 Development Tools
- ❑ Windows Server 2008 R2 with SharePoint 2010 Foundation, Visual Studio 2010, and the SharePoint 2010 SDK

It is worth noting that the Windows Phone 7 Emulator will not run on a machine running other virtualization software and as such, the Windows 7 machine can neither run on a virtual machine nor on other virtual machines while the emulator is running.

Chapters taken from *Microsoft SharePoint 2010 Development with Visual Studio 2010 Expert Cookbook* require that you have a 64-bit Windows development machine with lots of memory.

Who this book is for

This book is for developers who want to enhance their knowledge of SharePoint development to create sites with great user experience using a variety of tools.

Conventions

In this book, you will find a number of styles of text that distinguish between different kinds of information. Here are some examples of these styles, and an explanation of their meaning.

Code words in text are shown as follows: "We can include other contexts through the use of the include directive."

A block of code is set as follows:

```
$siteUrl = "http://intranet.contoso.com"
$snapin = Get-PSSnapin | Where-Object {$_.Name -eq 'Microsoft.
SharePoint.Powershell'}
if ($snapin -eq $null) {
Write-Host "Loading SharePoint Powershell Snapin"
Add-PSSnapin "Microsoft.SharePoint.Powershell"
}
```

When we wish to draw your attention to a particular part of a code block, the relevant lines or items are set in bold:

```
protected override void CreateChildControls()
{
  Control control = Page.LoadControl(_ascxPath);
  Controls.Add(control);
  _control = (control as AssetsBrowserWebPartUserControl);
  base.CreateChildControls();
}
```

Any command-line input or output is written as follows:

```
Add-PSSnapin "Microsoft.SharePoint.Powershell"
```

New terms and **important words** are shown in bold. Words that you see on the screen, in menus or dialog boxes for example, appear in the text like this: "Click **Site Actions** menu, and select the **New Page** item".

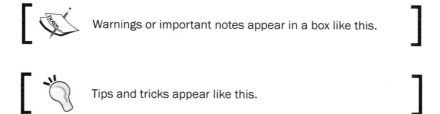

Warnings or important notes appear in a box like this.

Tips and tricks appear like this.

Reader feedback

Feedback from our readers is always welcome. Let us know what you think about this book—what you liked or may have disliked. Reader feedback is important for us to develop titles that you really get the most out of.

To send us general feedback, simply send an e-mail to feedback@packtpub.com, and mention the book title via the subject of your message.

If there is a book that you need and would like to see us publish, please send us a note in the **SUGGEST A TITLE** form on www.packtpub.com or e-mail suggest@packtpub.com.

If there is a topic that you have expertise in and you are interested in either writing or contributing to a book, see our author guide on www.packtpub.com/authors.

Customer support

Now that you are the proud owner of a Packt book, we have a number of things to help you to get the most from your purchase.

Downloading the example code

You can download the example code files for all Packt books you have purchased from your account at http://www.packtpub.com. If you purchased this book elsewhere, you can visit http://www.packtpub.com/support and register to have the files e-mailed directly to you.

This book is a compendium title which is extracted from five different best-selling books by Packt. The code bundles for these individual titles can be also downloaded from www.packtpub.com/support.

Errata

Although we have taken every care to ensure the accuracy of our content, mistakes do happen. If you find a mistake in one of our books—maybe a mistake in the text or the code—we would be grateful if you would report this to us. By doing so, you can save other readers from frustration and help us improve subsequent versions of this book. If you find any errata, please report them by visiting http://www.packtpub.com/support, selecting your book, clicking on the **errata submission form** link, and entering the details of your errata. Once your errata are verified, your submission will be accepted and the errata will be uploaded on our website, or added to any list of existing errata, under the Errata section of that title. Any existing errata can be viewed by selecting your title from http://www.packtpub.com/support.

Piracy

Piracy of copyright material on the Internet is an ongoing problem across all media. At Packt, we take the protection of our copyright and licenses very seriously. If you come across any illegal copies of our works, in any form, on the Internet, please provide us with the location address or website name immediately so that we can pursue a remedy.

Please contact us at copyright@packtpub.com with a link to the suspected pirated material.

We appreciate your help in protecting our authors, and our ability to bring you valuable content.

Questions

You can contact us at questions@packtpub.com if you are having a problem with any aspect of the book, and we will do our best to address it.

1
Understanding SharePoint Development Choices

This chapter is taken from *SharePoint 2010 Business Application Development Blueprints* (Preface) by Mike Oryszak. At the time of publication, this chapter is taken from an exciting new Packt title which is yet to be published.

SharePoint provides a robust platform that contains many services from which we can create business solutions. While many solutions can be configured using the included features, it is often necessary to develop customizations in order to meet all of the business requirements for a project. Customizations can come in many forms that range in complexity from simple visualizations in web part displays, custom forms, and timer jobs , all the way to a custom service application that extends the application to provide fully packaged solutions.

These customizations can be created using a number of different techniques so it is important to understand the strengths and limitations of each of the development paths. It is also important to understand the development tools that are available and what they can produce.

In the sections that follow you will find a brief overview of the different customization options that are available, tools that can be used to create them, as well as some additional considerations when choosing a development path.

Server-side development

The Server Object Model (Server OM) is an application programming interface that supports full interaction with all of the SharePoint configuration and data, and it is organized according to the conceptual system hierarchy which allows easy navigation for people familiar with SharePoint. All of the main objects are available with properties, methods, and sub-objects accessible. There is also a series of Context objects that make it easy to find or set your starting point such as the site the user is on, when the solution is called.

Frequently Used Objects and Collections include:

Object	Description
SPFarm	The object representation for the entire SharePoint system. Parent object to the SPServer and SPService collections.
SPSite	Represents a Site Collection
SPWeb	Represents a Web or Sub-site
SPList	Represents a List or Library
SPListItemCollection	Represents the items within a list or library
SPField	Represents a single field
SPListItem	Represents a single list item
SPContext	Represents current HTTPContext information including information on the current site and user.

All code has to be deployed to the server and references the SharePoint objects is loaded on the local server. Using the Server OM, you can build robust solutions and automate configuration changes. A few examples include custom Web Parts, Application Pages, Event Receivers, custom Timer Jobs, custom Workflows, custom Workflow Activities, custom web services, or even create a custom Service Application that can extend the services of the SharePoint platform.

With the 2010 version there are now two options for developing solutions; farm solutions and sandbox solutions.

Farm solutions

Creating farm solutions has been the traditional way to create solutions in SharePoint going back all the way to the earliest versions. The Server OM provides access to the system configuration and data allowing developers the ability to create solutions or automate configuration changes.

When deployed, the solution's objects are either loaded into the server's Global Assembly Cache (GAC) or into the 'bin' directory of the Web application(s). This allows farm solutions run in the same memory as SharePoint, which means the developer can have full access to the server, farm configuration, and content. These solutions do not have the overhead of the sandbox solution's process overhead and it also allows the developer to access additional caching features available inside of SharePoint to optimize the solution's performance. This does add risk though since poorly written or tested solutions can impact overall system performance or potentially crash the system.

Farm solutions can only be deployed by a Farm Administrator, and in many cases the Governance policy may also dictate a formal review or change management process to be followed before the Farm Administrator is allowed to deploy the solution.

Farm solutions are scoped for activation at a set level: **Farm**, **Web Application**, **Site Collection**, or **Web** allowing the developer to set it based on how and where the solution will be used. Take a look at the following figure for an illustration. A generally best practice is to scope a solution as narrowly as possible to provide more control on where it is activated. It is also important to note that solutions scoped for Site or Web can be activated by their respective owners based on site permissions.

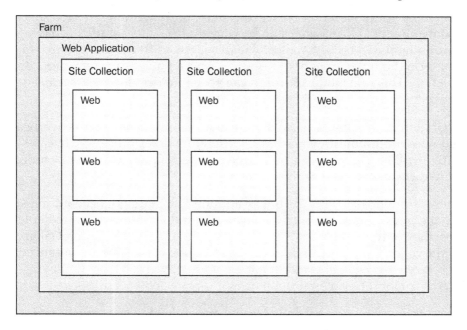

Good candidates for farm solutions include:

- Custom MasterPages, PageLayouts, and global CSS
- Complex Web Parts
- Complex Application Pages
- Complex Workflows
- Complex Event Receivers
- Global Navigation Providers
- Complex Cross-Site or Cross-Web Application Roll-ups

Sandboxed solutions

Sandboxed solutions were introduced with SharePoint 2010 and provide an interesting shift for custom solutions offering a path for user created and maintained server solutions. Unlike the farm solutions previously discussed, these are partially trusted solutions and there are some limitations. Where the farm solutions run in the same memory space as the main SharePoint services and application pools, Sandboxed solutions run in an isolated memory pool with resource quotas that can be managed by administrators. This means that poorly written or tested solutions cannot slow down or crash your main server processes. If a solution is having trouble running it will be automatically disabled. In addition, the resource throttling and quotas can limit the amount of resources each solution can consume within the site collection. This safe mode approach can speed up development cycle, but should not remove the need to properly test your solutions.

This separation does come at a cost though and there is some process overhead involved with communicating across the different worker processes. In cases where the solution will be actively used by a large number of people, it may be more difficult to meet any scalability requirements.

Unlike farm solutions, developers or site administrators do not need administrative access to the physical servers or to the farm's Central Administration to deploy their solutions; they only need access to upload the solution to the Solution Gallery for a specific site collection. This provides custom solution capabilities to organizations that have very strict change control policies or are prevented from deploying custom solutions as in cloud based environments.

Since the solutions are only partially trusted and uploaded to a specific site collection there are limitations. Sandboxed solutions cannot access resources outside of the farm, access a database directly, call unmanaged code, access resources in a different site collection, or write data to the local server.

For any solution that fits cleanly into a single site collection, and does not need to reach out to resources outside of that boundary, sandbox solutions offer additional flexibility. It is also important to note that a sandbox solution can also be deployed as a farm solution giving administrators the option of deploying it either way.

Good candidates for sandbox solutions include:

- Most web parts
- Event receivers
- Most Application Pages
- List Definitions

Connecting to SharePoint through web services

SharePoint also includes a comprehensive set of web services that can also be used to interact with system configuration and content. The available services cover both the base SharePoint functionality covered in the SharePoint Foundation version as well as the extended functionality available in SharePoint Server.

The services come in two formats; SOAP based services and new WCF based services that support REST.

Web Service	Version
Alerts	Foundation and Server
Authentication	Foundation and Server
Copy	Foundation and Server
Forms	Foundation and Server
Lists	Foundation and Server
Meetings	Foundation and Server
People	Foundation and Server
Permissions	Foundation and Server
SiteData	Foundation and Server
Users and Groups	Foundation and Server
Versions	Foundation and Server
Views	Foundation and Server
WebPartPages	Foundation and Server
Webs	Foundation and Server

Web Service	Version
PublishedLinksService	Server
Search	Server
UserProfileService	Server
Workflow	Server
SocialDataService	Server
TaxonomyClientService	Server

These services provide an effective integration option since they can be called from any network accessible computer written in any technology that can support the standard services. As an example, the integrations built into MS Office applications use these web services to integrate with SharePoint as well as the list extraction support built into SQL Server's Integration Services.

Good candidates for using SharePoint web services include:

- Consume data in InfoPath forms
- Integrating with SharePoint from non-SharePoint systems

Client-side development

Client-side development can be leveraged to provide rich, dynamic content and experiences. With Client-side development all of the code runs from the client which in most cases is the end user's web browser. The code is written in a scripting language like JavaScript, ECMAScript, or in the case of Silverlight, using XOML and references script libraries instead of server based objects.

There are two common options for interacting with SharePoint from client-side solutions; the Client Object Model and jQuery.

Client Object Model

The Client Object Model (Client OM) is an application programming interface that supports extensive, but not full interaction with the SharePoint configuration and data. It was added with the SharePoint 2010 release to provide an easy way to interact with SharePoint configuration and data without the need for code deployed to the server. It puts a simple wrapper around the previously discussed web services simplifying the interaction and removing the need to create and parse the XML needed to interact with the Web services. The client-side code can be called from Silverlight, ECMAScript, or via your .Net code.

The Client OM can be used to include the Ajax enabled features allowing content and data refreshes or loads without the need for a page post back which reloads or redirects the page.

The Client OM is limited in that it cannot connect or perform calls outside of the site context that it is called from. This means that it cannot be used for cross-site calls or aggregating content from multiple web applications or site collections.

There are also some functions available in the Server OM that are not supported in the Web services and therefore not supported in the Client OM due to security boundaries.

Frequently Used Objects and Collections include:

Object	Description
ClientContext	Represents current Context, and is used as the main entry point for interacting with the Client OM.
Site	Represents a Site Collection
Web	Represents a Web or Sub-site
WebCollection	Represents the collection of Webs within the Site Collection
List	Represents a List or Library
ListCollection	Represents the collection of lists within the Site Collection
ListItemCollection	Represents the items within a list or library
Field	Represents a single field
FieldCollection	Represents the collection of fields
ListItem	Represents a single list item

Good candidates for Client OM solutions include:

- Modular visualizations or content, similar to a web part
- Enhancing DataForm Web Parts
- Silverlight solutions
- Page level customizations and enhancements

Using jQuery

The jQuery library (`http://jquery.com/`) can be leveraged to support client-side development and Ajax enabled functions. This JavaScript based library is completely cross-browser compliant and offers a rich set of selectors and advanced support for animations that can be used to provide a much richer interface than static HTML. This library is completely platform independent, and there is nothing SharePoint specific about this library. Since there are a number of Ajax methods that make it easy to consume web services, you can use the library to interact with SharePoint through its web services.

In its base format, you would need advanced knowledge of all of SharePoint's web services. To help simplify the development effort the SPServices library (`http://spservices.codeplex.com/`) was created to provide a wrapper around SharePoint's web services. This library was created in the Sumer of 2009 originally for the SharePoint 2007 version, but it is also fully functional with SharePoint 2010. While it conceptually offers the same functionality as the Client OM, it could be used for solutions that need to be backward compatible with 2007 or in cases where there is a SPServices method not supported in the current Client OM.

Good candidates for jQuery Solutions include:

- Modular visualizations or content, similar to a web part
- Enhancing DataForm Web Parts
- Page level customizations

Deploying and managing client-side customizations

There are a number of ways to deploy and manage client-side code inside of SharePoint. You can add it directly to your SharePoint page using a tool like SharePoint Designer, or you can add it to a container such as the Content Editor Web Part that is included with each of the SharePoint versions. In cases where you use the Content Editor Web Part, you also have the option of linking to your content or script stored in any network accessible location.

It is important to consider how changes and versions will be managed. If you are adding code and functionality to pages, you should have versioning configured for the library the pages are in, as well as any libraries used to store your scripts. This will allow you to compare versions or to recover a prior version if things go wrong.

Many environments have very strict change management or deployment guidelines for any code that is deployed to the server by administrators. One of the big advantages to the client-side development approach is that system users with appropriate access can deploy their customizations themselves without the involvement of the administrators or change control group. This typically means that customizations can be created and deployed very quickly without all of the formality needed for the more advanced customizations. While there is some risk that a defective customization will cause an error or unexpected results, the impact is typically localized to the page the customization is used on or the content it interacts with.

SharePoint development tools

Microsoft has a number of tools that can be used to create business solutions including Visual Studio, SharePoint Designer, and InfoPath Designer.

Visual Studio

Visual Studio 2010 provides a robust environment for developing solutions for SharePoint 2010. Unlike previous versions, there is native support for most of the base project templates. It also natively supports the packaging and deployment process, producing the full feature and package objects and also supports automated deployment and retraction to/from the local SharePoint server to support development efforts.

Available Templates	
Visual Web Part	Business Data Connectivity Model
Web Part	Content Type
Application Page	List Definition From Content Type
Sequential Workflow	List Definition
State Machine Workflow	List Instance
Event Receiver	User Control
Module	

In addition to the default templates provided by Microsoft, there is an additional community driven project that can add additional or customized project templates under the Community Kit for SharePoint Development (CKS:Dev) project available on CodePlex (`http://cksdev.codeplex.com/`).

Available Templates	
Fluent UI Visual Web Part	Custom Action Group
Basic Site Page	Custom Action
Starter Master Page	Hide Custom Action
Branding	Delegate Control
Blank Site Definition	Basic Service Application
WCF Service	SharePoint PowerShell CommandLet
Full Trust Proxy Operation	SharePoint PowerShell Pipe Binding
SPMetal Definition	

In addition to any server-side development, Visual Studio can also provide a rich development experience for Client-side development of scripts and xsl, though it cannot be used to edit a SharePoint page directly or publish scripts to SharePoint outside of a SharePoint WSP package.

SharePoint Designer

SharePoint Designer 2010 is a free tool targeted to Site Administrators and Information Workers. It excels as a tool that can be used for site level administration and customization. Since it connects to and interacts directly with a specified site, customizations can be deployed directly by the user, without administrator assistance. This makes SharePoint Designer an incredibly important tool in either cloud environments or environments with a strict server change control policy.

Through SharePoint Designer, you can create or customize the following:

Customization	Description
DataForms	Add and configure the DataForm Web Part on a page. The control generates standard XSL for the user with multiple display options
Data Connections	Add and maintain Data Connections available on the site
External Content Types and External Lists	Define External Content Types and External Lists that can load Line of Business data for use on the site

Customization	Description
MasterPage, Page Layouts	Create or edit Master Pages and Page Layouts
Workflows	Create or edit workflows using the graphical interface

InfoPath Designer

InfoPath Designer 2010 is a tool that is included with the Office 2010 Professional Plus suite. It can be used to create electronic forms that can be submitted to a SharePoint library. The forms can configured to either open in the local InfoPath Filler client or with SharePoint Server Enterprise you have the option of deploying the forms as Web Enabled forms to Forms Services. InfoPath Designer can also be used to customize the default SharePoint list and library forms for New Item, Display Item, or Edit Item pages allowing much more robust forms far easier than creating custom Application Pages in Visual Studio.

The InfoPath Designer tool is targeted to Developers, Information Workers, and Power Users able to generate office forms and templates. It provides an easy to use graphical interface for defining form fields and easy to use property windows to configure business rules and back end data connections. It has the ability to easily connect to data sources including SharePoint lists, SQL databases, and web services including SharePoint's own web services.

When publishing the forms, you have the ability to publish it as a Content Type along with the ability to specify the form fields you would like to include as Site Columns or Library Columns. This allows you to map form fields and data to metadata available within the library. In many cases InfoPath forms are developed in conjunction with custom workflows to automate the form submission and processing previously handled by paper based processes.

For advanced cases, there is also support for including managed code inside of the InfoPath forms. While including this code complicates the overall development and deployment process, it does offer flexibility to organizations that do not have developers available to create custom Application Pages in Visual Studio. It is important to note that including managed code is not supported in Office 365 or on many cloud based environments.

Choosing a development path

In the previous sections we reviewed the capabilities along with some advantages and disadvantages of each of the development and customization paths. Choosing the right path for your solution requires that you consider your environment and the requirements of the solution.

Environment considerations

There are a number of environment variables to consider that have an immediate impact on your development options.

Cloud Environments

Since cloud based SharePoint environments do not support farm solutions, sandboxed solutions and client-side code represent the sole methods for creating customizations. Even if you are not in the cloud today, it would be a good idea to consider if that is a possibility in the next few years. If you have a simple solution that can be accommodated with either sandboxed solutions or client-side code, then it might be a good idea to *cloud proof* your customizations to reduce the hassle and rework later.

Governance, change management policies, and server access

In many organizations there is either governance or change management policies that can define capabilities or potentially rule out some of the development options. That should be given strong consideration before choosing a development path. In cases where there is a robust change management policy for anything deployed to the server, it can sometimes take weeks for changes to be deployed to the server after they have been developed and properly tested. Those constraints can make it very difficult to provide updates or respond to change, so in those cases it can be very important to choose a path where you can be responsive and deploy quickly.

It is also important to consider how your teams are organized and who has what access to the SharePoint system's Central Administration. In some organizations access is tightly controlled and given to a small set of administrators who do not create customizations. In other organizations the administrators are also the developers and have access to both create and deploy solutions as needed.

Solution reuse

When making a choice on the development path, it is also important to consider how or where the solution will be used. The approach may be completely different when developing a reusable solution expected to be deployed on sites throughout multiple farms, when compared to the approach for a simple solution intended to be used on only one site collection.

For the reusable solution it will be critical that updates be deployed centrally with a solution package update built within Visual Studio, but for a single use customization it may be acceptable to manually apply it where it is needed using either browser customizations, through SharePoint Designer, or with InfoPath Designer in the case of forms development.

Another example is when working on customizations to MasterPages and CSS. While this can effectively be applied to a single site collection using SharePoint Designer, it would be extremely difficult to try and maintain it manually across 1,000 site collections throughout the organization. Using Visual Studio to package and deploy the solutions will not only make the solution more maintainable, but it also gives the developer the option of including additional code that can automate additional tasks through the use of Feature Receivers and Event Receivers. Within the context of the existing example, this can include automatically setting the MasterPage when the feature is activated as well as when any new sites are provisioned.

Scalability of solutions

When you are architecting or designing business solutions it is important to consider the overall scalability requirements. Consider how many users will be using the system, and what the overall performance requirements are. Designing a feature to support ten concurrent users is much different than designing a feature for five hundred concurrent users. Also, in cases of content roll-up as the number of data sources or sites increase the performance of the feature will change substantially. In some cases even commercially available roll-up features fail completely when trying to aggregate content from more than one hundred sites.

Strongly typed server-side code, running in a capable environment, will always perform better than weakly typed client-side code. In addition to actual code execution, another downsides of client-side development is that since everything is running on the client, all of the content needs to be downloaded to the client. That means there is potentially extra content being transferred, but not displayed. In addition, client-side development does not have the ability to cache data the way server-side development does.

For simple solutions or in small environments, the scalability of the solution may not be a real concern and far less important than the value provided by the easy deployment options. For more complex or heavily used solutions, the scalability of server-side development should be given serious consideration.

Application lifecycle management

Application lifecycle management (ALM) is a software development process that supports the combined management of all application requirements, source, build, and testing processes. For organizations with a focus on ALM, there may be a requirement to include all formal projects and development in the ALM tool or environment such as Team Foundation Server (TFS). Development tools like Visual Studio provide full integration with standard ALM tools including TFS which means that solutions created in Visual Studio, using the Server OM will work transparently with ALM processes.

For client-side development or anything done in SharePoint Designer there is currently no support for ALM so things are not so easy. To support ALM with the other SharePoint development tools the developer will need to manually keep source files synchronized through a manual copy and paste process. This can make managing larger, more complex project using these tools and technologies a lot more tedious. In cases where you have a lot of code or a mixture of client and server code you can also consider deploying the client-side scripts to the server as part of a solution package, but in doing so you lose the flexibility and convenience of end user deployed customizations.

Summary

SharePoint developers have a rich set of development options and tools that can be leveraged to develop and deploy rich business solutions. These solutions have the potential to increase the overall value of SharePoint and to provide capabilities not available in many organizations.

For development options we covered server-side development with the Server OM for both farm and sandbox solutions, connecting to SharePoint through web services, and client-side development using either the Client OM or jQuery directly to provide a rich experience.

For tools we covered the robust features available in Visual Studio 2010, SharePoint Designer 2010, and InfoPath Designer 2010, and how the tools match up against the development options.

I encourage everyone to spend some time working through each of the development paths so that they can better understand for themselves the pros and cons of these options as well as how their personal skills can be best leveraged to build and maintain these solutions.

2
Building an Engaging Community Site

[
This chapter is taken from *SharePoint 2010 Business Application
Development Blueprints* (Chapter 4) by Mike Oryszak. At the time
of publication, this chapter is taken from an exciting new Packt
title which is yet to be published.
]

Organizations today are looking for ways to increase collaboration and to provide
more self-help resources through the use of tools like SharePoint. While it can be
fairly easy to build a department level collaboration site, it can be significantly harder
to build a cross-functional community site not tied to one specific department. This
chapter will attempt to highlight those challenges so that you can build a community
site that can keep people engaged and bring the collaboration levels that everyone is
looking for.

Community sites can be used to drive collaboration and self-help around a specific
topic or system. Examples could include business topics like Lean, Six Sigma, or
other Process Improvement methodologies, or for system support for various ERP,
HRIS, or IT systems. The management, education, and governance of SharePoint
itself make for a good community site focus, and will be the focus of this chapter.
Using this as a template though, there could be numerous community sites created
for an organization.

The community sites can provide a much better collaboration platform, and also
can provide user training and a help platform as well. When done properly, people
throughout the organization will be willing participants and can help provide that
support which better utilizes the company's resources and potentially provide more
relevant information. Community sites should be the future of collaboration and
perhaps for IT system support.

It is essential to start this process by defining what the goals for the site are, followed by defining the information architecture, content, and feature strategy.

Most community sites have varying levels of formality to the content. On the informal side it could be completely informal collaboration using tools like a note board, a threaded discussion list, perhaps a list of helpful links. Moving more towards the formal side you may also see Frequently Asked Question type lists or system and process documentation. As the community fills with content, it becomes more important to start highlighting popular or useful content.

The return on investment and value offered by community sites are tied directly to the level of user engagement and adoption. Therefore it is extremely important to consider this when designing the site, its features and content. One way to do that is to find community advocates or champions to help lead the cause and generate content. The great thing about this is that communities can grow significantly quicker with a bottom up, grassroots approach. Another thing to consider is to offer incentives to participate or even better, to build it into the job description and duties for various permissions Using the example of a IT System Support site, consider having a help desk person post content or answer discussion questions instead of just answering the phone. Chances are they can assist many more people in a given day, and those answers could continue to benefit the organization for months or years to come. I have come across organizations that will hold contents or offer incentives like premium parking spots, extra days off, or various items of swag as incentives for participation.

This chapter will provide an overview of configuration steps needed to create a base community site template along with example customizations that can be created to provide dynamic and relevant content which is a key ingredient to building an engaging community site solution. The covered solutions include:

- Enterprise Wikis
- Content Rollups
- Community Leaders Group
- Social Web Parts

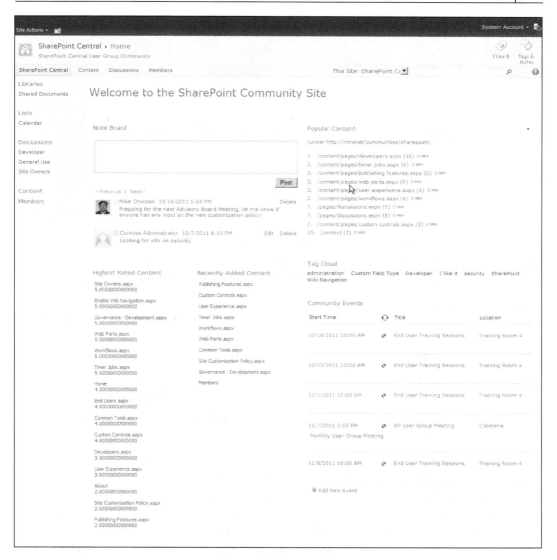

Creating the community site

To get started we will need to provision a new site collection using the Team Site Template, activate the supporting features, and create a landing page to support our community.

In this case I have selected a Team Site Template because it is a good generic building block for sites like this, and it can also be used to create Web Templates that can be used to provision additional sites.

Activating supporting features

After choosing a site template and provisioning the site collection, the next step is to activate the initial features needed to support the Intranet site. The robust feature deployment and activation system supported in SharePoint makes it very easy to fine-tune the functionality available within a site. In many cases these features may already be activated by default depending on your settings for the Web application and overall farm.

Following is a list of the features that should be activated on the site being configured:

Site collection features

- **Document ID Service**: Assigns IDs to documents in the site collection, which can be used to retrieve items independent of their current location

- **Search Server Web Parts**: This feature uploads all web parts required for Search Center

- **SharePoint Server Standard Site Collection features**: Features such as user profiles and search, included in the SharePoint Server Standard License

- **SharePoint Server Enterprise Site Collection features**: Features such as InfoPath Forms Services, Visio Services, Access Services, and Excel Services Application, included in the SharePoint Server Enterprise License

- **SharePoint Server Publishing Infrastructure**: Provides centralized libraries, content types, master pages, and page layouts, and enables page scheduling and other publishing functionality for a site collection

Site features

- **SharePoint Server Standard Site Collection features**: Features such as user profiles and search, included in the SharePoint Server Standard License

- **SharePoint Server Enterprise Site Collection features**: Features such as InfoPath Forms Services, Visio Services, Access Services, and Excel Services Application, included in the SharePoint Server Enterprise License

- **SharePoint Server Publishing**: Create a Web page library as well as supporting libraries to create and publish pages based on page layouts

For anyone who is not familiar with the publishing features, it is important to understand that the Document Libraries are setup for publishing, including the resources provisioned when the feature is activated such as the Style Library, will require that all changes be fully published for non-administrators to be able to view the most recent changes. If changes are made to pages, scripts, images, or CSS stylesheets included in any of these libraries and are not fully published you will see unexpected behaviors such as 404 errors, out of date content, or miscellaneous unexpected SharePoint page level errors.

Create and configure the Community Landing Page

With the Publishing features enabled at both the Site Collection and Web level, we can now create and configure our landing page.

From anywhere on the community site, perform the following steps:

1. Click **Site Actions** menu, and select the **New Page** item.
2. Provide a title for the page.
3. Click the **Create** button.

When the page is created it will open in edit mode and be ready for configuration. The next task is to set the appropriate Page Layout. In the **Page** tab of the ribbon is an action for the **Page Layout**. Within the selecting panel, a list of options will be displayed by category with an included thumbnail.

The **Welcome Page** category includes some great landing pages, and for this one we will select the **Blank Web Part Page** option as seen in the following screenshot:

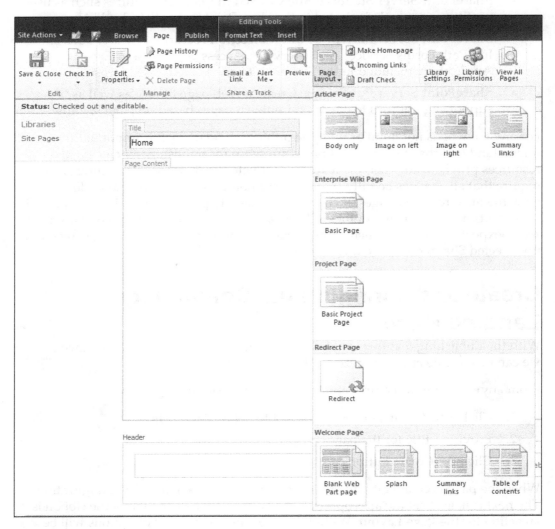

Next we will want to set the new page as the site's home page. In the **Page** tab of the ribbon is the **Make Homepage** action, as seen in the following screenshot. Click this action to set the new page as the site's home page.

Site permissions

Permissions management is one of the things that is typically different when working with community sites. Where a traditional department site is tied to a specific department and likely has an Active Directory security group, the community site is meant to be cross-functional including people from throughout the organization. Making that collaboration easy, especially for new members, often means taking a completely different approach.

The approach that I typically take is to identify the top most Active Directory groups that apply and then grant them Contributor permission level. That could be something like `<my domain>\domain` users which is a standard security group that will include all domain users. Letting everyone contribute by default will make the site easier to maintain and also better support collaboration and innovation.

Community members

One way to profile community advocates and members from throughout the organization is to find a way to profile them. A great way to do this is to define a user profile property that can track the communities that the person is associated with. This one field can be used to support all of the communities throughout the organization so it should only be created once. The great thing about this property is that it can be used to help find people within the user profiles, but also it can be used to display the members within the community site itself. In this section, we will define the custom user profile property and then create a custom page that lists people associated with the community.

Create Communities User Profile Property

To create a new Property, simply click the **New Property** menu item. Creating a new property requires a little more thought and planning since there are a number of different options and behaviors available. Following are the settings for each of the three fields.

From the **Manage User Properties** screen, click the **New Property** menu item as shown in the following screenshot:

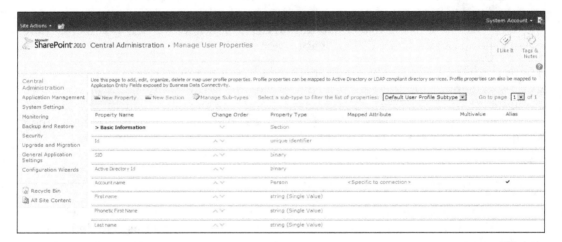

Communities Property Attributes

The Communities user profile property will be used to link a user to a specific community group. On the **New Property** screen, set the attributes as shown in the following table:

Property	Value
Name	Communities
Display Name	Communities
Type	String (Multi Value)
Length	250

Property	Value
Multivalue Separator	Semicolon
Default User Profile Subtype	Yes
Description	Community Site Membership
Policy Setting	Optional
Default Privacy Setting	Everyone
Edit Settings	Allow users to edit values for this property
Show in the profile properties section	Yes
Show on the Edit Details page	Yes

Map Communities as a Managed Property

To make it easier to retrieve people in specified groups we will identify the Communities property as a Managed Property. A managed property will set a formal mapping between a keyword and one or more metadata property fields.

To create the mapping perform the following steps:

1. Navigate to the Search Service Application.
2. Click the **Metadata Properties** link under the **Queries and Results** heading.
3. Provide a Property name value such as Communities and a description.
4. Under the Mappings to crawled properties section, click the **Add Mapping** button and search for the Communities field identified in the content type.
5. Select the People:Communities(Text) and click the **OK** button.

Configure the Member page

The Member page will display a listing of all of the group members using SharePoint's People Search and the People Core Results Web Part to execute a set query that looks at the Communities field previously defined.

Create the Member page

To create the Member page perform the following steps:

1. Click **Site Actions** menu, and select the **New Page** item.
2. Provide a title for the page.
3. Click the **Create** button.

Add the People Search Core Results Web Part

To add the People Search Core Results Web Part to the page perform the following steps:

1. Click the **Insert** tab of the Ribbon.

2. Select the **Web Part** action.

3. Select the **Search** category.

4. Select the **People Search Core Results** Web Part.

Configure members search query

To configure the pre-set members search query:

1. Edit the People Core Results web part properties.

2. Under the **Display Properties** group, change the **Default Results Sorting** to **Name**.

3. Set the **Results Per Page** value to 20.

4. If custom properties need to be displayed, they need to be added to the **Fetched Properties** field.

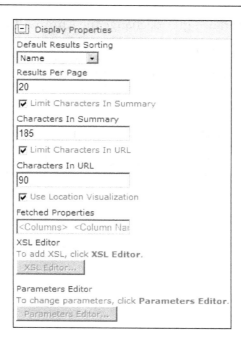

5. Under the **Results Query Options** group, change the **Cross-Web Part query ID**.

6. Change the **Fixed Keyword Query** to Communities:"SharePoint".

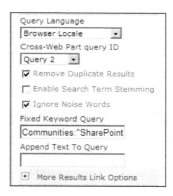

7. Under the **Appearance** group, change the **Chrome Type** field to **None**.

8. Click the **OK** button.

The Fixed Keyword Query value added in step 6 will perform a managed property search for the Communities field and look for matches with the value "SharePoint" which is the name of this community.

The final rendered view is displayed in the following screenshot:

Configuring social Web Parts

The social features included with SharePoint Server 2010 are intended to support collaboration and increase user engagement. Both the Note Board and Tag Cloud web parts are included to help support those social interactions.

Note Board

The Note Board allows users to pose a simple note such as a question they need help with, or some other note that may benefit the community. Any notes saved will be tied to the URL of the page it is on so it is important to understand that unlike a discussion board, there should be some thought put into which pages the note board is prominently placed.

To add a note board to the front page of the site perform the following steps:

1. Browse to the home page of the community site.
2. Click the **Site** Actions menu and select the **Edit Page** option.
3. Select the **Insert** ribbon tab.
4. Select the **Social Collaboration** category.
5. Select the **Note Board** web part as displayed in the following screenshot:

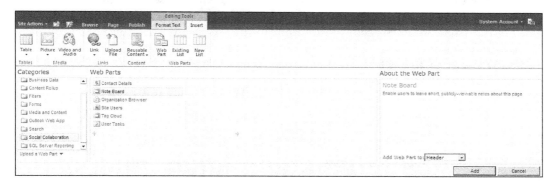

6. For the **Add Web Part** to option, select **Header**.
7. Click the **Add** button.

The following screenshot is an example of the Note Board:

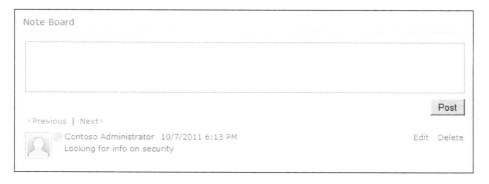

Tagging and Tag Clouds

The Tagging and Tag Cloud feature introduced with SharePoint Server 2010 is powered by the Managed Metadata Services and allows users to apply tags to any content including pages, documents, or list items. User can tag the item using any term they chose, but they are also given tag recommendations based on what other people tagged the document with. This informal metadata process provides a lot of flexibility better supporting informal or dynamic content, but it also provides a much more personalized experience which users tend to appreciate.

All tags that a user sets will be available to them in their profile page and MySites, and users also have the ability to subscribe to tags so that they receive updates when that tag is used. This is great for cases where maybe they are a Subject Matter Expert (SME) on a topic or perhaps a Product Manager responsible for a given product.

The Tag Cloud web part that ships with SharePoint Server 2010 offers three views to filter the available tags; By current user, By all users, and Under the current URL by all users. The appropriate selection will depend on the context of how you want to use the information. In the case of our community site, we want to make it easy for people to find information so we want people to be able to leverage the tags of other users on this particular site.

To add the Tag Cloud web part to the community site perform the following steps:

1. Browse to the home page of the community site.
2. Click the **Site Actions** menu and select the **Edit Page** option.
3. Select the **Insert** ribbon tab.
4. Select the **Social Collaboration** category.
6. Select the **Tag Cloud** web part as displayed in the following screenshot:

7. For the **Add Web Part to** option, select **Right**.

8. Click the **Add** button.

By default the Web part will display the current user's tags. To change that simply edit the Web part settings and change the **Show Tags** option to **Under the current URL for all users** as displayed in the following screenshot:

Configuring Rollup Web Parts

It is important that we continue to try and find effective ways to surface content so that it is as easy as possible for users to find and use the content. To do that we are going to leverage two additional web parts available in SharePoint server that can assist here. The Web Analytics Web Part and the Content Query Web Part.

Web Analytics Web Part – frequently accessed content

The Web Analytics Web Part leverages the Usage and Web Analytics system to provide content reporting to your authors and end users. In the past it has been difficult to provide an accurate list of frequently accessed content, but this web part provides the much needed information.

It is important to understand that this is pre-processed information that is generated based on the schedule configured for the Web Analytics reporting. This allows it to execute very fast, but the content may be up to 24 hours up to date so new content may not be displayed.

To configure the Web Analytics Web Part perform the following steps:

1. Browse to the home page of the community site.
2. Click the **Site Actions** menu and select the **Edit Page** option.
3. Select the **Insert** ribbon tab.
4. Select the **Content Rollup** category.
5. Select the **Web Analytics Web Part** as displayed in the following screenshot:

6. For the **Add Web Part to** option, select **Top Right**.
7. Click the **Add** button.
8. Edit the Web Part settings.
9. Change the Information to **Display** option to **Most Viewed Content**.
10. Ensure that the **Site Scope** option is set to **This Site and Subsites**.
11. Ensure that the **Period** option is set to **Proceeding 30 Days**.
12. Select the **Show Frequency** option.
13. Select the **Show Popularity Rank** option.
14. Select the **Show Popularity Rank Trend** option.
15. Under the Appearance section, change the Title field to **Popular Content**.

An example of the configured web part is shown in the following screenshot:

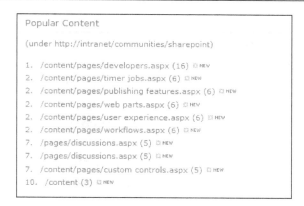

Content Query Web Part – new content

The Content Query Web Part allows you to do simple content rollups within a site collection. We are going to configure one that can be used to highlight new pages that are added to the site.

To configure the Content Query Web Part perform the following steps:

1. Browse to the home page of the community site.
2. Click the **Site Actions** menu and select the Edit Page option.
3. Select the **Insert** ribbon tab.
4. Select the **Content Rollup** category.
5. Select the **Content Query** as displayed in the following screenshot:

6. For the **Add Web Part** to option, select **Right**.

7. Click the **Add** button.

8. Edit the Web Part settings.

9. Under the **Query** section, List Type grouping, set the **Show items from this list type** field to the *Pages Library* option.

10. Under the **Presentation** section, Grouping and Sorting grouping, set the **Sort items by** field to the *Created* option.

11. Ensure that the **Show items in descending order** option is selected.

12. Under the **Styles** grouping, set the **Item Style** field to **Title, description, and document icon**.

13. Under the **Appearance** section, set the **Title** field to **Recently Added Content**.

14. Click the **OK** button.

An example of the configured web part is displayed in the following screenshot:

Content Query Web Part – highly rated content

Next we will add and configure another Content Query Web Part that will highlight the highest rated pages that are added to the site.

To configure the Content Query Web Part perform the following steps:

1. Browse to the home page of the community site.

2. Click the **Site Actions** menu and select the **Edit Page** option.

3. Select the **Insert** ribbon tab.

4. Select the **Content Rollup** category.

5. Select the **Content Query** as displayed in the following screenshot:

6. For the **Add Web Part to** option, select **Top Left**.

7. Click the **Add** button.

8. Edit the Web Part settings.

9. Under the **Query** section, List Type grouping, set the **Show items from this list type** field to the **Pages Library** option.

10. Under the **Presentation** section, Grouping and Sorting grouping, set t he **Sort items by** field to the **Rating (0-5)** option.

11. Ensure that the **Show items in descending order** option is selected.

12. Under the **Styles** grouping, set the **Item Style** field to **Title, description, and document icon**.

13. Under the **Fields to Display** grouping, **Description** field, add **Rating (0-5);** to the field listing to show the current Rating for the content.

14. Under the **Appearance** section, set the **Title** field to **Recently Added Content**.

15. Click the **OK** button.

An example of the configured web part is displayed in the following screenshot:

Creating an Enterprise Wiki

Using Wikis is a great way to collaborate on content within SharePoint. While most people still think in terms of documents, there are a number of advantages to using Wikis over individual documents. These advantages include the ability to link from one document to another easily, the ability to provide better change markup without the need to use Track Changes, and the ability to integrate other web parts or SharePoint content within the Wiki content.

The Enterprise Wikis introduced with SharePoint Server 2010 provides some much needed advances over the standard Wiki features. While the page editing and markup are the exact same, there are Page Layout changes that provided much better support especially for larger sets of content. The features include Page Ratings, Wiki Categories making it easier to tag and relate pages, and also Metadata Navigation.

This section will detail the recommended steps for configuring the Enterprise Wiki on our community site, explain the use of categories, activate the Metadata Navigation feature, and then configure a navigation scheme that will make it easier to find the content.

Configure Enterprise Wiki sub-site

When configuring a Wiki, it is important to consider where to place that content. It is possible to simply create a Wiki library on a given site, but when considering site topology in most cases it is more beneficial to create the Wiki as a sub-site in order to segment and manage the content separately if needed, but also in order to optimize content rollups and search.

To create an Enterprise Wiki as a sub-site perform the following steps:

1. From the community site, click the **Site Actions** menu.

2. Select the **New Site** option.

3. Select the **Enterprise Wiki** option.

4. In the right margin, click the **More Options** button.

5. Provide a **Title**.

6. Provide a **Description**.

7. Provide a **URL**.

8. Ensure the **Use the same permissions as parent site** option is selected which will ensure that users have the same permissions on the sub-site.

9. Under **Navigation Inheritance**, select the **Yes** option which will ensure that the navigation is consistent between the two sites.

10. Click the **Create** button to create the site.

An example of the Create Enterprise Wiki form is shown in the following screenshot:

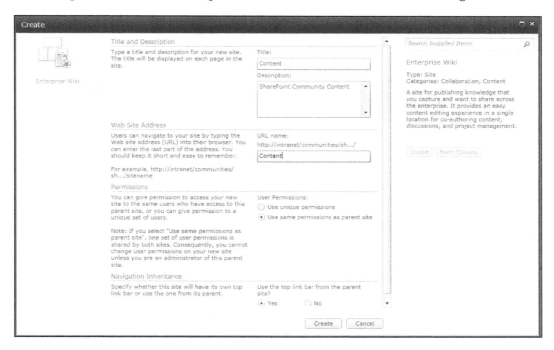

Use of categories

The categories make it easy to organize and locate your content. Where most site fields are editable only within the library, the Enterprise Wiki has the category field available directly on the Wiki page. When editing a page the taxonomy field is enabled and new categories can be added or selected. An example is shown in the following screenshot:

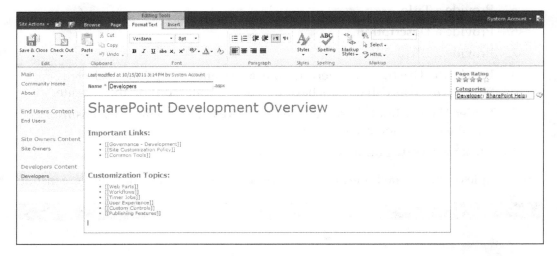

When browsing the pages, any identified categories will be displayed. Clicking one of the category values will lead to a special Category filtering page that will display all wiki pages in the library that match that category value.

It is important to keep in mind that the identified Categories are stored and interpreted differently than the tags that power the Tag Cloud web part previously configured. If you want pages to show up in the tag cloud, they also have to be tagged using the tagging feature.

Metadata Navigation

As the number of pages and the amount of content grows, finding that content in a large Wiki can get very challenging. One of the great features added with SharePoint Server 2010 is the Metadata Navigation feature. This feature can be used to browse items based on their tagged metadata. This feature however is not enabled by default so unless it is included as part of an automated site provisioning process, it will need to be enabled manually.

Activating the feature

To activate the Metadata Navigation feature perform the following steps:

1. From the Enterprise Wiki site, click **Site Actions**.

2. Select the **Site Settings** option.

3. Under the **Site Actions** group, click the **Manage Site Features** link.

4. Browse to the **Metadata Navigation and Filtering** feature and click the **Activate** button as shown in the following figure.

Configuring Metadata Navigation for Enterprise Wiki library

With the feature now activated on the site, we can configure its use within the Enterprise Wiki library.

To configure Metadata Navigation on the library perform the following steps:

1. From one of the Wiki pages, select the **Page** ribbon tab and select the **View All Pages** action as shown in the following screenshot:

2. Select the **Library Settings** action as shown in the following screenshot:

3. Under the **General Settings** category, click the **Metadata navigation settings** link as shown in the following figure:

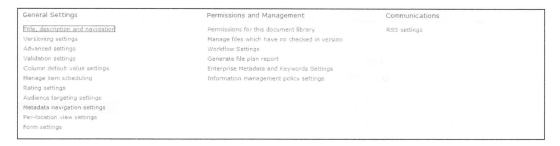

4. Select the **Folders** and **Wiki Categories** nodes.
5. Click the **Add** Button.
6. To **Configure Key Filters**, select the desired fields and click the **Add** button.
7. Click the **OK** button when finished to save your changes.

The Manage Navigation Settings screen is displayed in the following figure:

Using the feature

With Metadata Navigation now configured, whenever you are on a view page within the library you will see a Category navigation control added to the left side below the standard Quick Launch navigation. Selecting a tag will filter down the related Wiki Pages associated with that tag providing a quick and effective way of finding content. As you will see in the Site Navigation section that follows, it is possible to add navigation nodes to the top most common or important categories.

You will also notice that the **Key Filters** control is also displayed on the left hand side allowing for advanced filtering of any fields that were configured. This is especially helpful when looking for content by a specific author, or perhaps based on dates.

An example of the Metadata Navigation is displayed in the following screenshot:

Site Navigation

The Metadata Navigation features can provide a great way to find content within the libraries, but it is also important to consider the navigation employed when browsing the wiki pages as well.

The normal navigation settings page available by navigating through Site Actions, Navigation supports having Wiki pages added to the navigation automatically which may work fine with small Wikis, but does not work well if you have dozens or hundreds of Wiki pages. Generally I uncheck the Show Pages option for the Current Navigation section. This means that any navigation would have to be configured manually. This does take some on-going maintenance but will result in a much more usable system.

The general navigation should be determined by how the content is organized. Since the purpose of this Wiki is for content relating to SharePoint, a set of categories have been identified; Main, End User, Site Owner, Developer. For each of these categories, a Section Heading will be created that links to the main view of the library. This will allow users to click into the library to filter down available pages based on the category or topic. In this example, the heading for Main shows the full library, while the others start by selecting the identified tag.

Main section pages can be linked to directly as well as any other important pages. As new pages are added, the most important ones should be added to the navigation settings, but not too many as it will eventually get very cluttered.

An example of the Navigation Settings is available in the following screenshot:

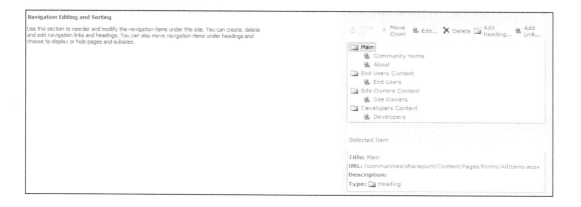

Summary

This section heavily leverages the out of the box web parts and features to assemble a rich and interactive community site.

The customizations are grouped as follows:

Browser based configuration

- Provision a Site Collection
- Configure Content Query Web Part (CQWP)
- Configure Web Analytics Web Part
- Configure People Core Results Web Part
- Configure Enterprise Wikis
- Configure Advanced Navigation
- Configure Note Board Web Part
- Configure Tag Cloud Web Part

There are a number of additional types of content that may be beneficial to a community that were not covered in detail within this chapter. Items configured but not covered include threaded discussions, community events, and community links. The key is to find content that is relevant and make it as easy as possible for participants to contribute.

An effective community site can greatly enhance collaboration, innovation, and provide a foundation for user self-service. Providing an engaging site requires a mix of good content, features, and the ability to personalize it to the communities needs.

3

PowerShell Scripting Methods and Creating Custom Commands

This chapter is taken from *Microsoft SharePoint 2010 and Windows PowerShell 2.0: Expert Cookbook* (Chapter 1) by Yaroslav Pentsarskyy.

In this chapter, we will cover:

- ▸ Setting up your Virtual Machine and running a test script
- ▸ Authoring, debugging, and executing script accessing farm settings with PowerGUI and PowerShell ISE
- ▸ Accessing advanced SharePoint 2010 functionality with external libraries
- ▸ Creating a custom PowerShell command (CmdLet)
- ▸ Creating a custom PowerShell Snap-In

Introduction

PowerShell as a scripting language will execute actions on your target environment. Scripting is not a new concept and PowerShell is definitely not a new language. However, PowerShell and SharePoint 2010 integrate very well. This integration allows administrators and developers to access not just a limited set of commands, but also to connect to SharePoint objects and libraries to take advantage of additional capabilities of SharePoint as a platform.

To ensure that we are on the same page while reading this book and trying out various recipes, we'll start by setting up your environment and verifying the setup by running a test script. After all, SharePoint relies on components, most of which we're going to be directly interacting with, and having a consistently configured environment will help in reducing any potential integration issues.

Although we can author our PowerShell scripts in Notepad and execute them in a PowerShell command-line environment, you can experience more advantages from authoring and debugging your scripts by using rich authoring environments, such as PowerGUI or PowerShell ISE. In this chapter, we'll see exactly what the benefits of using those environments are.

Whether you are creating a PowerShell script in a professional scripting environment or calling an existing script from a command line, you'll quickly notice that a default set of commands is definitely not enough to manage and work with your SharePoint system. When you have the need to author scripts accessing various other aspects of SharePoint functionality, you will need to use the additional libraries available to facilitate custom or out-of-the-box functionality required. This is a very common scenario for developers when building custom solutions for a variety of platforms. PowerShell, as a scripting language, really takes advantage of this concept allowing you to call functions from SharePoint and third-party libraries. In this chapter, we'll take a look at exactly how you can access advanced SharePoint 2010 functionality using external libraries.

As you become more familiar with authoring PowerShell scripts, you will realize that you can create a collection of reusable functionality which can be shared with others. That's when you can take advantage of sealing your custom functionality in a portable and sharable way. We'll take a look at how you can package your custom scripts as custom PowerShell CmdLets, as well as how to create a custom PowerShell Snap-In.

Setting up your Virtual Machine and running a test script

In this recipe, we'll ensure your development environment is configured properly.

Getting ready

To complete the recipes in this book, it's assumed you're running a system with SharePoint 2010 Server Standard installed. If not, it is recommended you download and install the 2010 Information Worker Demonstration and Evaluation Virtual Machine (RTM) Virtual Machine environment, if you do not have a compatible system set up. For the most current link to download this virtual environment, search Microsoft Download Center with the keyword **2010 IW demo RTM**.

By downloading the preceding environment, you will ensure all of the configurations and setups have been performed and your system is ready for using PowerShell with SharePoint. Whether you're using your own or a downloaded Virtual Machine, let's ensure PowerShell is enabled in your environment.

How to do it...

Let's see how you can get your virtual environment configured and run your first script using the following steps:

1. On the target Virtual Machine, ensure you are logged in with an administrator's role.

2. Click **Start | All Programs | Microsoft SharePoint 2010 Products | SharePoint 2010 Management Shell**.

3. Input `Get-ExecutionPolicy` and press *Enter* on your keyboard. PowerShell may return a value of `Restricted`.

4. Input `Set-ExecutionPolicy Unrestricted` and hit *Enter*.

 Ensure this policy is reverted back on your production environments to avoid the risk of malicious script execution.

5. Input the following command in the window:

```
Get-SPSite | Where-Object {$_.Url -eq "http://intranet.contoso.com"}
```

6. You should see a result that looks similar to the following screenshot:

```
Administrator: SharePoint 2010 Management Shell                          _ □ X
PS C:\Users\Administrator> Get-SPSite | Where-Object {$_.Url -eq "http://intrane
t.contoso.com">

Url

http://intranet.contoso.com
WARNING: More results were found in Get-SPSite but were not returned.  Use
'-Limit ALL' to return all possible results.


PS C:\Users\Administrator> _
```

How it works...

On Windows 2008 Server, PowerShell script execution policy is set to restrict script execution by default. As an administrator, you can choose to allow script execution by calling the `Set-ExecutionPolicy Unrestricted` command.

 For more information on options available for script execution policy and how it affects your environment, search TechNet with the keyword **Set-ExecutionPolicy**.

Once script execution is not restricted, we run a PowerShell command enumerating all of the SharePoint sites with the `http://intranet.contoso.com` URL. This assumes you have an existing site collection with such a URL. If you're using the downloadable environment from above, the site collection will be already set up for you. If you're running a site collection with a different URL, feel free to replace the value in this example.

There's more...

In this example, we assumed you were running a Virtual Machine downloaded from the Microsoft download site with all of the pre-set options. In this case, you may see that the execution policy has already been set to `unrestricted`. In this case, you don't need to set the value again.

Authoring, debugging, and executing script accessing farm settings with PowerGUI and PowerShell ISE

As you can see from the previous recipe, authoring and executing a PowerShell script is a simple task that can be done right from the command line. In this recipe, we'll take a look at how you can author and debug your PowerShell scripts using two of the most popular tools: **PowerShell ISE** and **PowerGUI**. Using these tools, we'll execute a script accessing farm settings of the SharePoint site.

Getting ready

First, let's ensure you have installed PowerShell ISE:

1. On the target Virtual Machine, click **Start | Administrative Tools | Server Manager**.
2. On the left-hand side panel of the **Server Manager** window, click the **Features** node.
3. In the main window of the Server Manager, click **Add Features**.

4. From the **Add Features** Wizard, ensure **Windows PowerShell Integrated Scripting Environment (ISE)** is selected. If it is selected and grayed out, as seen in the following screenshot, skip to Step 6 in this sequence.

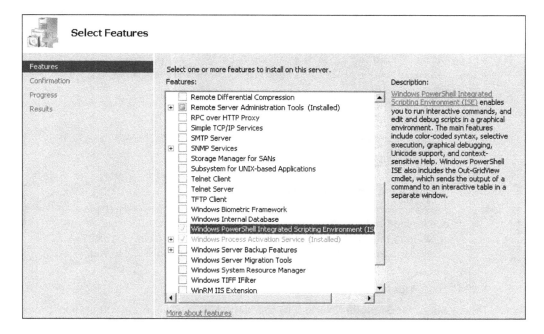

5. Click **Next** and **Install** on the following window to install the feature.

6. Upon installation completion, close the **Server Manager** window.

Let's now install PowerGUI:

1. Navigate to `http://www.powergui.org` or search the Internet with **PowerGUI**.

2. Download the latest version of PowerGUI installer.

3. Run the installation package on your development environment and install the PowerGUI tool using the default installation options.

Now that you have all of the tools installed, let's use PowerShell ISE and PowerGUI to author, debug, and execute our new script.

How to do it...

Let's see how PowerShell ISE and PowerGUI can help with your script authoring.

1. On your development environment, click **Start | All Programs | Accessories | Windows PowerShell | Windows PowerShell ISE**.

2. In the PowerShell ISE window's top section, type in the following script:

```
$siteUrl = "http://intranet.contoso.com"

$snapin = Get-PSSnapin | Where-Object {$_.Name -eq 'Microsoft.
SharePoint.Powershell'}
if ($snapin -eq $null) {
Write-Host "Loading SharePoint Powershell Snapin"
Add-PSSnapin "Microsoft.SharePoint.Powershell"
}

$site = Get-SPSite | Where-Object {$_.Url -eq $siteUrl}
$site.WebApplication.QueryFeatures("00BFEA71-EC85-4903-972D-
EBE475780106")
```

Downloading the example code

You can download the example code fles for all Packt books you have purchased from your account at `http://www.PacktPub.com`. If you purchased this book elsewhere, you can visit `http://www.PacktPub.com/support` and register to have the fles e-mailed directly to you.

3. Press *F5* on your keyboard.

4. Take a note of the results returned by the script which will contain multiple instances in the following format:

```
DefinitionId           : 00bfea71-ec85-4903-972d-ebe475780106
Parent                 : My
Properties             : {}
Definition             : SPFeatureDefinition
Name=FeatureDefinition/00bfea71-ec85-4903-972d-ebe475780106
Version                : 3.0.0.0
FeatureDefinitionScope : Farm
```

5. Now let's see the result with PowerGUI. On your development environment, click **Start | All Programs | PowerGUI | PowerGUI Script Editor**.

6. In the top section of the PowerGUI editor, insert the same code we used in step 2 of this sequence:

```
$siteUrl = "http://intranet.contoso.com"

$snapin = Get-PSSnapin | Where-Object {$_.Name -eq 'Microsoft.
SharePoint.Powershell'}
if ($snapin -eq $null) {
Write-Host "Loading SharePoint Powershell Snapin"
Add-PSSnapin "Microsoft.SharePoint.Powershell"
```

```
}

$site = Get-SPSite | Where-Object {$_.Url -eq $siteUrl}
$site.WebApplication.QueryFeatures("00BFEA71-EC85-4903-972D-
EBE475780106")
```

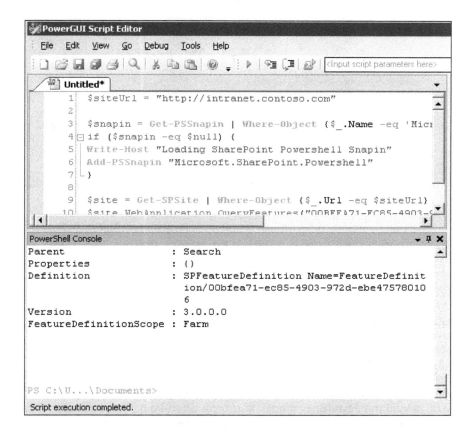

7. Press *F5* to execute your script.

8. Take a note of the same result set in the PowerShell Console window right below the editor, seen in the previous image.

9. Switch back to the script editor section of the screen and set your cursor on the last line of the code.

10. Press *F9* to set the breakpoint on the last line of the code.

11. Press *F5* to execute the script up to the breakpoint.

12. Take a note of the script editor window when the script has been executed up to the breakpoint. Your PowerGUI editor will look similar to the following screenshot:

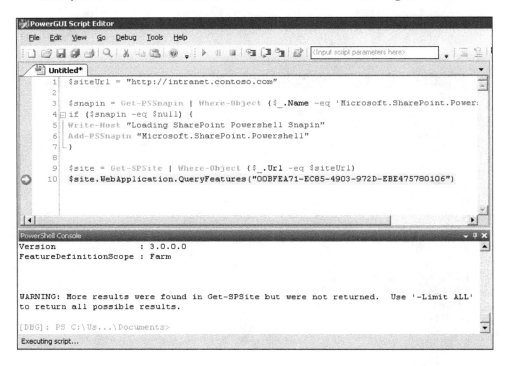

13. At this point you can press *F5* on your keyboard to continue execution.

How it works...

We launched the PowerShell ISE to execute our custom script. The first thing our script is going to do is load the PowerShell cmdlet library for SharePoint. This extension library holds various PowerShell functions allowing us to work with SharePoint objects from within PowerShell. Once the library is loaded, our script connects to our SharePoint site, `http://intranet.contoso.com,` and gets a hold of the current site. Further, the script calls a function which enumerates all of the SharePoint sites and their basic details which have a specified featured ID active in them, as seen in the following screenshot

```
PowerShell Console
Version                  : 3.0.0.0
FeatureDefinitionScope   : Farm

DefinitionId             : 00bfea71-ec85-4903-972d-ebe475780106
Parent                   : Marketing
Properties               : {}
Definition               : SPFeatureDefinition Name=FeatureDefinit
                           ion/00bfea71-ec85-4903-972d-ebe47578010
                           6
Version                  : 3.0.0.0
FeatureDefinitionScope   : Farm

DefinitionId             : 00bfea71-ec85-4903-972d-ebe475780106
Parent                   : New Products
Properties               : {}
Definition               : SPFeatureDefinition Name=FeatureDefinit
                           ion/00bfea71-ec85-4903-972d-ebe47578010
                           6
Version                  : 3.0.0.0
FeatureDefinitionScope   : Farm

DefinitionId             : 00bfea71-ec85-4903-972d-ebe475780106
Parent                   : Projects
Properties               : {}
Definition               : SPFeatureDefinition Name=FeatureDefinit
                           ion/00bfea71-ec85-4903-972d-ebe47578010
                           6
Version                  : 3.0.0.0
PS C:\Users\Administrator\Documents>
Script execution completed.
```

This function can be pretty handy when you're trying to locate problem features, or determine which site will be affected by the planned feature upgrade.

Our PowerShell script has been executed first in PowerShell ISE to see what capabilities you have in this Integrated Scripting Environment (ISE).

We then used PowerGUI to see how the same script can be executed and debugged. As you can see, PowerGUI has a few more features facilitating the script authoring process.

The debug option available in the script editor is particularly handy when your script doesn't quite yet work to your standards, and you want to figure out potential problems in it. If you're a developer, you already know all about debugging and its benefits.

Once you're satisfied with the script, you can execute it and run it on the current environment.

There's more

Let's take a look at how we can author and execute scripts with PowerGUI.

Script authoring with PowerGUI

One of the other advantages to PowerGUI is the ability to see values of variables in your script as it executes. The **Variables** panel is, by default, on the right-hand side of your **PowerGUI** window as seen here:

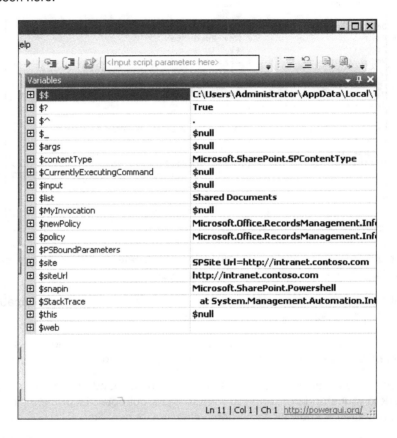

Without this panel, if you wanted to list the variable value, you would typically need to call it in a command line. If the variables in question are complex objects, you get to see the value of all the properties too, as shown in the following screenshot:

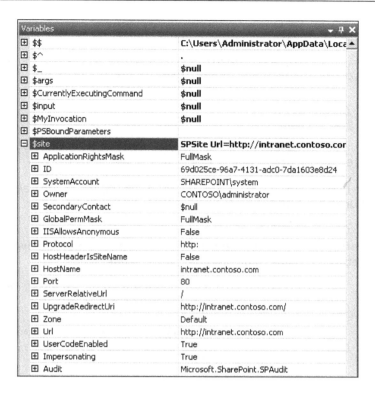

Also, to aid you with script authoring, PowerGUI has a collection of handy snippets which you can access with the **Edit | Insert Snippet** option.

For more tips on working with PowerGUI user interface and features, check out http://www. `Powergui.org`. For more tips on PowerShell ISE, search TechNet for Windows PowerShell Integrated Scripting Environment.

Accessing advanced SharePoint 2010 functionality with external libraries

In the previous recipe, we looked at some of the functionalities available to you in the PowerShell library, designed to help you access basic features in SharePoint. By using those features, you can access SharePoint objects and manipulate their properties. But what if you need to access the object model beyond what's available to you from the PowerShell snap-in for SharePoint? In this recipe, we'll take a look at how you can access more advanced features in SharePoint by referencing SharePoint assemblies and associated methods in those libraries.

Getting ready

In this example, we'll be using PowerGUI to execute our script. So log in to your environment with administrative privileges and launch PowerGUI.

How to do it...

The following steps will demonstrate how you can use some of the advanced SharePoint functions by referencing external assemblies in your PowerShell script:

1. Navigate to the test site URL: `http://intranet.contoso.com` and click on the **Shared Documents** library to access the library.

2. In the ribbon click **Library | Library Settings**.

3. Under **Permissions and Management** click **Information management policy settings as seen in the following screenshot:**.

```
List Information

Name:            Shared Documents
Web Address:     http://intranet/Shared Documents/Forms/AllItems.aspx
Description:     Share a document with the team by adding it to this do


General Settings                     Permissions and Management

Title, description and navigation    Permissions for this document
                                     library
Versioning settings
                                     Manage files which have no
Advanced settings                    checked in version

Validation settings                  Workflow Settings

Column default value settings        Enterprise Metadata and
                                     Keywords Settings
Manage item scheduling
                                     Generate file plan report
Rating settings
                                     Information management policy
Audience targeting settings          settings

Metadata navigation settings         Record declaration settings

Per-location view settings

Form settings
```

4. Select **Document** from the list of available content types.

5. Take note that none of the policies have been defined for this document library.

6. Switch to your PowerGUI scripting editor and enter the following script:

```
$siteUrl = "http://intranet.contoso.com"

$snapin = Get-PSSnapin | Where-Object {$_.Name -eq 'Microsoft.
```

```
SharePoint.Powershell'}

if ($snapin -eq $null) {
Write-Host "Loading SharePoint Powershell Snapin"
Add-PSSnapin "Microsoft.SharePoint.Powershell"
}

$site = Get-SPSite | Where-Object {$_.Url -eq $siteUrl}
$web =  $site.OpenWeb();
$list = $web.Lists["Shared Documents"];

$policy = [Microsoft.Office.RecordsManagement.InformationPolicy.
ListPolicySettings]($list);
if ($policy.ListHasPolicy -eq 0)
{

$policy.UseListPolicy = "true";
$policy.Update();
}

$contentType = $list.ContentTypes["Document"];
[Microsoft.Office.RecordsManagement.InformationPolicy.Policy]::Cre
atePolicy($contentType, $null);

$newPolicy = [Microsoft.Office.RecordsManagement.
InformationPolicy.Policy]::GetPolicy($contentType);

$newPolicy.Items.Add(
"Microsoft.Office.RecordsManagement.PolicyFeatures.Expiration",
"<Schedules nextStageId='3'>" +
"<Schedule type='Default'>" +
"<stages>" +
"<data stageId='1' stageDeleted='true'></data>" +
"<data stageId='2'>" +
"<formula id='Microsoft.Office.RecordsManagement.PolicyFeatures.
Expiration.Formula.BuiltIn'>" +
"<number>1</number>" +
"<property>Created</property>" +
"<period>years</period>" +
"</formula>" +
"<action type='action' id='Microsoft.Office.RecordsManagement.
PolicyFeatures.Expiration.Action.MoveToRecycleBin' />" +
"</data>" +
"</stages>" +
"</Schedule>" +
```

```
"</Schedules>");

$newPolicy.Update();
```

7. Press *F5* to execute the script, and then wait until the script executes.

8. Switch back to the policy setting page we accessed in step 5. Take note of the new policy added to the **Retention policy** where expiration has been enabled on the document library items, as seen in the following screenshot:

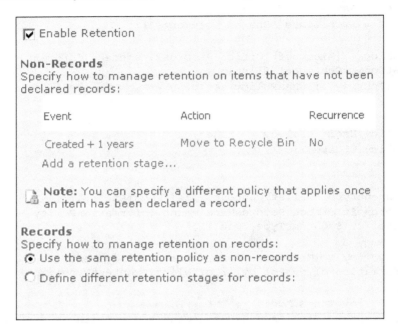

How it works...

The preceding code demonstrates how to take advantage of SharePoint class libraries to access functionality and methods available in those class libraries, and not directly available as PowerShell SharePoint script extensions. This recipe demonstrates basics behind accessing SharePoint object model using PowerShell. In this example, we created a new expiration policy on the document library of the team site on the development environment downloaded from Microsoft's download site http://intranet.contoso.com.

We started by accessing the site which we are interested in by using the PowerShell Get-SPSite method. We then accessed the current site at which the **SharePoint Documents** document library is hosted.

Next, we got hold of the current policy on the library in order to add a new instance of a policy.

We used the `CreatePolicy` method available in the `[Microsoft.Office.RecordsManagement.InformationPolicy.Policy]` namespace to create a policy for the library. This part demonstrates how the function is not available in the PowerShell syntax, but is available in the SharePoint library, and can be called in order to access some of the advanced functions in SharePoint.

The rest of the preceding code adds the definition of the policy we're trying to create on the library and adds the new policy object to the list of available policies.

When you execute this script, the newly defined policy will be added to the library on the site.

There's more

Let's take a look at how you can access external SharePoint libraries to execute more advanced PowerShell commands.

Accessing other SharePoint libraries and related functions

In this example, we looked at how you can create an expiration formula on the library, but there is plenty more you can do. To access functions in SharePoint libraries, you need to identify the object class and namespace those functions belong to so you can reference them in PowerShell.

If you search for the policy function class on TechNet you will find: `Microsoft.Office.RecordsManagement.InformationPolicy.Policy`. From there you can also determine various functions available to be called.

To call any of the functions, you would use the method we used in the preceding source code and reference the namespace first, followed by the class and function names.

Let's look at another example where we use PowerShell to connect to the current site and then change the status of features on the site.

1. Open PowerGUI, click **File | New** to create a new script.

2. Add the following code to the script window:

```
$siteUrl = "http://intranet.contoso.com"

$snapin = Get-PSSnapin | Where-Object {$_.Name -eq 'Microsoft.
SharePoint.Powershell'}
if ($snapin -eq $null) {
Write-Host "Loading SharePoint Powershell Snapin"
Add-PSSnapin "Microsoft.SharePoint.Powershell"
}

$site = Get-SPSite | Where-Object {$_.Url -eq $siteUrl}
$features = $site.FeatureDefinitions;
$features.get_Item("CustomFeature").Status = "Offline"
```

3.   Run the script from within PowerGUI by pressing *F5*.

4.   Verify the status of our `CustomFeature` which should be `Offline`.

Note that we did not have direct access to the `features` object but rather to its parent. Yet, by using PowerShell, we were able to call function on a child object allowing us to change the status of the feature on the site.

In this case, we set the feature to be `Offline`. Among other available options related to a feature status, we could choose the following: `Online`, `Disabled`, `Offline`, `Unprovisioning`, `Provisioning`, `Upgrading`.

As you can see, this method is handy when you need to disable defective features across many sites in your environment.

This example demonstrates how you can access other available libraries in SharePoint and even your own custom libraries to call functions from within them.

Creating a custom PowerShell command (CmdLet)

In this chapter, previous recipes have tackled accessing custom functions in other SharePoint libraries, and using those functions to perform various operations in our script. It's now time for us to see how we can create our own custom function executing some custom logic. Once the command has been created, it will be accessible from within PowerShell for users to call.

This is particularly handy when you're creating a collection of functions which perform frequent administrative tasks on your server.

Another example where you might want to create your own CmdLet is when you're planning to package those as custom offering for your customers to download and use on their environments.

Getting ready

To create a custom CmdLet, we will be using Visual Studio 2010 Professional. If you're using the virtualized environment we downloaded in the recipe, *Setting up your Virtual Machine and running a test script*, Visual Studio 2010 Professional will already be installed on your system. Otherwise, ensure you at least have the Professional version installed to continue with this recipe.

How to do it...

Let's take a look at how you can create your own CmdLet using the following steps:

1. From within your Visio Studio 2010, click **File | New | Project ....**
2. From **Installed Templates** select **Visual C# | Class Library**.
3. Leave the default name for the project as **ClassLibrary1** and click **OK**.
4. In the **Solution Explorer**, right-click **References | Add Reference** to add the following references:

   System.Management.Automation, *which can be found in a list of assemblies in the* **.NET** *tab.*

5. Also add a reference to **Microsoft.SharePoint**. *The reference can be found in the* **SharePoint** *tab as seen here:*

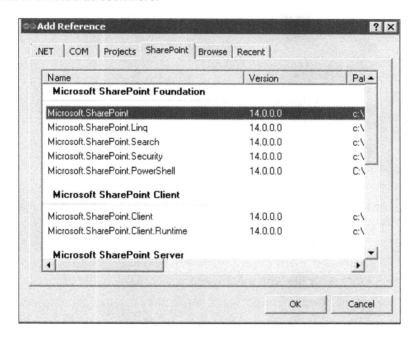

6. In the **Solution Explorer**, pick the **Class1.cs** and rename the file to **PowerShell Cmdlet1.cs**.
7. Replace the contents of the **PowerShell Cmdlet1.cs** with the following code:

```
using System.Management.Automation;
using Microsoft.SharePoint;

namespace PowerShellCmdlet1
```

```
    {
        [Cmdlet(VerbsCommon.Set, "WebTitle")]
        public class PowerShell_Cmdlet1 : Cmdlet
        {
            [Parameter()]
            public string siteUrl;

            [Parameter()]
            public string newTitle;

            protected override void ProcessRecord()
            {
                base.ProcessRecord();

                using (SPSite site = new SPSite(siteUrl))
                {
                    using (SPWeb web = site.OpenWeb())
                    {
                        web.Title = newTitle;
                        web.Update();
                        WriteObject("New Title: " + web.Title);
                    }
                }
            }
        }
    }
}
```

8. Right-click the project name **ClassLibrary1** and select **Properties**.

9. From the **Properties** page, pick the **Signing** tab and check the check mark titled **Sign the assembly**.

10. From the drop-down entitled **Choose a strong name key file**, pick **New** and provide key filename of your choice, which usually is safe to call **key.snk**.

11. Uncheck **Protect my file with a password** and click **OK**.

12. Your project will now have an assigned key as shown in the following screenshot:

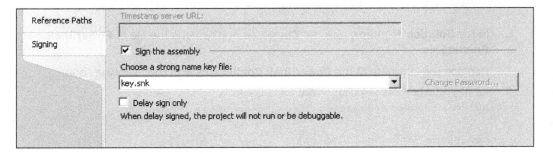

13. At this point, your Visual Studio **Solution Explorer** tree will look as in the following screenshot:

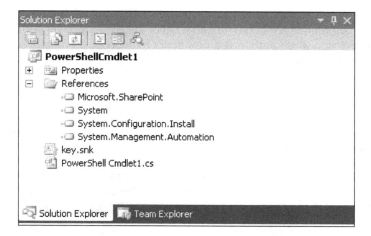

How it works...

At this stage, we have created a new class representing our CmdLet with Visual Studio solution. Visual Studio will produce an assembly file as an output of the solution once built.

Our solution has only one CmdLet functionality which is defined in `PowerShell_Cmdlet1`. You will notice the `[Cmdlet(VerbsCommon.Set, "WebTitle")]` part of the code defines the type of the command and the name of it.

 If you noticed, all of the PowerShell commands we have called so far have a naming convention of a `[Verb]-[Action]`. The verb in this case is either `Get` or `Set`. In fact, for the full list of available verbs, in your command let code, place the cursor over `VerbsCommon.Set` and press *F12*. Visual Studio will display all of the available verbs allowing you to find the one appropriate to the CmdLet you're creating.

The second part of the CmdLet declaration is the action of your function, which can be titled according to your preference.

 The best practice here is to name the command something descriptive to the action executed by it.

The actual functionality of the CmdLet is defined right below the CmdLet declaration, in our case, in the `PowerShell_Cmdlet1` class.

We started with a parameter declaration, which is an optional piece but often used. Since most PowerShell commands contain a reusable set of instructions to be performed on the object, it's very common when authoring a new script to accept parameters specifying an object. For PowerShell scripts interacting with SharePoint, this will be a URL of the site or list name, and so on. In our case, we'll capture the URL and the new title of the SharePoint site. The following function will use the parameters we supplied to connect to the URL we have identified, and rename the site title to the one defined.

The logic defined in `ProcessRecord` of our code handles all of the functionality our CmdLet will execute, and this is where you can code the functionality of your own CmdLet.

Finally, once the logic of our CmdLet has been created, we're prepared to make the functionality available in the PowerShell command line. Details of the CmdLet installation process are described in the *Creating a custom PowerShell Snap-In recipe*.

Due to the nature of CmdLet, before installing it on the system, we need to make sure the output DLL is signed with a strong name.

The purpose of signing the assembly with the strong name is to ensure the assembly can be dropped into the **Global Assembly Cache (GAC)**, where it can be consumed by the installation process.

See also

Creating a custom PowerShell Snap-In recipe in this chapter.

Creating a custom PowerShell Snap-In

As we've seen in the *Creating a custom PowerShell command (CmdLet)* recipe, the creation of PowerShell CmdLet is a process of defining the functionality you want to expose to the user, and sealing it as a .NET assembly. In this recipe, we'll take a look at how you install your custom CmdLet which directly involves the creation of a **PowerShell Snap-In.**

We have already used the PowerShell Snap-In when we referenced a set of SharePoint Set earlier in this chapter. In this case, we called the following command:

```
Add-PSSnapin "Microsoft.SharePoint.Powershell"
```

In this example, we'll use similar approach to call our custom Snap-In.

Getting ready

As trivial as it sounds, to create a Snap-In, you will need to create another class in the Visual Studio solution you created earlier to define your CmdLet. Your Snap-In solution doesn't need to contain both a Snap-In and a CmdLet. In fact, you can have them created in two separate solutions as long as your Snap-In references the CmdLet. In this example we'll add a Snap-In class to the existing CmdLet solution, which is very common when creating PowerShell CmdLet libraries.

How to do it...

We'll take a look at how you can create your own PowerShell Snap-In.

1. Switch to the Visual Studio 2010 solution you used to create a CmdLet earlier.

2. From the **Solution Explorer**, right-click the project name, **PowerShellCmdlet1** and select **Add | Class ...**.

3. In the **Solution Explorer,** pick the **Class1.cs** and rename the file to **PowerShell Cmdlet1.cs**

4. Rename the newly created class to **PowerShellCmdlet SnapIn1.cs**.

5. Open the class file created and replace the contents of the **PowerShellCmdlet SnapIn1.cs** with the following code:

```
using System.Collections.ObjectModel;
using System.ComponentModel;
using System.Management.Automation;
using System.Management.Automation.Runspaces;

namespace PowerShellCmdlet1
{
    [RunInstaller(true)]
    public class PowerShellCmdlet_SnapIn1 : CustomPSSnapIn
    {
        private Collection<CmdletConfigurationEntry> _cmdlets;

        /// <summary>
        /// The description of powershell snap-in.
        /// </summary>
        public override string Description
        {
            get { return "A Description of MyCmdlet"; }
        }

        /// <summary>
        /// The name of power shell snap-in
```

```csharp
        /// </summary>
        public override string Name
        {
            get { return "MyCmdlet"; }
        }

        /// <summary>
        /// The name of the vendor
        /// </summary>
        public override string Vendor
        {
            get { return ""; }
        }

         public override Collection<CmdletConfigurationEntry>
Cmdlets
        {
            get
            {
                if (null == _cmdlets)
                {
                    _cmdlets = new Collection<Cmdlet
                    ConfigurationEntry>();
                    _cmdlets.Add(new CmdletConfigurationEntry
                        ("Set-WebTitle", typeof(PowerShell_Cmdlet1),
"Set-WebTitle.dll-Help.xml"));
                }
                return _cmdlets;
            }
        }

    }
}
```

6. Right-click the project name **PowerShellCmdlet1** and select **Build**.

7. Right-click the project name **PowerShellCmdlet1** and select **Open Folder in Windows Explorer**.

8. In the folder opened, open the `bin\Debug` folder and locate the `PowerShellCmdlet1.dll`.

9. Click **Start | Run** on your development environment and open the Global Assembly Cache by typing `c:\windows\assembly`.

10. Drag-and-drop the `PowerShellCmdlet1.dll` to the `assembly` folder.

11. Open a PowerShell command line from **Start | All Programs | Accessories | Windows PowerShell | Windows PowerShell**.

12. Type in the following command to install our newly added Snap-In assembly. Ensure the path to your assembly is correct. In this example, our path is `C:\Users\Administrator\Documents\visual studio 2010\projects\PowerShellCmdlet1\PowerShellCmdlet1\bin\Debug`:

    ```
    PS> set-alias installutil $env:windir\Microsoft.NET\Framework\
    v2.0.50727\installutil
    ```

    ```
    PS> cd "C:\Users\Administrator\Documents\visual studio 2010\
    projects\PowerShellCmdlet1\PowerShellCmdlet1\bin\Debug"
    ```

    ```
    S> installutil PowerShellCmdlet1.dll
    ```

13. Now that our Snap-In has been installed, let's open our SharePoint test intranet site, `http://intranet.contoso.com`. Take note of the current site title.

14. Switch back to the PowerShell command-line window and register the new Snap-In:

    ```
    PS> Add-PSSnapin "MyCmdlet"
    ```

15. Let's change the title of the site by executing our custom CmdLet:

    ```
    PS> Set-WebTitle -siteUrl "http://intranet.contoso.com" -newTitle
    "Test Title"
    ```

16. Switch back to `http://intranet.contoso.com` and take note of the changed title.

How it works...

Since we have already created the actual CmdLet, we reused the same Visual Studio solution to add a Snap-In class. The Snap-In class will perform the role of installer. As you can see, the contents of the class declare the name and description on the CmdLet as well as a reference to CmdLet class. This information will further be used to identify your custom CmdLet.

Once the solution has been built and the solution library has been generated, we copied the library to GAC. We used `InstallUtil` to install and uninstall server resources by executing the installer components in our CmdLet library. By executing the `InstallUtil` command we will actually make the Snap-In available in the PowerShell command line.

Once installed, we can add the Snap-In and execute our custom CmdLet.

As you will notice, due to the fact that our custom Snap-In library will be placed into the GAC, the custom code executed will have access to most of the server resources. Because of the level of access, when downloading custom Snap-Ins ensure they come from a trusted source.

There's more

Let's take a look at how you can uninstall your Snap-In from the system as well as how Visual Studio templates can help you with Snap-In authoring.

Uninstalling a Snap-In from your system

Previously, we looked at how you can install the Snap-In so it's available to be called from the command line. You can also uninstall the Snap-In by using the uninstall key of the `InstallUtil` command. Here is a sample uninstall syntax for our Snap-In:

```
PS> installutil /u PowerShellCmdlet1.dll
```

It's quite common to need to uninstall the Snap-In. One common scenario includes the CmdLet authoring process. As you author your CmdLet and discover problems with it or would like to add more functionality, to have the new version available you would need to re-install the Snap-in on the environment.

Visual Studio CmdLet and Snap-In item templates

In this example, we looked at how you can install a custom PowerShell Snap-In by adding code to a Visual Studio solution. Since this is a fairly common task, there are a few templates available online which you're welcome to use to create core CmdLet and Snap-In code automatically. The core functionality will be your starting point which you can add your customizations to.

One of the templates you can try is available at *CodePlex*. The project is called PowerShell Visual Studio 2008 templates and recently was hosted at this URL: `http://psvs2008.codeplex.com`.

Although the version of this package is specifically designed for Visual Studio 2008, it is also compatible with Visual Studio 2010.

Once you download the package, open it on the development environment where you have Visual Studio installed, and install all of the suggested components, as seen in the following screenshot:

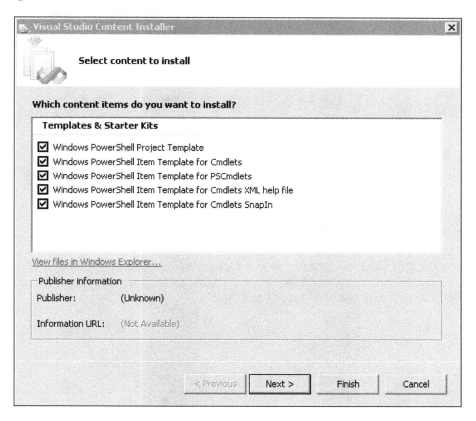

Once installed, to add a new instance of a template for CmdLet and Snap-In, simply right-click on the project name in **Solution Explorer**, and select **Add** | **New Item**.

From here, you need to pick the appropriate Snap-In or CmdLet template and click **Add** to create an initial version of the file, as seen in the following screenshot:.

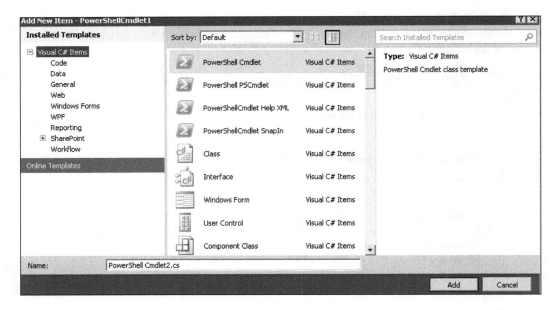

Whether you will be using components from the preceding template, or creating your own CmdLet classes, search MSDN with the keyword *Cmdlet Development Guidelines* for some handy tips and details on authoring your CmdLets.

4

Integrating Silverlight 4 with SharePoint 2010

This chapter is taken from *Microsoft Silverlight 4 and SharePoint 2010 Integration* (Chapter 1) by Gastón C. Hillar.

We want to include Silverlight 4 **RIAs (Rich Internet Applications)** in SharePoint 2010. RIAs provide rich experience for users, both through their browsers and outside them. Integrating Silverlight RIAs in SharePoint 2010 offers amazing opportunities to combine the power and flexibility offered by SharePoint with great user experiences. In fact, many interfaces shown in SharePoint 2010 are developed in Silverlight. We want to integrate Silverlight RIAs into SharePoint 2010. First, we must understand some of the fundamentals that are related to various tools and their configurations. In this chapter, we will cover many topics to help us understand the new tools and techniques involved in creating Silverlight RIAs for SharePoint 2010 sites. We will:

- Understand the benefits of integrating Silverlight with SharePoint
- Prepare the development environment to develop applications for SharePoint 2010 using Silverlight 4
- Prepare the SharePoint 2010 server to host Silverlight applications
- Create a Silverlight Line of Business RIA
- Learn to add a Silverlight RIA to a SharePoint site
- Understand the advantage of creating rich user experiences for SharePoint solutions
- Work with shared documents to store a Silverlight application in SharePoint sites

- Work with many Silverlight applications in a single page
- Learn the differences between client and server code

Understanding the benefits of integrating Silverlight with SharePoint

The following list shows many benefits of integrating Silverlight with SharePoint 2010:

- **Rich UX**: Silverlight RIAs can offer a rich user experience. You can take full advantage of the rich visual capabilities offered by Silverlight and include them in a SharePoint site. The rich and interactive content offers an incredible new world of possibilities in SharePoint. For example, you can offer an interactive balanced scorecard with animated graphs, rich navigation capabilities, and context menus.

- **Code runs on the client**: You can take advantage of the power of the client computers accessing the SharePoint server. You can use threading and asynchronous calls to offer responsive user interfaces and to take advantage of modern multi-core microprocessors found in client computers. You can offer great response times without the need to wait for the server to load another page. You can take advantage of rich controls, animations, and exciting multimedia effects. The processing removes load from the server and enables you to use both the server and the client in your solutions. Additionally, Silverlight 4 is cross-browser capable and we can take advantage of the improved Out of Browser features to create applications that interact with the SharePoint 2010 server but run in the Windows desktop, out of the Web browser.

- **Efficient applications**: As you can work with the power offered by the client, you can process data without the need to make requests to the server all the time. This way, you can create load-balanced solutions.

- **Access to the Client OM (Client Object Model)**: When you have to access data and services offered by the SharePoint 2010 server, you don't need to create your own complex infrastructure. There is no need to add additional layers. You can take advantage of the new Client Object Model, also known as Client OM. As you can work with asynchronous calls to the Client OM, you can still offer great responsive applications when consuming services from the server. Users can interact with SharePoint data without requiring server calls as they would from traditional pages. Lots of the processing can be pushed down to the client. This way, as previously explained, you can remove load from the SharePoint server and create load-balanced solutions.

- **Leverage your existing Silverlight knowledge, components, and applications**: You can build new capabilities quickly from existing Silverlight components and applications, integrating them with SharePoint 2010.

Considering the aforementioned benefits, we will work hard to learn all the possibilities offered by the integration of Silverlight and SharePoint 2010 in later parts of the book.

Creating a SharePoint solution

Now, when we design a new SharePoint 2010 solution, we will be able to consider Silverlight RIAs as new components for the global solution. We have to consider the aforementioned benefits of integrating Silverlight with SharePoint and decide which parts would be convenient to create as Silverlight RIAs.

This way, we can focus on preparing the SharePoint 2010 infrastructure and then we can access data and services offered by the server through Silverlight RIAs. For example, you can view the images found in an assets library defined in SharePoint through a Silverlight application.

 Once you start integrating Silverlight with SharePoint, you will find a new exciting way of enhancing SharePoint solutions.

Preparing the development environment

We want to take full advantage of modern technologies. First of all, we must install the latest tools and begin working on configurations. Later, we will be able to use our existing knowledge to create different kinds of RIAs for SharePoint 2010, using Silverlight 4 — the newest kid-on-the-block from Microsoft.

 Silverlight 4 is backward-compatible with its previous version, Silverlight 3. Therefore, when an example uses a feature found only in Silverlight 4, you will find a note explaining this situation. Most of the examples work for both Silverlight versions. However, we will also take advantage of some of the new features found in Silverlight 4.

The only requirements underpinning the development and integration of RIAs into SharePoint 2010 sites are understanding the basics of the C# programming language, ASP.NET, XAML code, and the Visual Studio IDE. We will cover any other requirements in our journey through the creation of many different kinds of RIAs to run in a SharePoint 2010 site. First, we must download and install various Silverlight development tools. We need Visual C# 2010 Professional, Premium, or Ultimate installed, in order to successfully complete the installations explained in the following section. Visual C# 2010 allows us to choose the desired Silverlight version (for example, version 3 or version 4). The following sections will show Visual Studio 2010 Ultimate screenshots. If you use other versions, some elements that appear in the screenshots could be different but the steps are all valid for the aforementioned versions.

Setting up the development environment

Follow these steps to prepare the development environment:

1. Download the following files:

Application's name	Download link	File name	Description
Silverlight 4 Tools for Visual Studio 2010	`http://www. microsoft.com/ downloads/details. aspx?FamilyID= eff8a0da-0a4d-48e8- 8366-6ddf2ecad801& displaylang=en`	`Silverlight4_ Tools.exe`	We must install Silverlight 4 Tools in order to create Silverlight 4 applications in the Visual Studio 2010 IDE, using XAML and C#. It will co-exist with previous Silverlight SDKs (Software Development Kits). This new version of Silverlight Tools also includes the WCF RIA Services package.

Application's name	Download link	File name	Description
Silverlight 4 Offline Documentation (in CHM format)	`http://www.microsoft.com/downloads/details.aspx?familyid=B6127B9B-968C-46C2-8CB6-D228E017AD74&displaylang=en`	`Silverlight_Documentation.EXE`	We must download and run this file to decompress its content, because we will need access to Silverlight 4 official documentation in due course.
Expression Blend for .NET 4	`http://www.microsoft.com/downloads/details.aspx?FamilyID=88484825-1b3c-4e8c-8b14-b05d025e1541&displaylang=en`	`Blend_Trial_en.exe`	This tool will enable us to create content that targets Silverlight 4 and to create rapid prototypes with the SketchFlow tool.
Silverlight Toolkit (Updated for Silverlight 4 compatibility)	`http://codeplex.com/Silverlight`	`Silverlight_4_Toolkit_April_2010.msi`	It is convenient to download the latest stable release. This toolkit provides a nice collection of Silverlight controls, components, and utilities made available outside the normal Silverlight release cycle. It will be really helpful to use these controls to provide even more attractive user interfaces. Besides, it includes more Silverlight themes.

2. Run the installers in the same order in which they appear in the above table and follow the steps to complete the installation wizards.

3. Once the installations have successfully finished, run Visual Studio 2010 or Visual Web Developer 2010 (or later).

4. Select **File | New | Project...** or press *Ctrl+Shift+N*. Select **Visual C# | Silverlight** under **Installed Templates** in the **New Project** dialog box. You will see many Silverlight templates, including **Silverlight Business Application** and **WCF RIA Services Class Library**, as shown in the following screenshot:

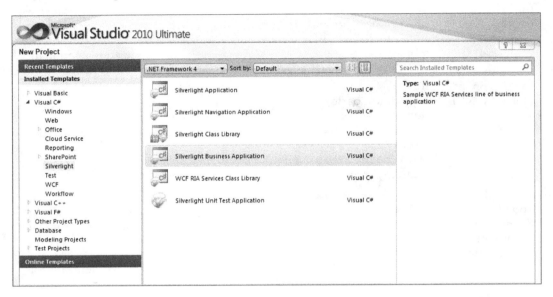

Discovering the rich controls offered by the Silverlight Toolkit

Silverlight Toolkit is a Microsoft project offering many rich controls, components, and utilities that can help us to enhance our Silverlight UI (User Interface). As we want to create a very attractive UI for SharePoint, it is convenient to get familiar with its features. Follows these steps to see the controls in action and to change the values for many of their properties.

1. Select **Start | All Programs | Microsoft Silverlight 4 Toolkit April 2010 | Toolkit Samples** and your default web browser will display a web page with a Silverlight application displaying a list of the controls organized in ten categories as follows:

    ° Controls
    ° Data
    ° DataForm
    ° Data Input

- ° DataVisualization
- ° Input
- ° Layout
- ° Navigation
- ° Theming
- ° Toolkit

 By default, the `default.htm` web page is located at `C:\Program Files (x86)\Microsoft SDKs\Silverlight\v4.0\Toolkit\ Apr10\Samples` in 64-bit Windows versions.

2. Click on a control name under the desired category and the right panel will display the control with different values assigned for its properties, creating diverse instances of the control. For example, the following screenshot shows many instances of the `Rating` control under the **Input** category.

3. Click on the buttons shown at the bottom of the Web page and you will be able to see both the XAML and the C# code used to create the sample for the control. For example, the following screenshot shows the XAML code for the `DataGrid` control example, `DataGridSample.xaml`. You can also click on `DataGridSample.xaml.cs` and check the C# part. This control appears under the **Data** category.

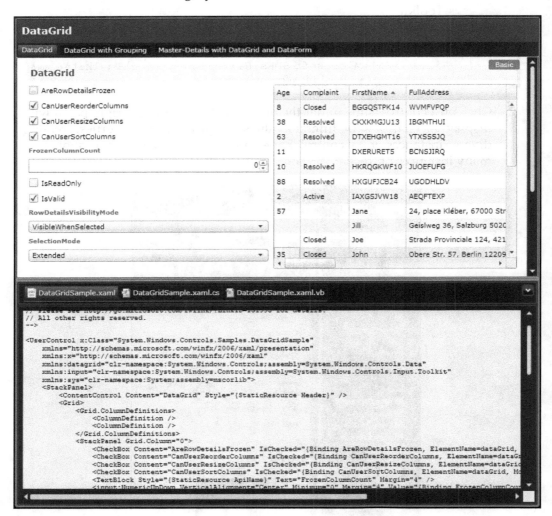

Browsing themes with sample controls

Silverlight Toolkit also includes 11 themes that allow us to change and improve the overall look-and-feel for our Silverlight UI. They are:

- Bubble Creme
- Bureau Black
- Bureau Blue
- Expression Dark
- Expression Light
- Rainier Purple
- Rainier Orange
- Shiny Blue
- Shiny Red
- Twilight Blue
- Whistler Blue

Click on **Theme Browser** under the **Theming** category and you will be able to select one of the themes shown in the previous list to preview the look-and-feel of many controls. The following screenshot shows the preview for the **Whistler Blue** theme:

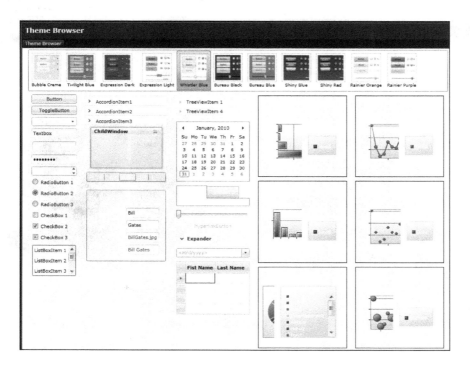

Preparing the server

So far, we have prepared the development environment. Now, it is time to make sure that we have the necessary configuration for the SharePoint 2010 server in which we are going to integrate Silverlight applications.

In order to complete all the examples that we will develop throughout this book, you must be an administrator of a SharePoint site collection. SharePoint Server 2010 or SharePoint Foundation 2010 must be installed in the same computer that runs Visual Studio 2010. You can check the necessary steps to perform a SharePoint Server 2010 or SharePoint Foundation 2010 installation for your development computer at `http://msdn.microsoft.com/en-us/library/ee554869.aspx`. Follow these steps to ensure that you are a site collection administrator:

1. Open your default web browser, view the SharePoint site, and log in with your username and password. You have to enter the SharePoint server URL. In our examples, we will use `http://xpsgaston` as our default SharePoint 2010 site. However, you have to replace it with your SharePoint 2010 site URL. Your default site will appear, in this case, `http://xpsgaston/SitePages/Home.aspx`, as shown in the following screenshot:

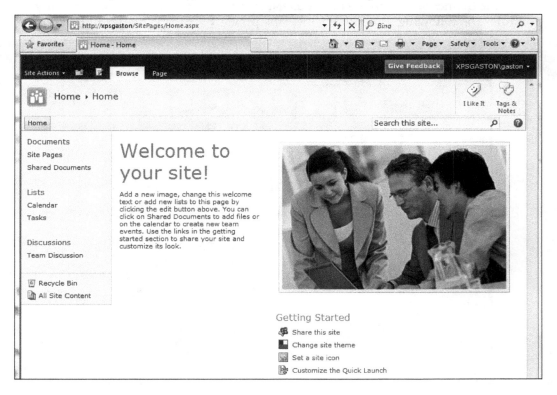

2. Click **Site Actions | Site Permissions** and a list of users with their permission levels will appear.

3. Now, click on **Site Collection Administrators** in the ribbon. A new dialog box with the names of the users with administrator rights on this site collection will appear.

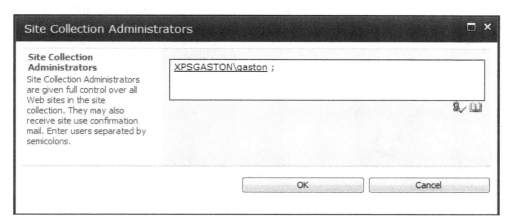

4. If your user name appears in the text box, you are a Site Collection Administrator.

 If you cannot see the **Site Collection Administrators** button in the ribbon, it means that you don't have site collection administrator privileges on the site. In this case, you have to request this permission from the SharePoint site administrator.

Browsing SharePoint Site collections

Once we have ensured that our username is a Site Collection Administrator, we can use **Server Explorer** in Visual Studio to browse a SharePoint site.

1. Start Visual Studio as a system administrator user. In Windows Server 2008 R2, 2008, and 2003, if you are already logged as Administrator on the machine you can simply run the application. However, in Windows 7 or Windows Vista, you can do it by right-clicking on its shortcut and selecting **Run as administrator** in the context menu that appears, as shown:

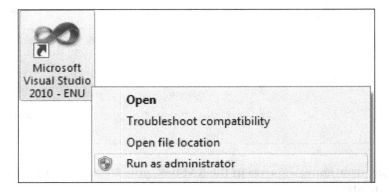

2. Activate the **Server Explorer** palette. If it isn't visible, you have to select **View | Server Explorer** in the main menu.

3. Click on the expand button for **SharePoint Connections**. If the name of your desired SharePoint 2010 server doesn't appear in the list, you can manually connect to the server. You can do it by right-clicking on **SharePoint Connections** and selecting **Add Connection...** in the context menu that appears. Then, you have to enter the URL for the server, for example, http://xpsgaston and click **OK** in the dialog box that appears. If your user has the previously explained privileges, the server will appear in the list.

4. Now, click on the expand button for the SharePoint server and you will be able to browse its different nodes. Every component of a SharePoint site is represented by a node in the **Server Explorer** tree view. You can inspect the properties for each node, as shown in the following screenshot:

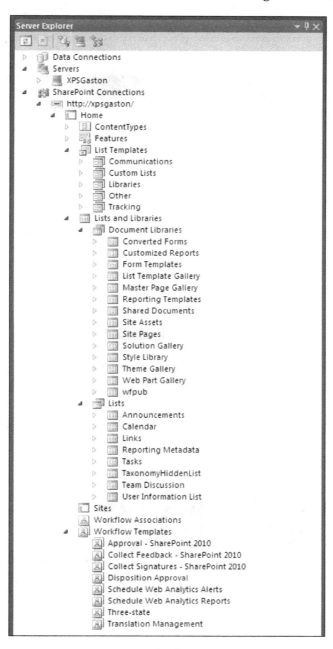

5. You can view some lists in your default web browser by right-clicking on a node and then selecting **View in Browser** in the context menu that appears. For example, you can do it for the node **Home | Lists and Libraries | Site Pages** and your default web browser will display all the pages. In this case, the URL shown is `http://xpsgaston/SitePages/Forms/AllPages.aspx`.

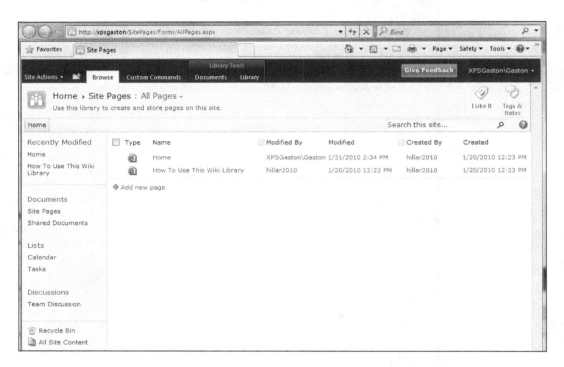

 Remember to run Visual Studio as a system administrator user in order to interact with SharePoint for all the examples covered in this book.

Creating a Silverlight LOB (Line-of-Business) RIA

Now, we are going to create a very simple Silverlight **LOB** (**Line-Of-Business**) RIA that retrieves data, displays a grid with a list of projects, and allows the users to navigate through the data. Then, we are going to integrate this Silverlight UI in SharePoint.

1. Create a new Visual C# project using the **Silverlight | Silverlight Application** template. Use `SilverlightProjects` as the project's name.

2. Deactivate the **Host the Silverlight application in a new Web site** checkbox in the **New Silverlight Application** dialog box. We want the Silverlight application to run in a simple HTML web page. As you have installed Silverlight 4 Tools, the dialog box will offer you a combo box with the possibility to choose the desired Silverlight version. Select **Silverlight 4** as we want to take advantage of the new features offered by this version.

3. Add a new XML file to the project, `Projects.xml`. The following lines define properties and values for five `project` instances. This way, we have some data in XML format for our simple LOB application.

```xml
<?xml version="1.0" encoding="utf-8" ?>
<projects>
  <project projectId="0">
    <title>Creating a Silverlight 4 UI</title>
    <estimatedDaysLeft>4</estimatedDaysLeft>
    <status>Delayed</status>
    <assignedTo>Jon Share</assignedTo>
    <numberOfTasks>5</numberOfTasks>
  </project>
  <project projectId="1">
    <title>Creating a Complex Silverlight LOB RIA</title>
    <estimatedDaysLeft>5</estimatedDaysLeft>
    <status>Delayed</status>
```

```xml
      <assignedTo>James Point</assignedTo>
      <numberOfTasks>35</numberOfTasks>
    </project>
    <project projectId="2">
      <title>Creating a New SharePoint Site</title>
      <estimatedDaysLeft>3</estimatedDaysLeft>
      <status>Delayed</status>
      <assignedTo>Vanessa Dotcom</assignedTo>
      <numberOfTasks>8</numberOfTasks>
    </project>
    <project projectId="3">
      <title>Installing a New SharePoint 2010 Server</title>
      <estimatedDaysLeft>3</estimatedDaysLeft>
      <status>Delayed</status>
      <assignedTo>Michael Desktop</assignedTo>
      <numberOfTasks>25</numberOfTasks>
    </project>
    <project projectId="4">
      <title>Testing the New Silverlight LOB RIA</title>
      <estimatedDaysLeft>4</estimatedDaysLeft>
      <status>Delayed</status>
      <assignedTo>Jon Share</assignedTo>
      <numberOfTasks>35</numberOfTasks>
    </project>
  </projects>
```

4. Add a new class to the project called `Project` in a new class file, `Project.cs`. The following lines define the new class, with six properties. This way, you will be able to create instances of this class to hold the values defined in the previously created XML file.

```csharp
public class Project
{
    public int ProjectId { get; set; }
    public string Title { get; set; }
    public int EstimatedDaysLeft { get; set; }
    public string Status { get; set; }
    public string AssignedTo { get; set; }
    public int NumberOfTasks { get; set; }
}
```

5. Open `MainPage.xaml`, define a new width and height for the `Grid` as `800` and `600`, add the following controls located in the **Toolbox** under **All Silverlight Controls**, and align them as shown in the screenshot. Remember that Visual Studio 2010 allows us to drag-and-drop controls from the toolbox to the Silverlight `UserControl` in the design view and it will automatically generate the XAML code.

    °   Two `Label` controls.

    °   One `DataGrid` control and set its name to `dataGridProjects`. Set its `AutoGenerateColumns` property to `true`.

    °   One `Slider` control, `sliGridFontSize`. Set its `Minimum` property to `8`, `Maximum` to `72`, and `Value` to `11`.

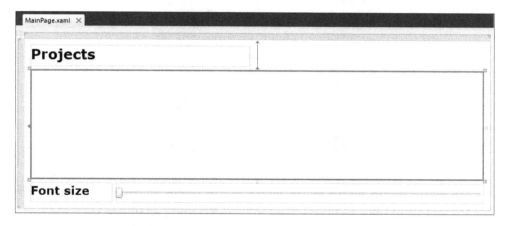

6. Apply data binding to the font size for the `DataGrid` control, `dataGridProjects`. In order to do so, select `dataGridProjects`, activate the **Properties** panel, display them in alphabetical order, right-click on the **FontSize** property, and select **Apply Data Binding** in the context menu that appears. Then, select `ElementName` in **Source**, `sliGridFontSize`, and then `Value` in **Path**. This way, when the user moves the slider, the font size for the data grid will change. The code that defines the data binding is as follows:

    ```
    FontSize="{Binding ElementName=sliGridFontSize, Path=Value}"
    ```

7. The complete XAML markup code for `MainPage.xaml` will be similar to the following lines:

```
<UserControl x:Class="SilverlightProjects.MainPage"
    xmlns="http://schemas.microsoft.com/winfx/2006/xaml/
      presentation"
    xmlns:x="http://schemas.microsoft.com/winfx/2006/xaml"
    xmlns:d="http://schemas.microsoft.com/expression/blend/2008"
    xmlns:mc="http://schemas.openxmlformats.org/markup-
      compatibility/2006"
    mc:Ignorable="d"
    d:DesignWidth="800" d:DesignHeight="600" xmlns:data=
      "clr-namespace:System.Windows.Controls;
      assembly=System.Windows.Controls.Data" xmlns:dataInput=
      "clr-namespace:System.Windows.Controls;
      assembly=System.Windows.Controls.Data.Input">

    <Grid x:Name="LayoutRoot" Background="White">
        <data:DataGrid AutoGenerateColumns="True" Height="491"
          HorizontalAlignment="Left" Margin="12,56,0,0"
          Name="dataGridProjects" VerticalAlignment="Top"
          Width="776" FontSize="{
          Binding ElementName=sliGridFontSize, Path=Value}" />

        <dataInput:Label Height="38" HorizontalAlignment="Left"
          Margin="12,12,0,0" Name="label1"
          VerticalAlignment="Top" Width="376"
          FontWeight="Bold" FontSize="24"
          Content="Projects" />

        <Slider Height="35" HorizontalAlignment="Left"
          Margin="158,553,0,0" Name="sliGridFontSize"
          VerticalAlignment="Top" Width="630" Value="11"
          Maximum="72" Minimum="11" />

        <dataInput:Label Content="Font size" FontSize="20"
          FontWeight="Bold" Height="35" HorizontalAlignment="Left"
          Margin="12,553,0,0" Name="label2"
          VerticalAlignment="Top" Width="140" />
    </Grid>
</UserControl>
```

8. Now, it is necessary to add code to retrieve data from the XML file and assign a value to the `ItemsSource` property of the `DataGrid` control. First, you have to add a reference to `System.Xml.Linq.dll`. Then, you can add the new `InitializeGrid` method and call it from the class constructor as shown in the following lines for `MainPage.xaml.cs`.

```
using System;
using System.Collections.Generic;
using System.Linq;
using System.Net;
using System.Windows;
using System.Windows.Controls;
using System.Windows.Documents;
using System.Windows.Input;
using System.Windows.Media;
using System.Windows.Media.Animation;
using System.Windows.Shapes;
// Added
using System.Xml.Linq;

namespace SilverlightProjects
{
    public partial class MainPage : UserControl
    {
        private void InitializeGrid()
        {
            XDocument docProjects =
                    XDocument.Load("Projects.xml");
            var projectsData = from el in
                    docProjects.Descendants("project")
                                select new Project
                                {
                                    ProjectId = Convert.
ToInt32(el.Attribute("projectId").Value),
                                    Title = Convert.ToString(el.
Element("title").Value),
                                    EstimatedDaysLeft = Convert.
ToInt32(el.Element("estimatedDaysLeft").Value),
                                    Status = Convert.ToString(el.
Element("status").Value),
                                    AssignedTo = Convert.
ToString(el.Element("assignedTo").Value),
                                    NumberOfTasks = Convert.
ToInt32(el.Element("numberOfTasks").Value)
                                };
            dataGridProjects.ItemsSource = projectsData;
        }

        public MainPage()
```

```
        {
            InitializeComponent();
            InitializeGrid();
        }
    }
}
```

9. Build and run the solution. The default web browser will appear showing a grid with headers and the five rows defined in the previously added XML file, as shown in the following screenshot:

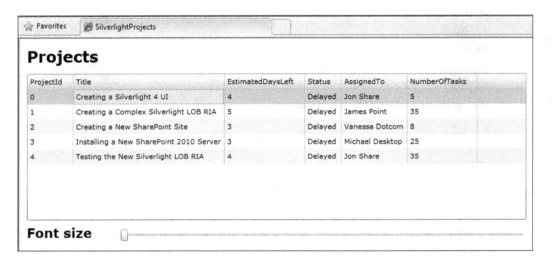

It is a very simple Silverlight LOB RIA displaying a data grid with rows that are read from the XML file included in the project, `Projects.xml`.

First, we added the XML file with the definitions for the five projects. Then, we added a class with the necessary properties to hold the values defined in this XML file.

The `InitializeGrid` method loads the projects from the `Projects.xml` XML file (embedded and compressed in the `.xap` file).

```
XDocument docProjects = XDocument.Load("Projects.xml");
```

Then, it uses a LINQ to XML query to create instances of the `Project` class and assign values to their properties. Finally, it assigns this query to the `ItemsSource` property of the `DataGrid`:

```
dataGridProjects.ItemsSource = projectsData;
```

C# 3.0 (Visual C# 2008) introduced LINQ and it is very useful for processing queries for many different data sources. The features of LINQ and its usage in real-life scenarios are described in depth in *LINQ Quickly (A Practical Guide to Programming Language Integrated Query with C#)* by N. Satheesh Kumar from Packt Publishing.

Creating rich User eXperiences (UX)

We can click on one of the headers and the grid will sort the data in ascending order. Then, we can click again to sort the data into descending order.

When we drag the slider located at the bottom, the font size for the grid will change, as shown in the following screenshot:

Projects	
ProjectId	**Title**
0	Creating a Silverlight 4 UI
1	Creating a Complex Silverlight
2	Creating a New SharePoint Site
3	Installing a New SharePoint 20
4	Testing the New Silverlight LOI

Font size

As previously explained, we can also take advantage of the themes included in Silverlight's Toolkit to offer the user a more exciting UI. Follow these steps to apply a theme to the main `UserControl` for the Silverlight UI:

1. Select **Start | All Programs | Microsoft Silverlight 4 Toolkit | Binaries** and Windows will open the folder that contains the Silverlight Toolkit binaries. By default, they are located at `C:\Program Files (x86)\Microsoft SDKs\Silverlight\v4.0\Toolkit\Apr10\Bin` in 64-bit Windows versions. Its parent folder contains the `Themes` sub-folder, `C:\Program Files (x86)\Microsoft SDKs\Silverlight\v4.0\Toolkit\Apr10\Themes`. In 32-bit Windows versions, the default folders are `C:\Program Files\Microsoft SDKs\Silverlight\v4.0\Toolkit\Apr10\Bin` and `C:\Program Files\Microsoft SDKs\Silverlight\v4.0\Toolkit\Apr10\Themes`.

2. Add a reference to `System.Windows.Controls.Theming.Toolkit.dll`. Remember that it is located in the aforementioned `Bin` sub-folder.

3. Add a reference to the DLL for the desired theme in the `Themes` sub-folder. For example, if you want to apply the `ShinyBlue` theme, add `System.Windows.Controls.Theming.ShinyBlue`, located in the aforementioned `Themes` sub-folder.

4. Add the following line to include the namespace that defines the theme in the `UserControl` defined in `MainPage.xaml`:

```
xmlns:shinyBlue=
    "clr-namespace:System.Windows.Controls.Theming;
    assembly=System.Windows.Controls.Theming.ShinyBlue"
```

5. Add the following line before the definition of the main `Grid`, `LayoutRoot`:

```
<shinyBlue:ShinyBlueTheme>
```

6. Add the following line after the definition of the main `Grid`, `LayoutRoot`:

```
</shinyBlue:ShinyBlueTheme>
```

This way, the `ShinyBlue` theme will be applied to the main `Grid`, `LayoutRoot` and all its child controls. It wasn't necessary to make great changes to offer a more attractive rich user experience. Let's see the revised look in the following screenshot:

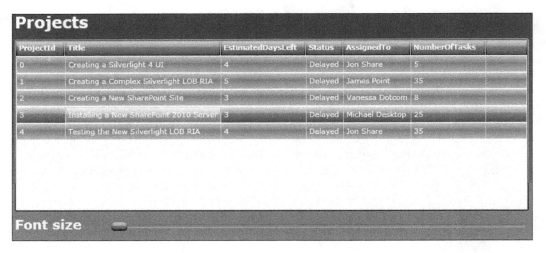

Building a Silverlight 4 RIA

When we build a Silverlight project, Visual Studio or Expression Blend creates many folders with a lot of sub-folders and files.

In this case, we want to add the simple Silverlight RIA to a page in SharePoint 2010. Thus, we are interested in the `SilverlightProjects.xap` file. This is a compressed file, that is, a ZIP file with a `.xap` extension, and it contains all the necessary files for the Silverlight application.

You can find this file in the `Debug` or the `Release` sub-folder, according to your active solution configuration. For example, if the project is located in a `SilverlightProjects` folder, the relative path for the release `SilverlightProjects.xap` file would usually be `...\SilverlightProjects\Bin\Release`. If you want to be sure about the location of the generated `.xap` file, you can follow these steps after building the project:

1. Activate the **Solution Explorer**.

2. Click on the **Show All Files** button, the second button located at the top of the **Solution Explorer** palette. Now, expand the `Bin` folder and then the `Debug` or `Release` sub-folder, according to your active solution configuration, as shown in the following screenshot:

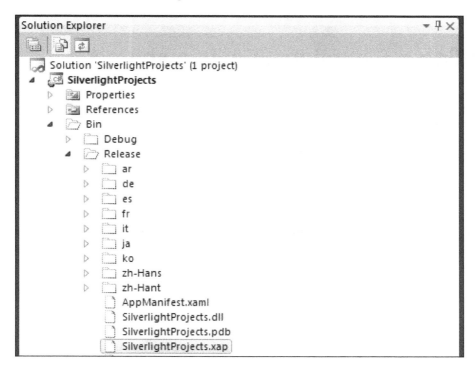

3. Right-click on the `SilverlightProjects.xap` file and, and select **Properties** in the context menu that appears or press *F4*. The **Properties** palette will appear and you will be able to see the value for its **Full Path** property. This way, you can get the exact path for this file, as shown in the next screenshot. You will need it later to integrate it with SharePoint.

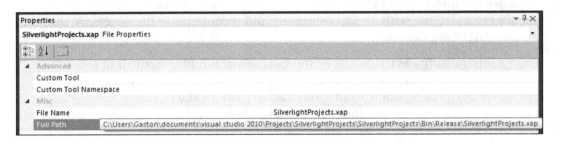

Adding a Silverlight Web Part

We now want to add the Silverlight RIA to a SharePoint site. This Silverlight application doesn't interact with the SharePoint services. It displays information about projects saved in the same `.xap` file.

In this case, we can add a **Silverlight Web Part** to a SharePoint site.

Adding a Silverlight RIA as a shared document

First, follow these steps to add the Silverlight RIA as a shared document in a SharePoint site:

1. Open your default web browser, view the SharePoint site, and log in with your username and password.

2. Click **Site Actions | View All Site Content** and SharePoint will display all sites, lists, and libraries in the active site.

3. Click on **Shared Documents** under **Documents** on the panel located at the left of the Web page. SharePoint will display the shared documents library. These are the documents shared with the team.

4. Click on **Add new document**. The **Upload Document** dialog box will appear. Click on the **Browse...** button and enter the full path for the SilverlightProjects.xap file. Then, click **Open** and the document's name will be the .xap file and its path, as shown in the next screenshot:

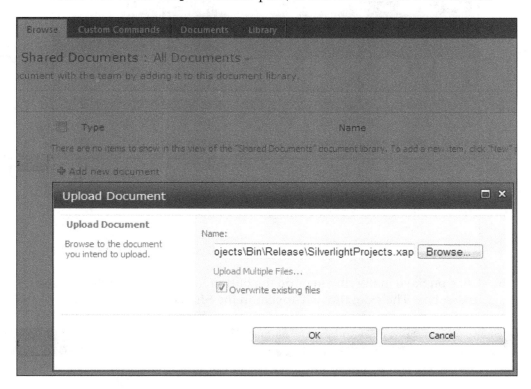

5. Click **OK**. Once the file finishes the upload process, the dialog box to define its properties as a shared document will appear. Enter `Silverlight projects` in **Title** and `Silverlight` in **Managed Keywords**.

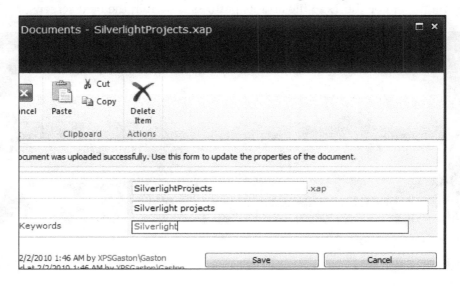

6. Click on **Save** in the ribbon or on the button located at the bottom of the dialog box. The `.xap` file will appear in the **Shared Documents** list.

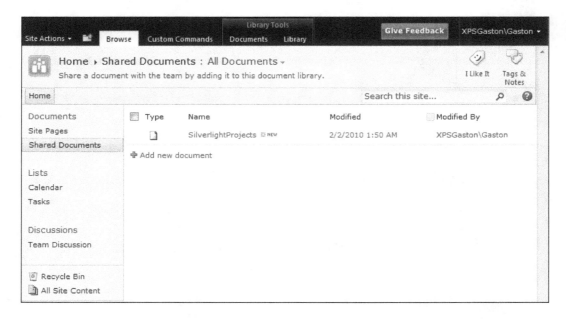

7. Right-click on the new document name, `SilverlightProjects`, and select **Copy Shortcut** from the context menu that appears. This way, you will copy the URL for this shared document in the clipboard and you will be able to paste it when SharePoint asks you for its URL. In this case, the copied URL is `http://xpsgaston/Shared%20Documents/SilverlightProjects.xap`.

Adding a Silverlight Web Part to display a Silverlight RIA

The `.xap` file is available as a shared document. Now, follow these steps to add a Silverlight Web Part to display the Silverlight RIA in a SharePoint site:

1. Click **Site Actions | New Page** and SharePoint will display a new dialog box requesting a name for the new page. Enter `Projects Grid` and click on **Create**. SharePoint will display the **Editing Tools** for the new page.

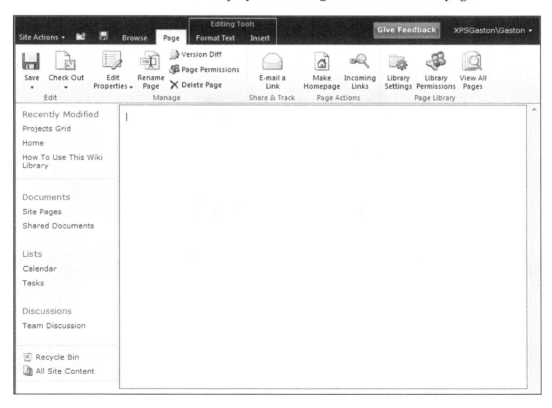

2. Click **Insert | Web Part** in the ribbon and a new panel will appear. Select **Media and Content** in **Categories** and then **Silverlight Web Part** in **Web Parts**, as shown in the following screenshot:

3. Click **Add**. The **Silverlight Web Part** dialog box will appear. Paste the previously copied URL for the shared document, the `.xap` file. In this case, it is `http://xpsgaston/Shared%20Documents/SilverlightProjects.xap`, as shown in the next screenshot:

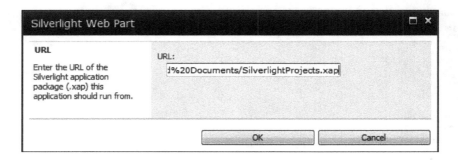

If you don't have the URL for the the .xap file copied to the clipboard, you can open a new tab or a new browser window and access the shared documents as previously explained. Then, you can right-click on the desired document name and select **Copy Shortcut** from the context menu that appears. This way, you will be able to paste the URL in the **Silverlight Web Part** dialog box.

4. Click **OK**.

 In certain SharePoint 2010 pre-release versions, the following error message could appear, **Could not download the Silverlight application or the Silverlight Plugin did not load. To re-configure the Web Part or to provide a different Silverlight application (.xap), open the tool pane and then click Configure.**

5. If the error appears, click on **open the tool pane** or click on the down arrow, located at the top and then select **Edit Web Part**.

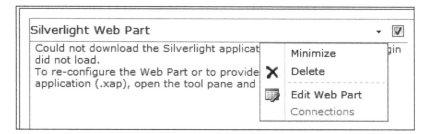

6. The **Silverlight Web Part** pane will appear on the right. It will enable us to define many properties that affect the appearance and behavior for the Silverlight UI.

7. Enter `Projects List Viewer` in **Title**.

8. Click on **Yes** in **Should the Web Part have a fixed height?** and enter `600` in **Pixels**.

9. Click on **Yes** in **Should the Web Part have a fixed width?** and enter `800` in **Pixels**.

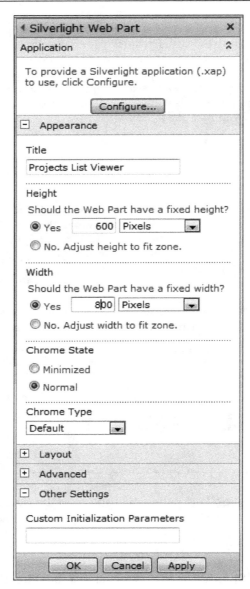

10. Click **OK**. The title for the Web Part will change but the same error message will appear. Don't worry about that.

11. Click on the **Save** button in the ribbon. Now, the new page will appear displaying the previously created Silverlight RIA. However, the title won't appear as expected, as shown in the next screenshot:

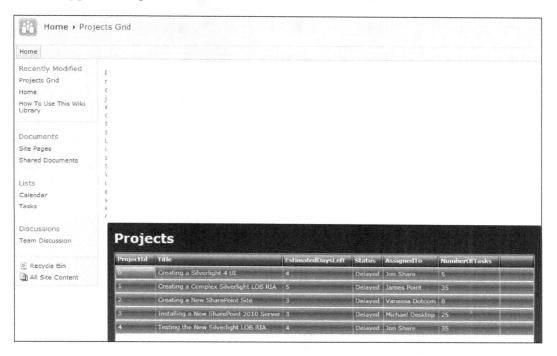

12. Click **Site Actions | Edit Page**. This time, SharePoint will display the Silverlight RIA alive in the editing mode instead of the previously shown error message.

13. Click on the down arrow, located at the top, and then select **Edit Web Part**. The **Silverlight Web Part** pane will appear on the right.

14. Click on **No. Adjust width to fit zone.** in **Should the Web Part have a fixed width?**

15. Click **OK** and then on the **Save** button in the ribbon. Now, the new page will appear displaying the previously created Silverlight RIA with the title appearing as expected.

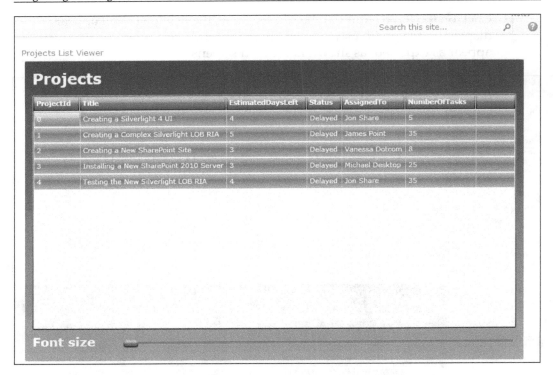

16. The Silverlight Web Part added to the page holds a running and active Silverlight application. Click on one of the grid rows and you will see the gradient animations for the selected theme. Click on a column header and the rows will be sorted according to it.

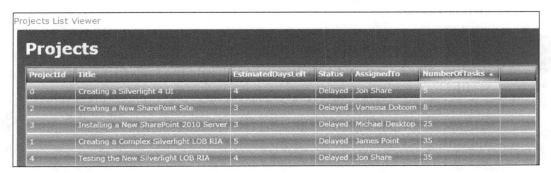

Working with many Silverlight Web Parts in a single page

Following the previously explained steps, we can upload many Silverlight RIAs as shared documents and then add various Silverlight Web Parts to a single page. For example, we can rename the `.xap` file for the previous version of the `SilverlightProjects` application, without the application of the theme, to `SilverlightProjectsNoTheme.xap`. Then, we can follow the necessary steps to edit the page and add it as a new Silverlight Web Part to allow the users to choose between the different looks-and-feels to display the list of active projects.

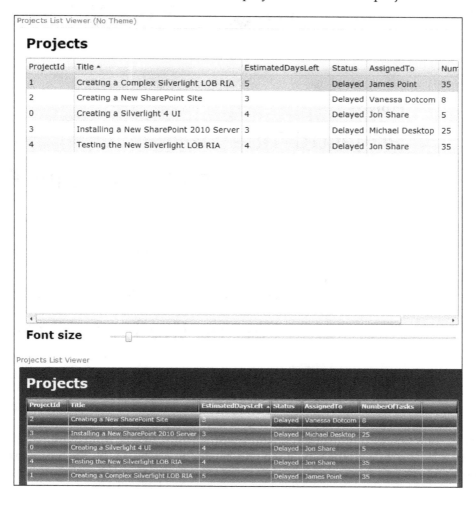

This way, you can make many Silverlight applications available to SharePoint users by following very simple steps. SharePoint 2010 added the new Silverlight Web Part to simplify adding Silverlight applications as part of SharePoint pages.

When the user moves the slider, the font size for the data grid will change, as previously experienced with the Silverlight RIA running in a simple web page. However, this time, the application is running as a Silverlight Web Part in a SharePoint site, as shown. Each Silverlight Web Part offers a very responsive application to the user because they don't have to wait for server responses to refresh the Web Part.

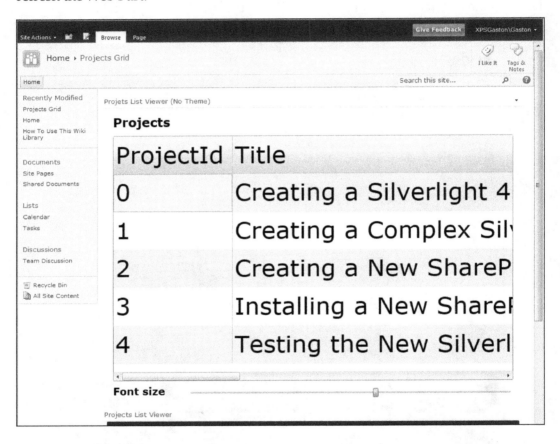

It is easy for a SharePoint user to consume a Silverlight Application. Now, all the users that have access to the new page will be able to interact with the Silverlight UIs added to this page.

It is possible to add Silverlight applications to SharePoint through many different alternatives:

- **As a Silverlight Web Part**
- **Included in a SharePoint Module**
- **Included in a SharePoint Visual Web Part**

The previous steps explained how to work with the first alternative.

Understanding client and server code

As previously explained, when we integrate Silverlight with SharePoint, there is going to be code running on both the client and the server. The Silverlight applications appear on the SharePoint pages. However, once the .xap files are downloaded, their code runs on the client. Each client will require the Silverlight 4 client runtime installed in order to be able to run the application. If it isn't installed, a message will appear indicating that it requires Silverlight.

When you see an animation in a Silverlight RIA, it is consuming processing power found in the client and it is not adding load to the SharePoint server. When you add code to interact with the SharePoint server, the requests consume processing power from the server. However, when the Silverlight application processes the results from a request this code is running on the client.

All the code that presents graphics on the screen runs on the client. When you move the mouse cursor over an element, the animations and the events run on the client. Therefore, you don't add huge processing power from the server when adding Silverlight applications to a SharePoint solution.

Summary

We learned a lot in this chapter about the integration of Silverlight 4 applications with SharePoint 2010 sites and solutions. Specifically, we prepared a development environment and the tools to work with Silverlight 4 RIAs. We configured the SharePoint 2010 server and added Silverlight Web Parts to a new page. We understood the differences between client and server code and the benefits of integrating Silverlight with SharePoint.

We created our first Silverlight RIA and then, we made it available in a SharePoint site. Now, we are ready to begin adding simple Silverlight RIAs as part of SharePoint solutions.

5

Interacting with Rich Media and Animations

 This chapter is taken from *Microsoft Silverlight 4 and SharePoint 2010 Integration* (Chapter 6) by Gastón C. Hillar.

We want to take advantage of Silverlight 4 features to work with rich media and perform animations. In this chapter, we will cover many topics related to retrieving digital assets from SharePoint libraries through the SharePoint Silverlight Client Object Model and consuming them in a Silverlight RIA. We will:

- Create and manage asset libraries in SharePoint 2010
- Access the digital assets in a SharePoint library from a Visual Web Part and a Silverlight RIA
- Create a SharePoint Visual Web Part that sends parameters and renders a Silverlight RIA
- Link a SharePoint Visual Web Part to a Silverlight RIA
- Add a SharePoint Visual Web Part in a web page
- Work with multiple interactive animations and effects
- Display and control videos
- Add background music from the assets library
- Change themes in Silverlight and SharePoint

Bringing life to business applications and complex workflows

So far, we have been able to interact with data from the SharePoint Server through the SharePoint Silverlight Client Object Model and WCF Data Services. Sometimes, we need to share, manage, and consume rich media, related to data.

SharePoint 2010 improves rich media management by introducing asset libraries and we can take advantage of this new feature by consuming it in a Silverlight RIA through the SharePoint Silverlight Client OM. Silverlight 4 offers outstanding features to create amazing User eXperiences (**UX**) when combining rich media with effects and animations.

Creating asset libraries in SharePoint 2010

SharePoint Server 2010 introduced a new asset library specially designed for managing and sharing digital assets and rich media files such as images, audio, and video. It is possible to combine workflows, routing, rules, and policies with asset libraries. However, in this case, we will focus on creating simple asset libraries to allow us to store images, videos, and audio files and we will consume them through the SharePoint Silverlight Client Object Model.

We will combine a new SharePoint Visual Web Part with a Silverlight RIA to allow users to select their desired asset library and to browse its images and videos with interactive animations and dazzling effects. The SharePoint Visual Web Part will display a drop-down list with the available asset libraries that store images, videos, or audio files and when the user selects one of them, the Silverlight RIA will use the capabilities offered by the Client OM to retrieve and display the digital assets. This way, with this new composite Web Part, it is going to be possible to create a new asset library and to upload the necessary images and videos to display, and the desired background music as an audio file. The Web Part will allow a user to interact with any asset library.

First, follow these steps to create two asset libraries in a SharePoint site:

1. Open your default web browser, view the SharePoint site, and log in with your username and password.
2. Click **Site Actions | More Options...** in the ribbon and the **Create** dialog box will appear.

3. Select **Library** under **Filter By:** and then **Asset Library** in **Installed Items**, as shown in the following screenshot:

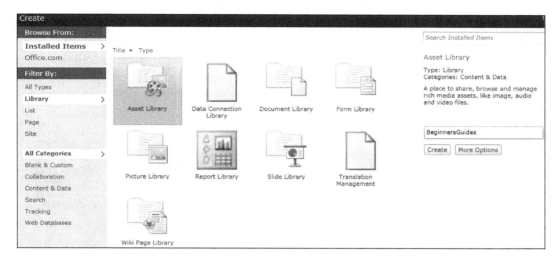

4. Enter `BeginnersGuides` in the **Name** textbox.

5. Click on **More Options**. SharePoint will display a new panel with additional options for the new asset library.

6. Enter `Beginner's Guides` in **Description** and select **Yes** in **Display this list on the Quick Launch?**

7. Click on **Create**; SharePoint will create the new asset library with no digital assets and it will appear in the Quick Launch for the SharePoint site.

8. Now, follow the aforementioned steps (1 to 7) to create another asset library. Use `Cookbooks` as the **Name** and **Description** for this new asset library.

Adding content to an assets library

Follow these steps to prepare and add images, videos, and audio files to the previously created asset libraries.

1. Prepare two folders, BeginnersGuides and Cookbooks. Add many JPG and/ or PNG images to these folders. Add a **WMV (Windows Media Video)** video file and an **MP3** audio file to both folders. The following screenshot shows an example of the contents of the BeginnersGuides folder with 17 JPG images, a WMV video file, and an MP3 audio file:

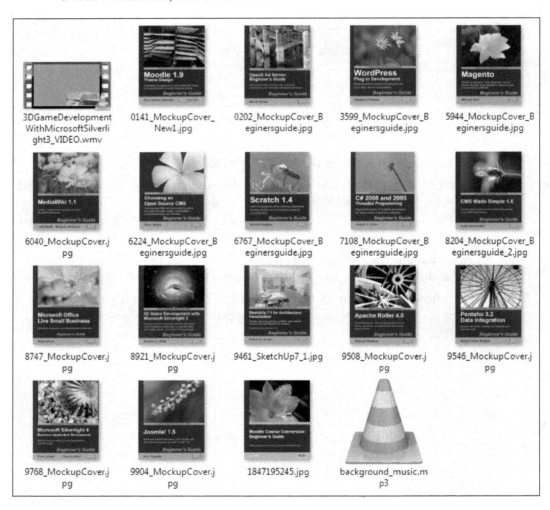

By default, SharePoint 2010 establishes 50 MB as the maximum upload file size setting. This setting specifies the maximum size of a file that a user can upload to the server. If a user tries to upload a file larger than the specified maximum upload size, the upload will fail.

2. Click on the hyperlink for the `BeginnersGuides` asset library in the Quick Launch for the SharePoint site.

3. Click on **Add new item**. The **Upload document** dialog box will appear. Click on **Upload Multiple files...** and a panel to which to drag files and folders will appear.

4. Open an Explorer window and navigate to your `BeginnersGuides` folder. Select all the files within the folder and drag-and-drop them in the **Drag files and folder here** panel within the **Upload Document** dialog box. All the file names will appear in the panel.

5. Click on **OK** and SharePoint will upload all the dropped files to the previously created asset library. Click on **Done** and the new digital assets will appear in the asset library. By default, SharePoint will display a thumbnail preview for the image files:

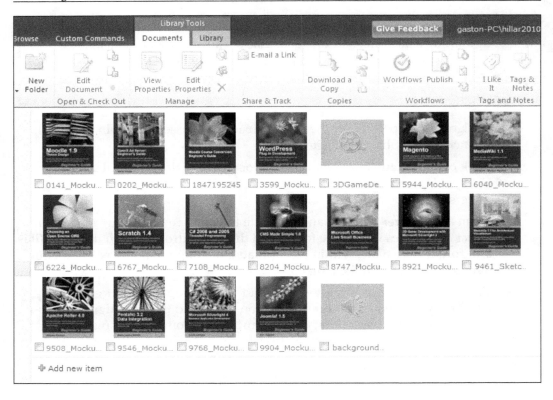

6. Click on one of the thumbnails for the images and a bigger thumbnail will appear with detailed properties for the digital asset:

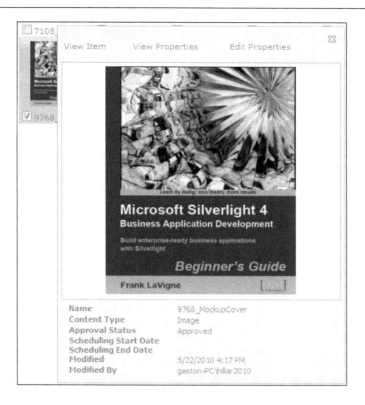

7. Click on **Edit Properties**, located at the top of the bigger thumbnail preview; a new dialog box will appear and you will be able to edit many properties related to the digital asset. The **Content Type** drop-down list will display **Image**, because SharePoint automatically recognized the digital asset as an image. As we uploaded many images dragging and dropping them to the panel, SharePoint assigned the name but it didn't set values for `Title`, `Keywords`, `Comments`, `Author`, and `Copyright`. You can use this dialog box to set the values for these properties in order to organize the contents of the asset library. Then, click on **Save**.

8. Now, follow the aforementioned steps (1 to 7) to add an audio file, images, and videos to the other asset library, Cookbooks. Remember to upload the files stored in the Cookbooks folder.

We added images, videos and audio files to the two asset libraries, BeginnerGuides and Cookbooks, in the SharePoint site. Now, we can browse the asset libraries' structure and then create an interactive Silverlight RIA capable of consuming the uploaded digital assets.

Browsing the structure for SharePoint Asset Libraries

Once we have created the two asset libraries in SharePoint, we can use Server Explorer in Visual Studio to analyze the new asset libraries' structures.

1. Start Visual Studio as a system administrator user.

2. Activate the **Server Explorer** palette by clicking on **View | Server Explorer**.

3. Click on the expand button for **SharePoint Connections** and then on the expand button for the SharePoint server. You will be able to browse its different nodes.

4. Expand **Lists and Libraries** and then **Document Libraries** for the Site Collection in which you created the new asset libraries. Remember that the default Site Collection is **Home**. There are asset libraries and document libraries within **Document Libraries** and therefore, it is going to be necessary to use a smart filter to display the right asset library names in the drop-down list that the user will use to select the desired asset library with pictures, videos, and audio files.

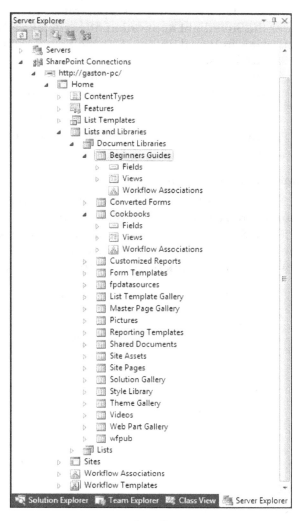

Controlling the rich media library by using controls in a Visual Web Part

This time, we are going to create a new solution in Visual Studio that will include two new projects:

- A SharePoint 2010 Visual Web Part, `SPAssetsBrowserWebPart`
- A Silverlight application project, `SLAssetsBrowser`

SharePoint is built on top of **ASP.NET**, and therefore, a **Visual Web Part** inherits key features from the ASP.NET Web Part architecture. The Visual Web Part will display the available asset libraries with videos, pictures, and/or audio files in a SharePoint site and it will send the selected asset library as a parameter to the Silverlight host control that will render the Silverlight application. We will take advantage of one of the new project templates in Visual Studio 2010, the Visual Web Part project template, which enables us to visually design a Web Part that can be deployed to SharePoint. The necessary steps to display a Silverlight application within the Visual Web Part are a bit complex but the flexibility offered by this combination is worth the effort.

Follow these steps to create the new Visual Web Part that accesses the available asset libraries in a SharePoint site:

1. Stay in Visual Studio as a system administrator user.
2. Select **File | New | Project...**. Expand **Other Project Types** and select **Visual Studio Solutions** under **Installed Templates** in the **New Project** dialog box. Then, select **Blank Solution**, make sure that **.NET Framework 4** version is selected, and enter `AssetsBrowser` as the project's name and click **OK**. Visual Studio will create a blank solution with no projects.

3. Right-click on the solution's name in **Solution Explorer** and select
   Add | New Project... from the context menu. Expand **Visual C#** and
   then expand **SharePoint** and select **2010** under **Installed Templates** in
   the **Add New Project** dialog box. Then, select **Visual Web Part**, enter
   SPAssetsBrowserWebPart as the project's name, and click **OK**. The
   SharePoint Customization Wizard dialog box will appear.

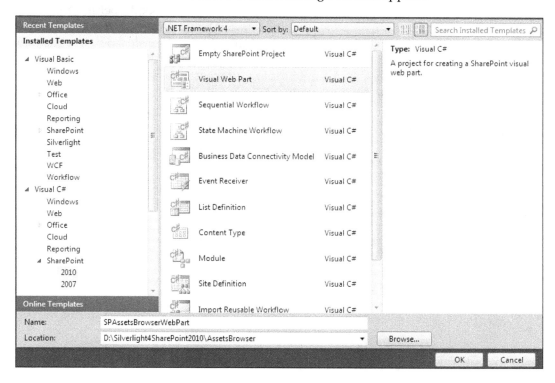

4. Enter the URL for the SharePoint server and site in **What local site do you
   want to use for debugging?**

5. Click on **Deploy as a farm solution**. Sandboxed solutions don't support
   the Visual Web Parts and therefore, it is necessary to deploy projects
   that include them as a **farm solution**. Then, click on **Finish** and the new
   SPAssetsBrowserWebPart empty SharePoint 2010 Visual Web Part project
   will be added to the solution. The code editor will open the source code
   for the VisualWebPart1UserControl.ascx UserControl (System.Web.
   UI.UserControl). This UserControl defines the UI for the Visual Web Part
   and it has a code-behind file, VisualWebPart1UserControl.ascx.cs.

6. Right-click on the VisualWebPart1 folder in **Solution Explorer** and select
   Delete in the context menu. Click **OK** in the confirmation dialog box.

7. Now, right-click on the recently added project's name in **Solution Explorer**, `SPAssetsBrowserWebPart`, and select **Add | New Item...** in the context menu. Expand **Visual C#** and then expand **SharePoint** and then select **2010** under **Installed Templates** in the **New Item** dialog box. Then, select **Visual Web Part**, enter `AssetsBrowserWebPart` in **Name**, and click **OK**. The code editor will open the source code for the `AssetsBrowserWebPart.ascx` UserControl (`System.Web.UI.UserControl`). Its new code-behind file is `AssetsBrowserWebPartUserControl.ascx.cs`. Renaming a Visual Web Part can be a very complex process and therefore, it is easier to delete the default `VisualWebPart1` folder and add a new Visual Web Part item with the desired name. This way, Visual Studio will create the container folder and all its related files with the new name.

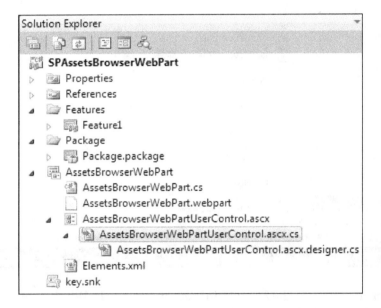

8. Switch to the **Design** view for the `AssetsBrowserWebPart.ascx` UserControl and use the **Toolbox** to drag-and-drop the following server controls. The names for the server controls are assigned in the `ID` property in the **Properties** window.

   ° One `Label` control, `Label1`. Set its `Text` property to `Select the Asset Library` to display.

- ° One `DropDownList` control, `cboDocumentLibraries`. Set
  its `AutoPostBack` property to `true`. This way, the page will
  automatically **post back** to the server after the user changes
  the selection for this drop-down list.

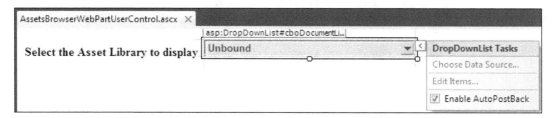

9. Now, open the code-behind file for the `AssetsBrowserWebPart.ascx`
    UserControl, `AssetsBrowserWebPartUserControl.ascx.cs` and add
    the following `using` statements.

    ```
    using Microsoft.SharePoint;
    using Microsoft.SharePoint.WebControls;
    ```

10. Add the following public property for the
    `AssetsBrowserWebPartUserControl` partial class.

    ```
    public string SelectedList { get; private set; }
    ```

11. Add the following lines to the `Page_Load` event. This code will run at the
    server when a user requests the Visual Web Part for the first time and each
    time a postback occurs. Thus, it is necessary to run different code when it
    is a postback by checking the Boolean value of the `IsPostBack` property.
    When the code runs for the first time (`IsPostBack == false`), it will add
    the titles for the lists of `SPBaseType.DocumentLibrary` type with at least one
    item (`libraryList.RootFolder.ItemCount > 0`) and with content types of
    `Picture`, `Image`, `Audio`, or `Video`.

    ```
    if (!IsPostBack)
    {
      var _context = SPContext.Current;
      var documentLibraries =
      _context.Web.GetListsOfType(SPBaseType.DocumentLibrary);
      foreach (SPList libraryList in documentLibraries)
      {
        if ((libraryList.RootFolder.ItemCount > 0) &&
          ((libraryList.ContentTypes[0].Name == "Picture") ||
          (libraryList.ContentTypes[0].Name == "Image") ||
          (libraryList.ContentTypes[0].Name == "Audio") ||
    ```

```
        (libraryList.ContentTypes[0].Name == "Video")))
        {
          // The list has at least 1 element
          cboDocumentLibraries.Items.Add(
          new ListItem(libraryList.Title));
        }
      }
      // Select the first item in the dropdown list
      cboDocumentLibraries.SelectedIndex = 0;
    }
    SelectedList = cboDocumentLibraries.SelectedValue;
```

12. Go back to the **Design** view for `AssetsBrowserWebPartUserControl.ascx` and define a `SelectedIndexChanged` event handler for the `cboDocumentLibraries DropDownList` and add the following code in it. This way, when the user selects a different item in the drop-down list, the `SelectedList` property will hold the name for the new list that has been selected.

```
    SelectedList = cboDocumentLibraries.SelectedValue;
```

13. Now, open the `AssetsBrowserWebPart.cs` code file within the `AssetsBrowserWebPart` folder. This file defines the `AssetsBrowserWebPart` class as a subclass of `WebPart`. Its original code defines a path for the `UserControl`, `AssetsBrowserWebPartUserControl.ascx`, that this `WebPart` subclass will load and add to the `Controls ControlCollection`. This way, the `WebPart` renders the `UserControl`. The following lines show the original code for this file.

```
using System;
using System.ComponentModel;
using System.Web;
using System.Web.UI;
using System.Web.UI.WebControls;
using System.Web.UI.WebControls.WebParts;
using Microsoft.SharePoint;
using Microsoft.SharePoint.WebControls;
namespace SPAssetsBrowserWebPart.AssetsBrowserWebPart
{
    [ToolboxItemAttribute(false)]
    public class AssetsBrowserWebPart : WebPart
    {
        // Visual Studio might automatically update this path when you
        change the Visual Web Part project item.
```

```
    private const string _ascxPath = @"~/_CONTROLTEMPLATES/
SPAssetsBrowserWebPart/AssetsBrowserWebPart/
AssetsBrowserWebPartUserControl.ascx";
        protected override void CreateChildControls()
        {
          Control control = Page.LoadControl(_ascxPath);
          Controls.Add(control);
        }
      }
  }
```

14. Add the following private variable to the `AssetsBrowserWebPart` class. This variable will hold a reference to the `Control` instance cast as `AssetsBrowserWebPartUserControl`. This way, it will be possible to access the value for the `SelectedList` public property to send it as a parameter to the Silverlight host control in the `OnPreRender` method.

```
private AssetsBrowserWebPartUserControl _control;
```

15. Add the following lines in the `CreateChildControls` method to save the reference to the `AssetsBrowserWebPartUserControl` instance.

```
protected override void CreateChildControls()
{
  Control control = Page.LoadControl(_ascxPath);
  Controls.Add(control);
  _control = (control as AssetsBrowserWebPartUserControl);
  base.CreateChildControls();
}
```

16. Override the `OnPreRender` event to add the Silverlight host control that will load and display the Silverlight RIA and it will send the selected asset library title as a parameter. The highlighted lines define the `.xap` file location and the parameter called `Name`.

```
protected override void OnPreRender(EventArgs e)
{
  var name = _control.SelectedList;
  string webUrl = SPContext.Current.Web.Url;
  string renderHost = @"<div id='silverlightControlHost'>
  <object data='data:application/x-silverlight-2,'
type='application/x-silverlight-2' width='100%' height='100%'>
    <param name='source' value='/_catalogs/wp/SLAssetsBrowser.xap'/>
    <param name='background' value='white' />
    <param name='minRuntimeVersion' value='4.0.50303.0' />
```

```
<param name='autoUpgrade' value='true' />
<param name='initParams' value='Name=" + name.Trim() + @"' />
<a href='http://go.microsoft.com/fwlink/?LinkID=149156
&v=4.0.50303.0' style='text-decoration:none'>
<img src='http://go.microsoft.com/fwlink/?LinkId=161376'
alt='Get Microsoft Silverlight' style='border-style:none'/>
</a>
</object><iframe id='_sl_historyFrame' style='visibility:hidden;
height:0px;width:0px;border:0px'></iframe></div>";
LiteralControl host = new LiteralControl(renderHost);
Controls.Add(host);
base.OnPreRender(e);
}
```

The values for the `renderHost` string define a Silverlight control host. You can check the test page generated by Visual Studio for the Silverlight application to find the most up to date definition.

Once you have built your application, click on the **Show All Files** button in **Solution Explorer**. Then, expand the `Bin\Debug` folder for your Silverlight project. You will find many folders and files; open the HTML file that ends with `TestPage.html`, in our example, `SLAssetsBrowserTestPage.html`. You can copy from `<div id="silverlightControlHost">` to `</div>` and you can assign this value to `renderHost` to create a Silverlight host control. However, you have to change the following line that defines the path for the `.xap` file:

```
<param name="source" value="SLAssetsBrowser.xap"/>
```

It has to be replaced with the path for the `.xap` file inside the SharePoint `_catalogs/wp` folder.

```
<param name='source' value='/_catalogs/wp/SLAssetsBrowser.xap'/>
```

In this case, then, it was necessary to add a parameter after the last `param name`, because we want to send a specific value to the Silverlight RIA.

Creating a Silverlight RIA rendered in a SharePoint Visual Web Part

Follow these steps to create the new Silverlight RIA that loads the images, videos, and audio from the asset library selected in the Visual Web Part that renders this application and sends the selected name as a parameter:

1. Stay in Visual Studio as a system administrator user.

2. Select **File | New | Project....** Expand **Visual C#** and select **Silverlight** under **Installed Templates** in the **New Project** dialog box. Then, select **Silverlight Application**, enter SLAssetsBrowser as the project's name, choose **Add to Solution** in the **Solution** drop-down list, and click **OK**.

3. Deactivate the **Host the Silverlight application in a new Web site** checkbox in the **New Silverlight Application** dialog box and select **Silverlight 4** in **Silverlight Version**. Then, click **OK**. Visual Studio will add the new Silverlight application project to the existing solution.

4. Follow the necessary steps to add the following two references to access the SharePoint 2010 Silverlight Client OM:
   ° Microsoft.SharePoint.Client.Silverlight.dll
   ° Microsoft.SharePoint.Client.Silverlight.Runtime.dll

5. Open App.xaml.cs and add the following using statement:

   ```
   using Microsoft.SharePoint.Client;
   ```

6. Replace the code in the StartUp event handler with the following lines. The code stores the value for the Name parameter, specified by the Visual Web Part in the string that creates the Silverlight host control, in the parameterName local variable. Then, it creates a new instance of MainPage sending this value as a parameter to the constructor.

   ```
   private void Application_Startup(object sender, StartupEventArgs e)
   {
       string parameterName = e.InitParams["Name"];

       this.RootVisual = new MainPage(parameterName);
       ApplicationContext.Init(e.InitParams,
         System.Threading.SynchronizationContext.Current);
   }
   ```

7. Select **Start | All Programs | Microsoft Silverlight 4 Toolkit April 2010 | Binaries** and Windows will open the folder that contains the Silverlight Toolkit binaries. By default, they are located at `C:\Program Files (x86)\Microsoft SDKs\Silverlight\v4.0\Toolkit\Apr10\Bin` in 64-bit Windows versions, and at `C:\Program Files\Microsoft SDKs\Silverlight\v4.0\Toolkit\Apr10\Bin` in 32-bit Windows versions.

8. Add a reference to `System.Windows.Controls.Toolkit.dll`. Remember that it is located in the aforementioned `Bin` sub-folder. This way, we will have access to the `WrapPanel` control.

9. Open `MainPage.xaml` and activate the **Toolbox**. Right-click on the **All Sivlerlight Controls** header and select **Choose Items...** in the context menu. The **Choose Toolbox Items** dialog box will appear with the **Silverlight Components** tab activated. Make sure that the checkbox located at the left of the **WrapPanel** item in the **Name** column is checked. This way, the **Toolbox** will display the `WrapPanel` control and you will be able to add it by dragging and dropping it to the desired location within the design view.

10. Define a new width and height for the `Grid`, 800 and 600, and add the following controls. The following lines show the XAML that defines all the controls and some effects for the `lblLibraryName` Label and the `wrapPanel` WrapPanel.

    ○ One `Label` control, `lblLibraryName`, located at the top
    ○ One `ScrollViewer` control, `scrollViewer`
    ○ One `WrapPanel` control, `wrapPanel`, within the `ScrollViewer` control
    ○ One `Label` control, `lblStatus`, located at the bottom
    ○ One `ProgressBar` control, `pgbLoadingStatus`, located at the bottom

```
<UserControl x:Class="SLAssetsBrowser.MainPage"
 xmlns="http://schemas.microsoft.com/winfx/2006/xaml/presentation"
          xmlns:x="http://schemas.microsoft.com/winfx/2006/xaml"
      xmlns:d="http://schemas.microsoft.com/expression/blend/2008"
xmlns:toolkit="http://schemas.microsoft.com/winfx/2006/xaml/
presentation/toolkit"
    xmlns:mc="http://schemas.openxmlformats.org/markup-
compatibility/2006"
   mc:Ignorable="d"
   d:DesignHeight="600" d:DesignWidth="800"  xmlns:sdk="http://
schemas.microsoft.com/winfx/2006/xaml/presentation/sdk">
  <Grid x:Name="LayoutRoot" Loaded="LayoutRoot_Loaded"
Width="Auto" Height="Auto">
  <sdk:Label Height="28" HorizontalAlignment="Left"
Margin="12,12,0,0" Name="lblLibraryName" VerticalAlignment="Top"
Width="776" FontSize="20" FontWeight="Bold" >
    <sdk:Label.Effect>
      <DropShadowEffect ShadowDepth="5" Color="Orange" />
    </sdk:Label.Effect>
  </sdk:Label>
  <ProgressBar Height="22" HorizontalAlignment="Left"
Margin="12,554,0,0" Name="pgbLoadingStatus"
VerticalAlignment="Top" Width="776" />
  <sdk:Label Height="22" HorizontalAlignment="Left"
Margin="12,534,0,0" Name="lblStatus" VerticalAlignment="Top"
Width="776" Content="Status" />
    <ScrollViewer Height="487" HorizontalAlignment="Left"
Margin="12,41,0,0" Name="scrollViewer" VerticalAlignment="Top"
Width="776">
      <toolkit:WrapPanel Name="wrapPanel" Width="Auto"
Height="Auto" RenderTransformOrigin="0.497,0.493">
        <toolkit:WrapPanel.Effect>
          <DropShadowEffect ShadowDepth="10"/>
        </toolkit:WrapPanel.Effect>
      </toolkit:WrapPanel>
    </ScrollViewer>
  </Grid>
</UserControl>
```

11. You can also define the effects in Expression Blend without having to edit the XAML code. You can do so by right-clicking on `MainPage.xaml` and selecting **Open in Expression Blend...** in the context menu. This way, you will be able to work with the additional effects offered by this tool.

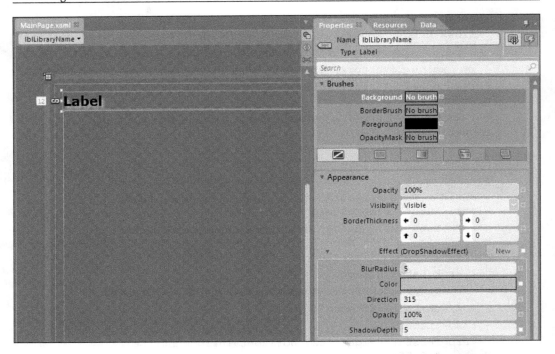

 There are many open source projects that provide additional effects that you can use in your RIAs, such as Silverlight.FX, `http://projects.nikhilk.net/SilverlightFX`.

12. Open `MainPage.xaml.cs`. Now, it is necessary to add a `using` statement to include the `Microsoft.SharePoint.Client` namespace, as we want to work with the SharePoint Silverlight Client OM. We also have to work with the `BitmapImage` class, included in `System.Windows.Media.Imaging`.

Add the following lines of code:

```
using Microsoft.SharePoint.Client;
using SP = Microsoft.SharePoint.Client;
using System.Windows.Media.Imaging;
```

Add the following seven private variables:

```
private ClientContext _context;
private SP.List _documents;
private string _assetLibraryName;
private int _maxImageWidth = 150;
```

```
private int _imageMargin = 5;
// The background music can be added just once
private bool _backgroundMusicAdded = false;
// The current document to load
private int _documentToLoad;
```

13. Replace the `MainPage` constructor with this new constructor that receives the asset library name as a parameter, assigns its value to the `_assetLibraryName` private variable, and displays it in the `lblLibraryName` Label.

```
public MainPage(string assetLibraryName)
{
  InitializeComponent();
  _assetLibraryName = assetLibraryName;
  lblLibraryName.Content = assetLibraryName;
}
```

We are going to work with three media file types, `Audio`, `Video`, and `Picture`. Add the following code to define an enumeration and a method that returns the media file type according to the received file name's extension:

```
private enum MediaFileType
{
  Audio,
  Video,
  Picture
}


private MediaFileType GetMediaFileType(string fileName)
{
  switch (System.IO.Path.GetExtension(fileName).ToUpper())
  {
    // It isn't necessary to add break;
    // after each line because the code
    // exits with the return statement
    case ".JPG":
    return MediaFileType.Picture;
    case ".JPEG":
    return MediaFileType.Picture;
    case ".GIF":
    return MediaFileType.Picture;
```

```
        case ".WMA":
        return MediaFileType.Audio;
        case ".MP3":
        return MediaFileType.Audio;
        case ".AAC":
        return MediaFileType.Audio;
        case ".WMV":
        return MediaFileType.Video;
        case ".MP4":
        return MediaFileType.Video;
        default:
        return MediaFileType.Picture;
    }
}
```

14. Add the following event handlers that will define and start animations when the user right-clicks on a button that displays an image or a video:

```
private void imageButton_MouseRightButtonDown(object sender,
MouseButtonEventArgs e)
{
  // This ensures that Silverlight won't show up
  // the default Silverlight context menu
  e.Handled = true;
  var hlButton = (sender as HyperlinkButton);
  var image = hlButton.Content as Image;
  // Add a doubleAnimation for a MaxWidth animation
  var doubleAnimMaxWidth = new DoubleAnimation();
  doubleAnimMaxWidth.Duration =
    new Duration(TimeSpan.FromSeconds(6));
  doubleAnimMaxWidth.From = image.ActualWidth;
  doubleAnimMaxWidth.To = scrollViewer.ActualWidth -
    (_imageMargin * 2);
  doubleAnimMaxWidth.FillBehavior = FillBehavior.HoldEnd;
  // Create a new Storyboard to handle the MaxWidth animation
  var storyboardMaxWidth = new Storyboard();
  storyboardMaxWidth.Children.Add(doubleAnimMaxWidth);
  Storyboard.SetTarget(doubleAnimMaxWidth, image);
  Storyboard.SetTargetProperty(doubleAnimMaxWidth,
    new PropertyPath("MaxWidth"));
  storyboardMaxWidth.AutoReverse = true;
  storyboardMaxWidth.RepeatBehavior = new RepeatBehavior(1);
  // Add a doubleAnimation for a MaxHeight animation
```

```
var doubleAnimMaxHeight = new DoubleAnimation();
doubleAnimMaxHeight.Duration = new
  Duration(TimeSpan.FromSeconds(6));
doubleAnimMaxHeight.From = image.ActualHeight;
  doubleAnimMaxHeight.To = scrollViewer.ActualHeight -
    (_imageMargin * 2);
doubleAnimMaxHeight.FillBehavior = FillBehavior.HoldEnd;
// Create a new Storyboard to handle the MaxHeight animation
var storyboardMaxHeight = new Storyboard();
storyboardMaxHeight.Children.Add(doubleAnimMaxHeight);
Storyboard.SetTarget(doubleAnimMaxHeight, image);
Storyboard.SetTargetProperty(doubleAnimMaxHeight,
  new PropertyPath("MaxHeight"));
storyboardMaxHeight.AutoReverse = true;
storyboardMaxHeight.RepeatBehavior = new RepeatBehavior(1);
// Start the previously defined storyboards
storyboardMaxWidth.Begin();
storyboardMaxHeight.Begin();
}


private void videoButton_MouseRightButtonDown(object sender,
MouseButtonEventArgs e)
{
  // This ensures that Silverlight won't show up
  // the default Silverlight context menu
  e.Handled = true;
  var hlb = (sender as HyperlinkButton);
  var element = hlb.Content as MediaElement;
  // Add a doubleAnimation for a MaxWidth animation
  var doubleAnimMaxWidth = new DoubleAnimation();
  doubleAnimMaxWidth.Duration = new
    Duration(TimeSpan.FromSeconds(9));
  doubleAnimMaxWidth.From = element.ActualWidth;
  doubleAnimMaxWidth.To = scrollViewer.ActualWidth -
    (_imageMargin * 2);
  doubleAnimMaxWidth.FillBehavior = FillBehavior.HoldEnd;
  // Create a new Storyboard to handle the MaxWidth animation
  var storyboardMaxWidth = new Storyboard();
  storyboardMaxWidth.Children.Add(doubleAnimMaxWidth);
  Storyboard.SetTarget(doubleAnimMaxWidth, element);
```

```
Storyboard.SetTargetProperty(doubleAnimMaxWidth,
    new PropertyPath("MaxWidth"));
storyboardMaxWidth.AutoReverse = true;
storyboardMaxWidth.RepeatBehavior = new RepeatBehavior(1);
// Add a doubleAnimation for a MaxHeight animation
var doubleAnimMaxHeight = new DoubleAnimation();
doubleAnimMaxHeight.Duration = new
    Duration(TimeSpan.FromSeconds(9));
doubleAnimMaxHeight.From = element.ActualHeight;
doubleAnimMaxHeight.To = scrollViewer.ActualHeight -
    (_imageMargin * 2);
doubleAnimMaxHeight.FillBehavior = FillBehavior.HoldEnd;
// Create a new Storyboard to handle the MaxHeight animation
var storyboardMaxHeight = new Storyboard();
storyboardMaxHeight.Children.Add(doubleAnimMaxHeight);
Storyboard.SetTarget(doubleAnimMaxHeight, element);
Storyboard.SetTargetProperty(doubleAnimMaxHeight,
    new PropertyPath("MaxHeight"));
storyboardMaxHeight.AutoReverse = true;
storyboardMaxHeight.RepeatBehavior = new RepeatBehavior(1);
// Start the previously defined storyboards
storyboardMaxWidth.Begin();
storyboardMaxHeight.Begin();
}
```

Add the following event handler that will restart the reproduction of a video after it ends:

```
private void media_MediaEnded(object sender, RoutedEventArgs e)
{
    var media = (sender as MediaElement);
    // It is necessary to stop it or to set its Position to
TimeSpan.Zero
    media.Stop();
    // Play again
    media.Play();
}
```

15. Add the following two methods that add and return a `HyperlinkButton` to the `wrapPanel` WrapPanel with an image and a video:

```
private HyperlinkButton AddImage(string url)
{
    var image = new Image();
```

```
            image.MaxWidth = _maxImageWidth;
            image.Stretch = Stretch.Uniform;
            var bitmapImage = new BitmapImage(new Uri(url,
                UriKind.Absolute));
            image.Source = bitmapImage;
            var imageButton = new HyperlinkButton();
            imageButton.Visibility = System.Windows.Visibility.Collapsed;
            imageButton.Margin = new Thickness(_imageMargin);
            imageButton.Content = image;
            imageButton.NavigateUri = new Uri(url);
            imageButton.MouseRightButtonDown += new
                MouseButtonEventHandler(imageButton_MouseRightButtonDown);
            imageButton.TargetName = "_blank";
            imageButton.Cursor = Cursors.Hand;
            // Add the new Hyperlink button with the image
            // to the WrapPanel wrapPanel
            wrapPanel.Children.Add(imageButton);
            return imageButton;
        }

    private HyperlinkButton AddVideo(string url)
    {
      MediaElement media = new MediaElement();
      media.MaxWidth = (_maxImageWidth * 3);
      media.Stretch = Stretch.UniformToFill;
      media.Source = new Uri(url, UriKind.Absolute);
      media.AutoPlay = true;
      media.MediaEnded += new RoutedEventHandler(media_MediaEnded);
      var videoButton = new HyperlinkButton();
      videoButton.Visibility = System.Windows.Visibility.Collapsed;
      videoButton.Margin = new Thickness(_imageMargin);
      videoButton.Content = media;
      videoButton.NavigateUri = new Uri(url);
      videoButton.MouseRightButtonDown += new
        MouseButtonEventHandler(videoButton_MouseRightButtonDown);
      videoButton.TargetName = "_blank";
      videoButton.Cursor = Cursors.Hand;
      // Add the new Hyperlink button with the video
      // to the WrapPanel wrapPanel
      wrapPanel.Children.Add(videoButton);
      return videoButton;
    }
```

16. Add the following method that defines and starts animations for the `HyperlinkButton` that displays an image or a video received as a parameter:

```
private void AddImageVideoAnimation(HyperlinkButton hlButton)
{
  // Add a projection to the button
  var projection = new PlaneProjection();
  hlButton.Projection = projection;
  // Add a doubleAnimation for a Projection's RotationZ animation
  var doubleAnimProjectionZ = new DoubleAnimation();
  doubleAnimProjectionZ.Duration = new
    Duration(TimeSpan.FromSeconds(5));
  doubleAnimProjectionZ.From = 0.0;
  doubleAnimProjectionZ.To = 360.0;
  doubleAnimProjectionZ.FillBehavior = FillBehavior.HoldEnd;
  // Create a new Storyboard to handle the Projection's RotationZ
animation
  var storyboardProjectionZ = new Storyboard();
  storyboardProjectionZ.Children.Add(doubleAnimProjectionZ);
  Storyboard.SetTarget(doubleAnimProjectionZ, projection);
  Storyboard.SetTargetProperty(doubleAnimProjectionZ,
    new PropertyPath("RotationZ"));
  // Add a doubleAnimation for a Projection's RotationY animation
  var doubleAnimProjectionY = new DoubleAnimation();
  doubleAnimProjectionY.Duration = new
    Duration(TimeSpan.FromSeconds(3));
  doubleAnimProjectionY.From = -45.0;
  doubleAnimProjectionY.To = 45.0;
  doubleAnimProjectionY.FillBehavior = FillBehavior.HoldEnd;
  doubleAnimProjectionY.RepeatBehavior = RepeatBehavior.Forever;
  doubleAnimProjectionY.AutoReverse = true;
  // Create a new Storyboard to handle the Projection's RotationY
animation
  var storyboardProjectionY = new Storyboard();
  storyboardProjectionY.Children.Add(doubleAnimProjectionY);
  Storyboard.SetTarget(doubleAnimProjectionY, projection);
  Storyboard.SetTargetProperty(doubleAnimProjectionY,
    new PropertyPath("RotationY"));
  // Add a doubleAnimation for an Opacity animation
  var doubleAnimOpacity = new DoubleAnimation();
  doubleAnimOpacity.Duration = new
    Duration(TimeSpan.FromSeconds(5));
  doubleAnimOpacity.From = 0.0;
```

```
doubleAnimOpacity.To = 1.0;
doubleAnimOpacity.FillBehavior = FillBehavior.HoldEnd;
// Create a new Storyboard to handle the Opacity animation
var storyboardOpacity = new Storyboard();
storyboardOpacity.Children.Add(doubleAnimOpacity);
Storyboard.SetTarget(doubleAnimOpacity, hlButton);
Storyboard.SetTargetProperty(doubleAnimOpacity,
  new PropertyPath("Opacity"));
// Start the previously defined storyboards
storyboardProjectionZ.Begin();
storyboardOpacity.Begin();
storyboardProjectionY.Begin();
hlButton.Visibility = System.Windows.Visibility.Visible;
}
```

17. Add the following method that plays an audio file as background music for the application. It will just play background music once, no matter the number of times it is called.

```
private void AddBackgroundMusic(string url)
{
  if (_backgroundMusicAdded)
  {
    // Background music already loaded
    return;
  }
  _backgroundMusicAdded = true;
  MediaElement backgroundMusic = new MediaElement();
  LayoutRoot.Children.Add(backgroundMusic);
  backgroundMusic.Volume = 0.8;
  backgroundMusic.Source = new Uri(url);
  backgroundMusic.Play();
}
```

18. Now, it is necessary to add code to connect to the SharePoint server, connect to the lists, retrieve data from the assets library name stored in _assetLibraryName, request its files, and process each picture, video, and audio file to add it to the wrapPanel WrapPanel. These methods will run in the UI thread. Replace "http://gaston-pc" with the SharePoint website's URL.

```
private void Connect()
{
  // Runs in the UI Thread
```

```
  lblStatus.Content = "Started";
  // Replace http://gaston-pc with
  // your SharePoint 2010 Server URL and Site
  _context = new SP.ClientContext(new Uri("http://gaston-pc",
UriKind.Absolute));
  _context.Load(_context.Web);
  _context.ExecuteQueryAsync(OnConnectSucceeded, null);
}


private void ConnectLists()
{
  // Runs in the UI Thread
  lblStatus.Content = "Web Connected. Connecting to Lists...";
  _context.Load(_context.Web.Lists);
  _context.ExecuteQueryAsync(OnConnectListsSucceeded, null);
}

private void GetListData()
{
  // Runs in the UI Thread
  lblStatus.Content = "Lists Connected. Getting List data...";
  _documents = _context.Web.Lists.GetByTitle(_assetLibraryName);
  _context.Load(_documents);
  _context.Load(_documents.RootFolder);
  // Request the files
  _context.Load(_documents.RootFolder.Files);
  _context.ExecuteQueryAsync(OnGetListDataSucceeded, null);
}


private void LoadItems()
{
  // Runs in the UI Thread
  lblStatus.Content = String.Format("Loading {0} items...",
    _documents.RootFolder.Files.Count);
  pgbLoadingStatus.Maximum = _documents.RootFolder.Files.Count;
  pgbLoadingStatus.Value = 0;
  _documentToLoad = 0;
  // Clear the WrapPanel children
  wrapPanel.Children.Clear();
  foreach (File file in _documents.RootFolder.Files)
  {
```

```
    _context.Load(file);
    _context.ExecuteQueryAsync(
    OnLoadItemsSucceeded,
    OnLoadItemsFailed);
  }
}


private void ShowItem()
{
  // Runs in the UI Thread
  lblStatus.Content = String.Format("Processing item # {0}",
    _documentToLoad);
  string fileName =
  _documents.RootFolder.Files[_documentToLoad].Name;
  string Url = _context.Url + _documents.RootFolder.Files
    [_documentToLoad].ServerRelativeUrl;
  switch (GetMediaFileType(fileName))
  {
    case MediaFileType.Audio:
    AddBackgroundMusic(Url);
    break;
    case MediaFileType.Picture:
    var imageButton = AddImage(Url);
    AddImageVideoAnimation(imageButton);
    break;
    case MediaFileType.Video:
    var videoButton = AddVideo(Url);
    AddImageVideoAnimation(videoButton);
    break;
  }
  // Update the progress bar
  pgbLoadingStatus.Value++;
  _documentToLoad++;
  if (_documentToLoad >= _documents.RootFolder.Files.Count)
  {
    // All documents loaded
    lblStatus.Content = "Displaying animations for all the
documents.";
  }
}
```

19. Most of the methods added in the previous step execute asynchronous queries to the SharePoint server. Both the successful and failed requests fire asynchronous callbacks that are going to run in another thread, different from the UI thread. Hence, if you have to update the UI, it is necessary to invoke the code to run in the UI thread. The following methods, which are going to be fired as asynchronous callbacks, schedule the execution of other methods to continue with the necessary program flow in the UI thread:

```
private void ShowErrorInformation(ClientRequestFailedEventArgs
args)
{
  MessageBox.Show("Request failed. " + args.Message + "\n" +
    args.StackTrace + "\n" +
  args.ErrorDetails + "\n" + args.ErrorValue);
}

private void OnConnectSucceeded(Object sender,
  SP.ClientRequestSucceededEventArgs args)
{
  // This callback isn't called on the UI thread
  Dispatcher.BeginInvoke(ConnectLists);
}

private void OnConnectListsSucceeded(Object sender, SP.ClientReque
stSucceededEventArgs args)
{
  // This callback isn't called on the UI thread
  Dispatcher.BeginInvoke(GetListData);
}

private void OnGetListDataSucceeded(Object sender, SP.ClientReques
tSucceededEventArgs args)
{
  // This callback isn't called on the UI thread
  Dispatcher.BeginInvoke(LoadItems);
}

private void OnLoadItemsFailed(Object sender,
SP.ClientRequestFailedEventArgs args)
{
  // This callback isn't called on the UI thread
  // Invoke a delegate and send the args instance as a parameter
  Dispatcher.BeginInvoke(() => ShowErrorInformation(args));
}
```

```
private void OnLoadItemsSucceeded(Object sender, SP.ClientRequestS
ucceededEventArgs args)
{
  // This callback isn't called on the UI thread
  Dispatcher.BeginInvoke(ShowItem);
}
```

20. Add the following line to the `LayoutRoot_Loaded` event:

    ```
    Connect();
    ```

We created a new Silverlight RIA that receives an asset library name as a parameter from the Visual Web Part that renders this application. When the user selects an asset library from a drop-down list in the Visual Web Part, the Silverlight RIA will load the images, videos, and audio from the chosen asset library. We added the necessary code to create an application that displays the images and videos with many animations and effects.

Linking a SharePoint Visual Web Part to a Silverlight RIA

Follow these steps to link the previously created Visual Web Part, `AssetsBrowserWebPart`, with this new Silverlight RIA, `SLAssetsBrowser`. This way, the Silverlight RIA will be part of the package that contains the Visual Web Part.

1. Stay in Visual Studio as a system administrator user.

2. Expand the SharePoint Visual Web Part folder, `AssetsBrowserWebPart`, in the **Solution Explorer**.

3. Now, right-click on `AssetsBrowserWebPart` and select **Properties** in the context menu that appears. You will see the values for its properties in the **Properties** panel.

4.. In the **Properties** palette, click the ellipsis (**...**) button for the **Project Output References** property. The **Project Output References** dialog box will appear.

5. Click on **Add** below the **Members:** list. The SharePoint 2010 Visual Web Part's project name, `SPAssetsBrowserWebPart`, will appear as a new member.

6. Go to its properties, shown on the list located at the right. Select the Silverlight application project's name, `SLAssetsBrowser`, in the **Project Name** drop-down list.

7. Select Element File in the **Deployment Type** drop-down list. The following value will appear in **Deployment Location**, {SharePointRoot}\Template\ Features\{FeatureName}\AssetsBrowserWebPart\. The following screenshot shows the dialog box with the explained values:

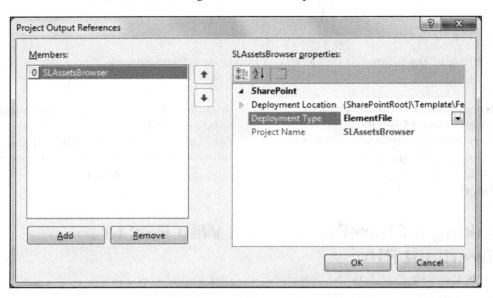

8. Click **OK**. The SharePoint Visual Web Part project now includes a reference to the Silverlight application project, SLTasksViewer. However, it is still necessary to add a line to the Elements.xml file to make the Silverlight RIA be part of the Visual Web Part.

9. Open the Elements.xml file. The following lines are the initial contents of this XML file. They describe the elements that compose this SharePoint 2010 Visual Web Part.

```
<?xml version="1.0" encoding="utf-8"?>
<Elements xmlns="http://schemas.microsoft.com/sharepoint/" >
  <Module Name="AssetsBrowserWebPart" List="113"
    Url="_catalogs/wp">
    <File Path="AssetsBrowserWebPart\AssetsBrowserWebPart.webpart"
Url="AssetsBrowserWebPart.webpart" Type="GhostableInLibrary" >
      <Property Name="Group" Value="Custom" />
    </File>
  </Module>
</Elements>
```

10. Add the highlighted line before `</Module>`. The new contents of this XML file will include a reference to the linked Silverlight project `.xap` file, `SLAssetsBrowser.xap`. This is a new element for this SharePoint 2010 Visual Web Part. During the deployment process, the `SLAssetsBrowser.xap` file will be located in the `AssetsBrowserWebPart` folder in the **SharePoint package file**, also known as the **WSP package**, because it has a `.wsp` extension. Thus, the WSP package will also deploy the Silverlight application to the SharePoint server.

```
<?xml version="1.0" encoding="utf-8"?>
<Elements xmlns="http://schemas.microsoft.com/sharepoint/" >
  <Module Name="AssetsBrowserWebPart" List="113" Url="_catalogs/
wp">
    <File Path="AssetsBrowserWebPart\AssetsBrowserWebPart.webpart"
Url="AssetsBrowserWebPart.webpart" Type="GhostableInLibrary" >
      <Property Name="Group" Value="Custom" />
    </File>
    <!-- Added -->
    <File Path="AssetsBrowserWebPart\SLAssetsBrowser.xap"
      Url="SLAssetsBrowser.xap" />
    <!-- EOF Added -->
  </Module>
</Elements>
```

11. Remember to enable Silverlight debugging instead of the default script debugging capabilities.

12. Right-click on the solution's name in **Solution Explorer** and select **Properties** from the context menu that appears. Select **Startup Project** in the list on the left, activate **Single startup project**, and choose the SharePoint Visual Web Part project's name in the drop-down list below it, `SPAssetsBrowserWebPart`. This way, the solution is going to start with the SharePoint project and not with the Silverlight application. This is very important because it will allow us to debug the Silverlight application when it runs in a SharePoint site. Then, click **OK**.

13. Expand **Features | Feature1** in Solution Explorer and double-click on `Feature1.feature`. Visual Studio will display a new panel with the feature title, description, scope, and its items. The feature will include three files in the **Items in the feature** list, `AssetsBrowserWebPart`, `AssetsBrowsersWebPartUserControl.ascx` and `Elements.xml`.

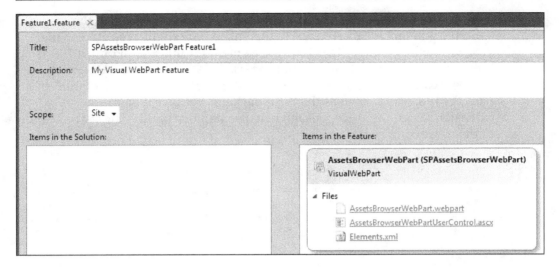

14. Build and deploy the solution.

Adding a SharePoint Visual Web Part in a Web Page

Now that the WSP package has been deployed to the SharePoint site, follow these steps to create a new web page and add the Visual Web Part that includes and renders the Silverlight RIA. In this case, it isn't necessary to upload the .xap file, because it was already deployed with the WSP package.

1. Open your default web browser, view the SharePoint site, and log in with your username and password.

2. Click **Site Actions | New Page** and SharePoint will display a new dialog box requesting a name for the new page. Enter AssetsBrowser and click on **Create**. SharePoint will display the editing tools for the new page.

3. Click **Insert | Web Part** in the ribbon and a new panel will appear. Select **Custom** in **Categories** and then the previously deployed Visual Web Part name, AssetsBrowserWebPart, in **Web Parts**.

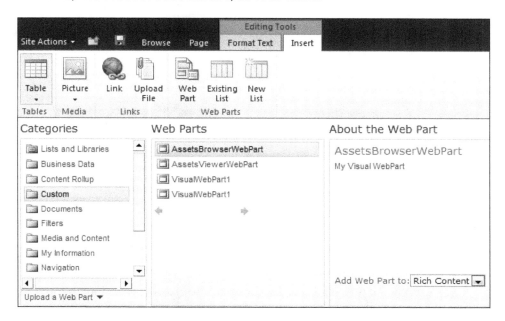

4. Click **Add**. The **Select the Asset Library to display** legend and the drop-down list will appear. Click on the down arrow, located at the top, and then select **Edit Web Part**. The **AssetsBrowserWebPart** pane will appear at the right. It will enable us to define many properties that affect the appearance and behavior for this Visual Web Part that renders a Silverlight RIA.

5. Enter Assets Browser in **Title**.

6. Click on **Yes** in **Should the Web Part have a fixed height?** and enter 700 in **Pixels**.

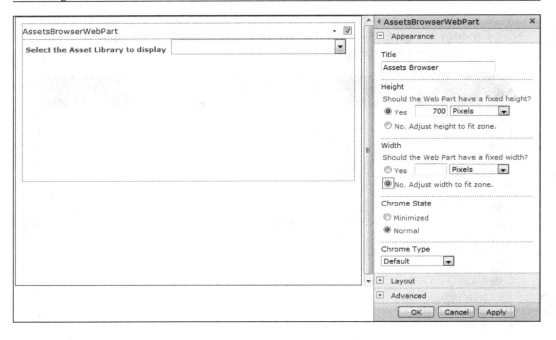

7. Click on **No. Adjust width to fit zone.** in **Should the Web Part have a fixed width?**, and then on **OK**.

8. Click on the **Save** button in the ribbon. Now, the new page will appear displaying the previously created Visual Web Part. This Web Part is going to display the drop-down list of asset libraries with pictures, videos, and audio files. The Silverlight RIA will appear below the drop-down list displaying the images and videos found in the first asset library in the drop-down list with interactive animations and dazzling effects. It is going to load and then it will display its different status values in the label located at the bottom:

   ° **Started**

   ° **Web Connected. Connecting to Lists...**

   ° **Lists Connected. Getting List data...**

   ° **Loading n items...**

   ° **Processing item #x...**, where x is the number of picture, video or audio file being processed

   ° **Displaying animations for all the documents. (this should be Bullet end)**

The following screenshot shows this value for the label and the Silverlight RIA displaying the images and videos for the chosen asset library.

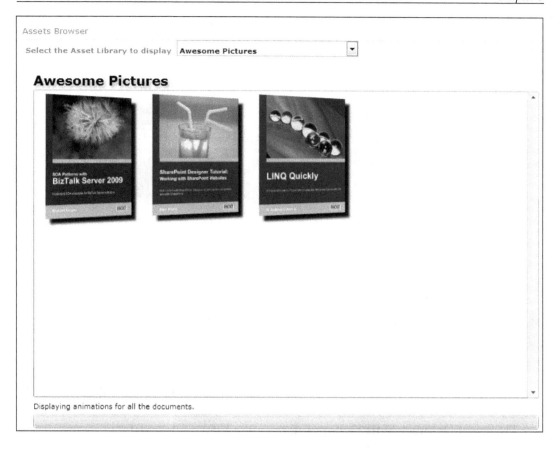

9. Now, go back to Visual Studio and open the code-behind
   file for `AssetsBrowserWebPartUserControl.ascx`,
   `AssetsBrowserWebPartUserControl.ascx.cs`. Insert a breakpoint in
   the first line of the `Page_Load` event handler, `if (!IsPostBack)`. Insert
   another breakpoint in the line of code of the `cboDocumentLibraries_
   SelectedIndexChanged` event handler, `SelectedList =
   cboDocumentLibraries.SelectedValue;`.

```
protected void Page_Load(object sender, EventArgs e)
{
    if (!IsPostBack)
    {
        var _context = SPContext.Current;
        var documentLibraries = _context.Web.GetListsOfType(SPBaseType.DocumentLibrary);
        foreach (SPList libraryList in documentLibraries)
        {
            if ((libraryList.RootFolder.ItemCount > 0) &&
                ((libraryList.ContentTypes[0].Name == "Picture") ||
                 (libraryList.ContentTypes[0].Name == "Image") ||
                 (libraryList.ContentTypes[0].Name == "Audio") ||
                 (libraryList.ContentTypes[0].Name == "Video")))
            {
                // The list has at least 1 element
                cboDocumentLibraries.Items.Add(new ListItem(libraryList.Title));
            }
        }
        // Select the first item in the dropdown list
        cboDocumentLibraries.SelectedIndex = 0;
    }
    SelectedList = cboDocumentLibraries.SelectedValue;
}

protected void cboDocumentLibraries_SelectedIndexChanged(object sender, EventArgs e)
{
    SelectedList = cboDocumentLibraries.SelectedValue;
}
```

10. Open `AssetsBrowserWebPart.cs` and insert a breakpoint in the first line of the `OnPreRender` event handler.

11. Select **Debug | Start Debugging** from the Visual Studio's main menu or press *F5* to start debugging the solution.

12. Visual Studio will display a new window for your default web browser with the server and Site Collection in which you deployed the WSP package.

13. Enter the URL for the previously added page that contains the Visual Web Part in the Web browser. This way, the ASP.NET code for the Visual Web Part will start running and Visual Studio will stop in the breakpoint established in the `Page_Load` event handler in the code-behind file, `AssetsBrowserWebPartUserControl.ascx.cs`.

14. Inspect the value for `IsPostBack` and it will be `false`, because it is the first time that the Visual Web Part is rendered. Thus, the method will run the code to add the titles of the document libraries that have pictures, images, audio, or video files. The first item for the `cboDocumentLibraries` DropDownList will be selected as the default library and the `SelectedList` property is going to save the selected title. Run the code step-by-step to understand the execution flow.

15. Then, Visual Studio will stop in the breakpoint established in the OnPreRender event handler, in AssetsBrowserWebPart.cs. The renderHost string will include a line that defines the value for the Name parameter. This parameter will specify a string with the value stored in the SelectedList public property. In this method, the code defines a new LiteralControl instance initialized with the renderHost string and adds it to the Controls ControlCollection.

16. Press *F5* and the Web browser will display the Silverlight RIA with the first asset library contents.

17. Now, select a different asset library to display in the drop-down list located at the top of the Visual Web Part. This way, the ASP.NET code for the Visual Web Part will start running again, performing a postback, and Visual Studio will stop in the breakpoint established in the Page_Load event handler in the code-behind file, AssetsBrowserWebPartUserControl.ascx.cs.

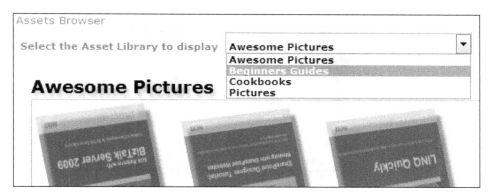

18. Inspect the value for IsPostBack and it will be true because it is a postback for the UserControl. Thus, the method won't run the code to add the titles of the document libraries to the drop-down list. It will just run the line that sets the SelectedList property to the selected title. Run the code step-by-step to understand the execution flow.

19. Then, Visual Studio will stop in the breakpoint established in the OnPreRender event handler, in AssetsBrowserWebPart.cs. The renderHost string will include a line that defines the new value for the Name parameter, held in the previously explained SelectedList public property. This way, the new LiteralControl instance will add a Silverlight RIA with a different parameter value.

20. Press *F5* and the Web browser will display the Silverlight RIA with the new asset library contents. The images and the videos will appear with animations and effects.

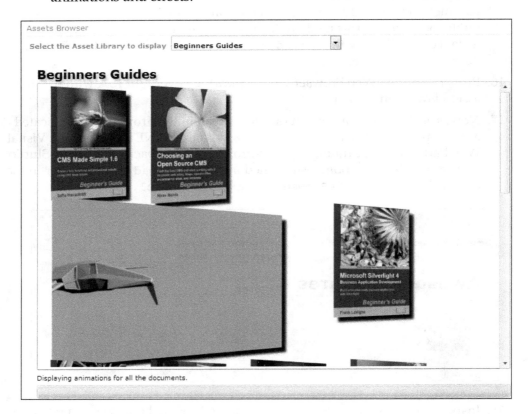

We added the SharePoint Visual Web Part to a new Web page in the SharePoint Site Collection. Then, we used Visual Studio to debug the Visual Web Part and we learned how Visual Web Parts renders a Silverlight RIA with parameters. We inserted many breakpoints to analyze the postback performed by the UserControl within the Visual Web Part.

Organizing controls in a containing box

The Silverlight RIA displays a WrapPanel control, wrapPanel, within a ScrollViewer, scrollViewer. The WrapPanel control works as a container and it locates its child elements in sequential positions from left to right, in columns, when its Orientation property is set to Horizontal. At the edge of the containing box, it breaks the content to the next row and therefore, it simplifies the organization of HyperlinkButton controls.

As we don't know the number of rows that will be necessary to display all the pictures and videos in the `WrapPanel` control, the `ScrollViewer` control defines a scrollable viewport. When the content of the `WrapPanel` is not entirely visible, the `ScrollViewer` will display scrollbars to allow the user to move the content area that is visible. The visible content is known as, **viewport** and all of the content included in the `ScrollViewer` is known as the **extent**.

The XAML markup in `MainPage.xaml` defines a `DropShadowEffect` for the `WrapPanel` control, with its `ShadowDepth` property set to 10. This way, all the `HyperlinkButton` controls added as `wrapPanel`'s children will inherit this effect and will drop a shadow with a depth of 10 pixels.

```
<ScrollViewer Height="487" HorizontalAlignment="Left"
Margin="12,41,0,0" Name="scrollViewer" VerticalAlignment="Top"
Width="776">
   <toolkit:WrapPanel Name="wrapPanel" Width="Auto" Height="Auto"
RenderTransformOrigin="0.497,0.493">
      <toolkit:WrapPanel.Effect>
        <DropShadowEffect ShadowDepth="10"/>
      </toolkit:WrapPanel.Effect>
   </toolkit:WrapPanel>
</ScrollViewer>
```

Reading files from an assets library

The `GetListData` method requests the asset library, a special list, specified in `_assetLibraryName`, and loads it, its `RootFolder` `Folder`, and its `RootFolder.Files` `FileCollection`.

```
_documents = _context.Web.Lists.GetByTitle(_assetLibraryName);
_context.Load(_documents);
_context.Load(_documents.RootFolder);
_context.Load(_documents.RootFolder.Files);
```

After the successful asynchronous execution of the queries, the `LoadItems` method clears the children for the `wrapPanel` `WrapPanel`. Then, it runs an asynchronous query to load each `File` in the asset library, `_documents`, `RootFolder.Files` `FileCollection`.

```
wrapPanel.Children.Clear();
foreach (File file in _documents.RootFolder.Files)
{
  _context.Load(file);
  _context.ExecuteQueryAsync(
          OnLoadItemsSucceeded,
            OnLoadItemsFailed);
}
```

Each successful asynchronous query will schedule the ShowItem method to run in the UI thread. The first time this method is called, _documentToLoad is set to 0 and the code in this method will increment _documentToLoad each time it finishes processing a file. The method retrieves the file name, stored in the Name property for the File instance to determine the media file type and saves it in the local fileName string. Then, it computes an absolute Url to access the file, _context.Url concatenated with the ServerRelativeUrl property for the File instance, and saves it in the local Url string.

```
string fileName = _documents.RootFolder.Files[_documentToLoad].Name;
string Url = _context.Url + _documents.RootFolder.Files[_documentToLoad].ServerRelativeUrl;
```

Working with interactive animations and effects

A switch statement considers the results of the GetMediaFileType method that receives the fileName string as a parameter. As previously explained this method determines the media file type according to the extension and returns a MediaFileType as a result.

If the file type is MediaFileType.Picture, the method calls the AddImage method with the Url string as a parameter and it saves the HyperlinkButton instance returned by this method in imageButton. Then, it calls the AddImageVideoAnimation with imageButton as a parameter.

```
case MediaFileType.Picture:
  var imageButton = AddImage(Url);
  AddImageVideoAnimation(imageButton);
    break;
```

The AddImage method creates a new Image instance, sets values for its MaxWidth and Stretch properties, creates a BitmapImage, bitmapImage, with the absolute Uri from the URL received as a parameter, url, and assigns bitmapImage to the image.Source property.

```
var image = new Image();
image.MaxWidth = _maxImageWidth;
image.Stretch = Stretch.Uniform;
var bitmapImage = new BitmapImage(new Uri(url, UriKind.Absolute));
image.Source = bitmapImage;
```

Then, the code creates a new invisible `HyperlinkButton`, imageButton, and sets its `Content` property to the previously created `Image` instance, image. When imageButton becomes visible, it will show the bitmap image. The `NavigateUri` property for imageButton is set to a new `Uri` from the URL received as a parameter, url. The `TargetName` property is set to `_blank`, and therefore, when the user clicks the `HyperlinkButton`, the Web browser will open a new window and will display the image from the URL.

The code attaches an event handler to the `MouseRightButtonDown` event that occurs when the user clicks the right mouse button and the mouse pointer is over the `Hyperlinkbutton`. It assigns a new `MouseButtonEventHandler` that will fire the `imageButton_MouseRightButtonDown` method. This method runs an animation for the `Hyperlinkbutton`.

```
var imageButton = new HyperlinkButton();
imageButton.Visibility = System.Windows.Visibility.Collapsed;
imageButton.Margin = new Thickness(_imageMargin);
imageButton.Content = image;
imageButton.NavigateUri = new Uri(url);
imageButton.MouseRightButtonDown += new MouseButtonEventHandler(imageB
utton_MouseRightButtonDown);
imageButton.TargetName = "_blank";
imageButton.Cursor = Cursors.Hand;
```

Finally, it is necessary to add the `HyperlinkButton` as a child to the `wrapPanel` `WrapPanel` and return the instance. As previously explained, `wrapPanel` will take care of organizing the layout of all the `HyperlinkButton` instances added as children.

```
wrapPanel.Children.Add(imageButton);
return imageButton;
```

At this point, the `HyperlinkButton` is invisible, because its `Visibility` property was set to `System.Windows.Visibility.Collapsed`. However, when the `AddImage` method returns, the `AddImageVideoAnimation` receives the `HyperlinkButton` control as a parameter, hlButton, and brings life to the image that it displays.

Firstly, it adds a `PlaneProjection` instance to the `HyperlinkButton`, hlButton, by setting its `Projection` property to a new `PlaneProjection` instance, projection. `PlaneProjection` is a subclass of the `Projection` class. The latter allows describing how to project a 2D object in the 3D space by using perspective transforms. Then, the code will run an animation with the values that define the perspective transform for hlButton.

```
var projection = new PlaneProjection();
hlButton.Projection = projection;
```

The `RotationX`, `RotationY`, and `RotationZ` properties for a `PlaneProjection` instance specify the number of degrees to rotate the `HyperlinkButton` in the space. The `LocalOffsetX` and `LocalOffsetY` properties specify the distance the `HyperlinkButton` is translated along each axis of the `HyperlinkButton`'s plane.

Then, the code defines three `DoubleAnimation` (`System.Windows.Media. Animation.DolubleAnimation`) instances and adds them as children of their corresponding `Storyboard` (`System.Windows.Media.Animation.Storyboard`) instances. A `DoubleAnimation` instance allows us to animate the value of a `Double` property between two target values specified by their `From` and `To` properties. It uses a linear interpolation over a specified duration, specified by the `Duration` property. Each `Storyboard` instance defines a container timeline that provides object and property targeting information for its child `DoubleAnimation` instance. The code creates the `DoubleAnimation` and `Storyboard` instances summarized in the following table:

DoubleAnimation instance	Storyboard instance	Animates	From	To	Duration (seconds)
doubleAnim ProjectionZ	storyboard ProjectionZ	projection. RotationZ	0.0	360.0	5
doubleAnim ProjectionY	storyboard ProjectionY	projection. RotationY	45.0	45.0	3
doubleAnim Opacity	storyboard Opacity	hlButton. Opacity	0.0	1.0	5

The following lines create the `doubleAnimProjectionZ DoubleAnimation` and set its properties. The `FillBehavior` property is set to `FillBehavior.HoldEnd` to specify that the animation must hold its value after it reaches the end of its active period. This way, the target property for this animation will remain at its end value after the animation ends and it won't revert to its non-animated value.

```
var doubleAnimProjectionZ = new DoubleAnimation();
doubleAnimProjectionZ.Duration = new Duration(TimeSpan.
FromSeconds(5));
doubleAnimProjectionZ.From = 0.0;
doubleAnimProjectionZ.To = 360.0;
doubleAnimProjectionZ.FillBehavior = FillBehavior.HoldEnd;
```

The next lines create the `Storyboard` instance and add `doubleAnimProjectionZ` as a child. Then, it is necessary to set the target object and the target property by calling the static methods `Storyboard.SetTarget` and `Storyboard.SetTargetProperty` with `doubleAnimProjectionZ` as its first parameter.

```
var storyboardProjectionZ = new Storyboard();
storyboardProjectionZ.Children.Add(doubleAnimProjectionZ);
Storyboard.SetTarget(doubleAnimProjectionZ, projection);
Storyboard.SetTargetProperty(doubleAnimProjectionZ, new
PropertyPath("RotationZ"));
```

The animations defined in `doubleAnimProjectionZ` and `doubleAnimOpacity` will run just one. However, `doubleAnimProjectionY` will run forever and it will auto reverse its execution, because its `RepeatBehavior` is set to `RepeatBehavior.Forever` and `Autoreverse` to `true`. Once it reaches the value specified by `To` for `projection.RotationY`, it will start a new animation from this value to the value specified by `From`, in the reverse direction.

```
doubleAnimProjectionY.RepeatBehavior = RepeatBehavior.Forever;
doubleAnimProjectionY.AutoReverse = true;
```

Once the method defines all the properties for the `DoubleAnimation` and `Storyboard` instances, it applies the animations associated with each Storyboard to their targets and initiates them by calling the `Begin` method.

```
storyboardProjectionZ.Begin();
storyboardOpacity.Begin();
storyboardProjectionY.Begin();
hlButton.Visibility = System.Windows.Visibility.Visible;
```

It is also possible for a single `Storyboard` instance to have many `DoubleAnimation` or other `Animation` subclasses as children. In this case, we used an independent `Storyboard` instance for each animation, because we want to have full control over each one to allow us to start and/or stop each animation to experience different alternatives for the UX in the future. However, if we just need to start all the animations at the same time, we can create a single `Storyboard` instance, add all the `DoubleAnimation` instances as their children, set the `Target` and `TargetProperty` for each `DoubleAnimation`, and call the `Begin` method.

When you open the page that contains the Visual Web Part, the Silverlight RIA will display all the hyperlink buttons that display images and videos with dazzling movements. doubleAnimProjectionY will run forever. The following screenshot shows one of the frames for the animations:

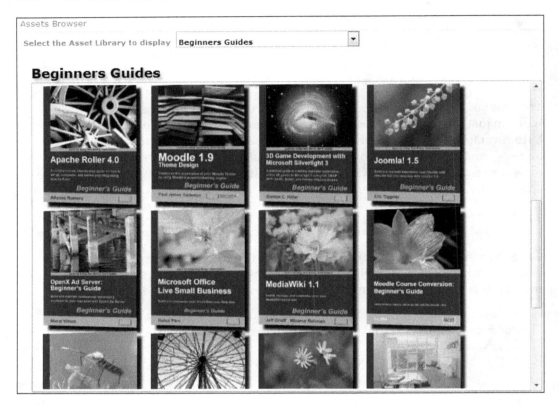

When you click on a dancing image, an animated `Hyperlink` button, the Web browser will open a new window with the image displayed with its full size. When you right-click on a dancing image, the code in the `imageButton_MouseRightButtonDown` method will run and the image will go on performing the same animation but it will also grow and then stretch. The container `WrapPanel` will make sure that the different elements displayed reorganize as the hyperlink button grows and stretches. The following picture shows one of the frames for the animation.

The `imageButton_MouseRightButtonDown` method receives two parameters, `object sender` and `MouseButtonEventArgs e`. The first line sets the `Handled` property for `e` to `true`. This way, it ensures that Silverlight won't show the default Silverlight context menu that appears when the user right-clicks within the Silverlight application area.

```
e.Handled = true;
```

As we attached this method as an event handler for the `MouseRightButtonDown` event for a `HyperlinkButton`, `sender` can be cast to `HyperlinkButton`, `hlb` and we can access its `Content` property to access its associated `Image` and store its reference in `image`.

```
var hlButton = (sender as HyperlinkButton);
var image = hlButton.Content as Image;
```

Then, the code defines two `DoubleAnimation` instances and adds them as children of their corresponding `Storyboard` instances. The code creates the `DoubleAnimation` and `Storyboard` instances summarized in the following table.

DoubleAnimation instance	Storyboard instance	Animates	From	To	Duration (seconds)
doubleAnim MaxWidth	storyboard MaxWidth	image. MaxWidth	image. Actual Width	scrollViewer. ActualWidth - (_imageMargin * 2)	6
doubleAnim MaxHeight	storyboard MaxHeight	image. MaxHeight	Image. Actual Height	scrollViewer. ActualHeight - (_imageMargin * 2)	6

Both `DoubleAnimation` instances have their `AutoReverse` property set to `true` and `RepeatBehavior` set to `RepeatBehavior(1)`. This means that the image will grow and then it will auto-reverse the animation to stretch to its original width and height.

Once the method defines all the properties for the `DoubleAnimation` and `Storyboard` instances, it applies the animations associated with each `Storyboard` to their targets and initiates them by calling the `Begin` method.

```
storyboardMaxWidth.Begin();
storyboardMaxHeight.Begin();
```

You can right-click on many images and the animation will run for all these images. The following screenshot shows one of the frames for the animation.

Adding and controlling videos

When the file type is `MediaFileType.Video`, the `ShowItem` method calls the `AddVideo` method with the `Url` string as a parameter and it saves the `HyperlinkButton` instance returned by this method in `videoButton`. Then, it calls the `AddImageVideoAnimation` with `videoButton` as a parameter.

```
case MediaFileType.Video:
  var videoButton = AddVideo(Url);
  AddImageVideoAnimation(videoButton);
  break;
```

The `AddVideo` method creates a new `MediaElement` instance, `media`, and sets values for its `MaxWidth` and `Stretch` properties. Then, it assigns the absolute `Uri` from the URL received as a parameter, `url`, to the `media.Source` property.

```
MediaElement media = new MediaElement();
media.MaxWidth = (_maxImageWidth * 3);
media.Stretch = Stretch.UniformToFill;
media.Source = new Uri(url, UriKind.Absolute);
```

Then, the code sets the `AutoPlay` property to `true` to automatically start the playback of the video specified in the `Source` property. The code attaches an event handler to the `MediaEnded` event that occurs when the video finishes. It assigns a new `RoutedEventHandler` that will fire the `media_MediaEnded` method. This method plays the video again from the beginning and therefore, the video is going to play forever while the Silverlight RIA performs all the animations.

```
media.AutoPlay = true;
media.MediaEnded += new RoutedEventHandler(media_MediaEnded);
```

Then, the code creates a new invisible `HyperlinkButton`, `videoButton`, and sets its `Content` property to the previously created `MediaElement` instance, `media`. When `videoButton` becomes visible, it will show the video being reproduced. The `NavigateUri` property for `videoButton` is set to a new `Uri` from the URL received as a parameter, `url`. The `TargetName` property is set to `_blank` and therefore, when the user clicks the `HyperlinkButton`, the Web browser will open the video from the URL in the default player associated with the file extension.

The code attaches an event handler to the `MouseRightButtonDown` event that occurs when the user clicks the right mouse button and the mouse pointer is over the `Hyperlinkbutton`. It assigns a new `MouseButtonEventHandler` that will fire the `videoButton_MouseRightButtonDown` method. This method runs the previously explained animation for the `Hyperlinkbutton`. This animation is very similar to the one explained for the `imageButton_MouseRightButtonDown` method.

```
var videoButton = new HyperlinkButton();
videoButton.Visibility = System.Windows.Visibility.Collapsed;
videoButton.Margin = new Thickness(_imageMargin);
videoButton.Content = media;
videoButton.NavigateUri = new Uri(url);
videoButton.MouseRightButtonDown += new MouseButtonEventHandler(videoB
utton_MouseRightButtonDown);
videoButton.TargetName = "_blank";
videoButton.Cursor = Cursors.Hand;
```

Finally, it is necessary to add the `HyperlinkButton` as a child to the `wrapPanel` `WrapPanel` and return the instance.

```
wrapPanel.Children.Add(videoButton);
return videoButton;
```

At this point, the `HyperlinkButton` is invisible, because its `Visibility` property was set to `System.Windows.Visibility.Collapsed`. However, when the `AddVideo` method returns, the `AddImageVideoAnimation` receives the `HyperlinkButton` control as a parameter, `hlButton`, and brings life to the video that it displays, as explained for the images.

The following screenshot shows one of the frames for the animated
`HyperlinkButton` reproducing the video and growing after the user right-clicked
on it:

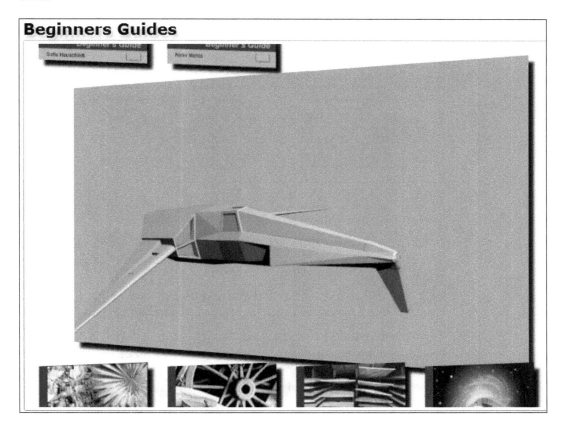

We defined the horizontal reproduction area for the video to be `_maxImageWidth * 3`
pixels and we assigned the `UniformToFill` value to the `Stretch` property. Thus, the
`MediaElement` resizes the original to fill the container's dimensions while preserving
the video's native aspect ratio.

The following screenshot shows the results of using the four possible values in the
`Stretch` property with the same original video:

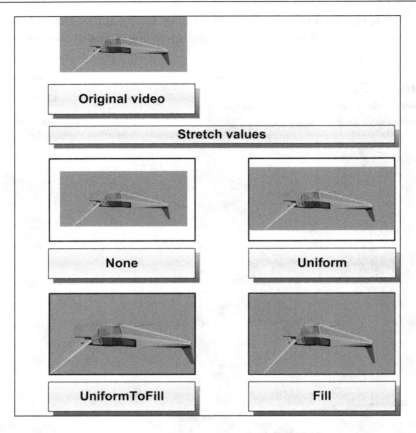

The following table explains the results of using the aforementioned values:

Stretch value	Description	Aspect ratio
None	The video preserves its original size.	Preserved
Uniform	The video is resized to fit in the destination dimensions.	Preserved
UniformToFill	The video is resized to fill the destination dimensions. The video content that does not fit in the destination rectangle is clipped.	Preserved
Fill	The video is resized to fill the destination dimensions.	Not preserved

Video formats supported in Silverlight 4

Silverlight 4 supports the video encodings shown in the following table:

Encoding name	Description and restrictions
None	Raw video
YV12	YCrCb(4:2:0)
RGBA	32-bit Red, Green, Blue, and Alpha
WMV1	Windows Media Video 7
WMV2	Windows Media Video 8
WMV3	Windows Media Video 9
WMVA	Windows Media Video Advanced Profile (non-VC-1)
WMVC1	Windows Media Video Advanced Profile (VC-1)
H.264 (ITU-T H.264 / ISO MPEG-4 AVC)	H.264 and MP43 codecs; base main and high profiles; only progressive (non-interlaced) content and only 4:2:0 chroma sub-sampling profiles

 Silverlight 4 doesn't support interlaced video content.

If we want to use a video with an encoding that does not appear in the previously shown table in a Silverlight RIA, we will have to convert it to one of the supported formats before uploading it to a SharePoint assets library.

Adding and controlling sounds and music

When the file type is `MediaFileType.Audio`, the `ShowItem` method calls the `AddBackgroundMusic` method with the `Url` string as a parameter.

```
case MediaFileType.Audio:
  AddBackgroundMusic(Url);
  break;
```

The `AddBackgroundMusic` method checks whether it was called before (`_backgroundMusicAdded == true`) before running the rest of the code, because it doesn't want to reproduce two audio files as the background music. If `_backgroundMusicAdded` is `true`, it assigns `true` to `_backgroundMusicAdded`.

The code creates a new MediaElement instance, backgroundMusic, adds it to a parent container, LayoutRoot, and sets its Volume property to 80% (0.8). The Volume ranges from 0 to 1. It uses a linear scale.

```
_backgroundMusicAdded = true;
MediaElement backgroundMusic = new MediaElement();
LayoutRoot.Children.Add(backgroundMusic);
```

Then, it assigns the absolute Uri from the URL received as a parameter, url, to the backgroundMusic.Source property and calls the Play method to start reproducing the audio file with the specified volume level. The background music will be reproduced just once.

```
backgroundMusic.Volume = 0.8;
backgroundMusic.Source = new Uri(url);
backgroundMusic.Play();
```

Audio formats supported in Silverlight 4

Silverlight 4 supports the audio encodings shown in the following table:

Encoding name	Description and restrictions
LPCM	Linear 8 or 16-bit Pulse Code Modulation.
WMA Standard	Windows Media Audio 7, 8, and 9 Standard.
WMA Professional	Windows Media Audio 9 and 10 Professional; Multichannel (5.1 and 7.1 surround) is automatically mixed down to stereo. It supports neither 24-bit audio nor sampling rates beyond 48 kHz.
MP3	ISO MPEG-1 Layer III.
AAC	ISO Advanced Audio Coding; AAC-LC (Low Complexity) is supported at full fidelity (up to 48 kHz). HE-AAC (High Efficiency) will decode only at half fidelity (up to 24 kHz); Multichannel (5.1) audio content is not supported.

If we want to use an audio file with an encoding that does not appear in the previously shown table, we will have to convert it to one of the supported formats before uploading it to a SharePoint assets library.

Changing themes in Silverlight and SharePoint

The Visual Web Part is a great candidate for applying the themes included in Silverlight's Toolkit to offer the user a more exciting UI.

1. Stay in Visual Studio as a system administrator user.

2. Add a reference to `System.Windows.Controls.Theming.Toolkit.dll`. Remember that it is located in the `Bin` sub-folder

3. Add a reference to the DLL for `System.Windows.Controls.Theming.ShinyRed` in the `Themes` sub-folder. This way, we are going to be able to apply the `ShinyRed` theme.

4. Add the following line to include the namespace that defines the theme in the `UserControl` defined in `MainPage.xaml`:

   ```
   xmlns:shinyRed="clr-namespace:System.Windows.Controls.
   Theming;assembly=System.Windows.Controls.Theming.ShinyRed"
   ```

5. Add the following line before the definition of the main `Grid`, `LayoutRoot`:

   ```
   <shinyRed:ShinyRedTheme>
   ```

6. Add the following line after the definition of the main `Grid`, `LayoutRoot`:

   ```
   </shinyRed:ShinyRedTheme>
   ```

7. This way, the `ShinyRed` theme will be applied to the main `Grid`, `LayoutRoot`, and all its child controls. Build and deploy the solution and open the page that displays the Visual Web Part. The Silverlight RIA looks really more attractive. However, the colors displayed by the rest of the SharePoint UI don't match the `ShinyRed` theme colors.

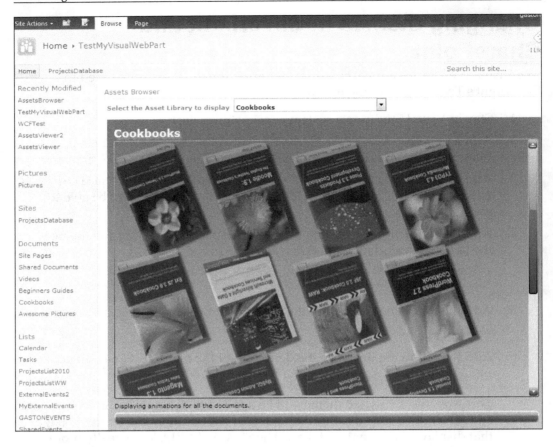

8. Click **Site Actions | Site Settings** and a list of customization options organized by categories will appear.

9. Click on **Site theme** under **Look and Feel**. A page that allows us to change the fonts and color scheme for our site will appear.

10. Select the `Municipal` theme in the list located at the right. This theme uses a color scheme that is appropriate for Silverlight applications that use the `ShinyRed` theme.

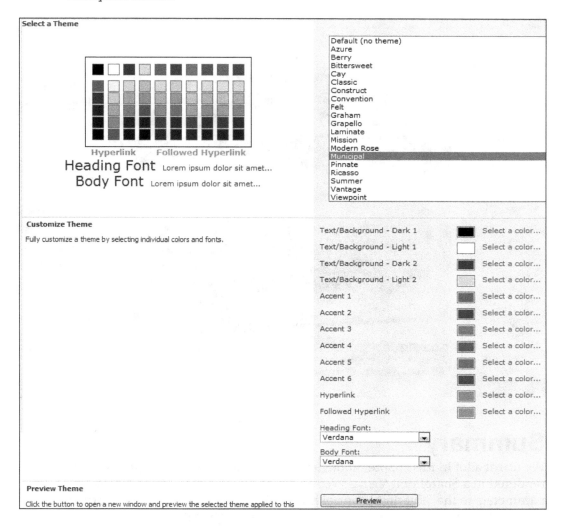

11. Click on **Preview** and the Web browser will open a new window with your site's home page with the new color schemes and fonts that the selected theme defines.

12. Close this window and click on **Apply**. SharePoint will apply the new theme to the pages that haven't been individually themed. The new theme won't affect the site's layout.

13. Now, refresh the page that displays the Visual Web Part and the combination of a new SharePoint theme with the theme applied to the Silverlight RIA will look really nice.

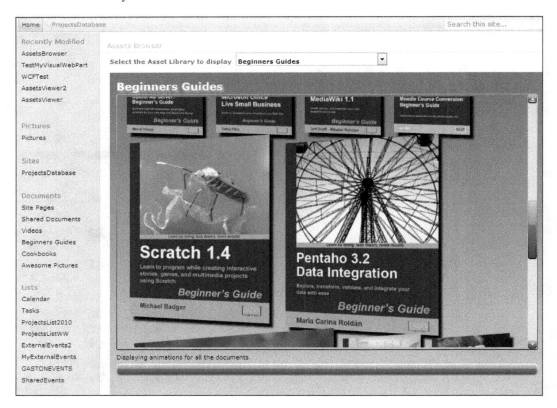

Summary

We learnt a lot in this chapter about accessing asset libraries in a Silverlight RIA rendered in a SharePoint Visual Web Part. Specifically, we were able to send parameters to the Silverlight control host to define the desired asset library to display. We took advantage of Silverlight 4 rich media features to add effects and interactive animations to the images and videos.

We have learned many alternatives to integrate Silverlight 4 with SharePoint 2010 and we have understood the great possibilities offered by Silverlight RIAs in SharePoint sites. Now, we are ready to create enhanced Silverlight User eXperiences combined with the powerful SharePoint 2010 services.

6

List Definitions and Content Types

 This chapter is taken from *Microsoft SharePoint 2010 Development with Visual Studio 2010 Expert Cookbook* (Chapter 4) by Balaji Kithiganahalli.

In this chapter, we will cover:

- Creating a site column
- Extending an existing content type
- Creating a custom content type using an object model
- Associating a document template to a content type
- Associating a workflow to a content type
- Creating an external content type
- Creating a list definition

Introduction

Content type is defined as a reusable collection of metadata, a workflow, and other settings for a category of items which encapsulate data requirements and enable standardization.

In SharePoint, content is stored in some type of list in the site. Content can be pictures, documents, contacts, tasks, or custom items that you store in a list. You can specify in the SharePoint list what kind of content that it can store. Out of the box, SharePoint provides templates that you can use to create lists or libraries that store specific contents like documents or pictures or contacts. This is achieved through content types. For example, a document library is intended for storing documents like word, PDF or excel documents where as a contacts list stores contacts. SharePoint makes this distinction by having different content types associated with these lists.

Apart from defining the type of content a list can store, content types can also have metadata properties and processes associated with the content. For example, a project proposal can have a word document that describes the project in a specific format and has certain metadata properties like the department that it belongs to, the cost associated with the the project, project start and end date, and any workflows that the document has to follow through in order to get an approval. Taken together the document, the metadata properties, and the workflows will become a content type.

The content types can be reused. This is when you define a content type at a site collection level or site level and you can use it in different sites or lists in the same site using the content type. For example, if you create the project proposal content type at the site level, you can create multiple document libraries that use the content type. This way you can create different project proposal lists (or document libraries) for each of the departments in your company and have a consistent format across the company. Apart from this, you can customize it at the list level for each of the departments in the previous example without affecting the parent content type.

Out of the box, SharePoint provides several content types. The following image shows the categories of the content types that come with SharePoint server:

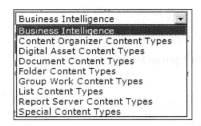

The list definition is a schema for defining lists in the SharePoint site. The list definition provides list structure with content type that is used in it. A list can have multiple content types which means it can have our example project proposal content type and also a resume content type. But each item in the list can only be associated with one content type. That is, the document in our example can only be a project proposal or resume but not both. The list is just a place holder for the content types.

 The other term that is used with Lists is list templates. They are very similar to list definitions. They mainly differ in how they are created. List templates are created by the end users using SharePoint UI by using an existing list as a starting point for the pattern. SharePoint designer also uses the term list templates. In Visual Studio terminology, it is always called **List Definitions**.

All content types in SharePoint are inherited from a parent content type. Whenever we create a new content type, we have to specify the parent content. All the attributes and settings of the parent content type are inherited in the child content type. When we make changes to the parent content type, the children are also updated with those changes. But when you make changes on the child content type, it does not affect the parent content type.

At the root of this inheritance is the System content type. This does not have any columns. Next in the inheritance is Item content type. We can derive content types from an Item content type but not directly from the System.

As indicated earlier, content types include metadata information as well. These metadata are stored as columns in the list or document library. These columns can be site columns or list columns. Site columns as the name suggests are created at the site level and can be reused in different lists.

A site column in SharePoint has the following four important parts:

▶ Column name
▶ Column type
▶ Column group
▶ Additional settings

Column name is a required attribute for a column. Column type provides information about its data type, that is, the type of information that the column can store like a number or text. The following screenshot shows the data types that SharePoint supports on the site columns:

The type of information in this column is:
- Single line of text
- Multiple lines of text
- Choice (menu to choose from)
- Number (1, 1.0, 100)
- Currency ($, ¥, €)
- Date and Time
- Lookup (information already on this site)
- Yes/No (check box)
- Person or Group
- Hyperlink or Picture
- Calculated (calculation based on other columns)
- Full HTML content with formatting and constraints for publishing
- Image with formatting and constraints for publishing
- Hyperlink with formatting and constraints for publishing
- Summary Links data
- Rich media data for publishing
- Managed Metadata

A column group is not a required attribute but provides a way to organize your custom site columns. In additional settings, we can define whether a column is required or not, the maximum number of characters, currency format, and so on.

Visual Studio 2010 provides templates to create content types and list definitions. These templates allow you to create content types using declarative XML. You can always use an empty SharePoint project to create content types via a SharePoint object model. In this chapter, we will create content types using both code and declarative XML.

Creating a site column

A site column is the building block for creating a content type. In this recipe, we will create a site column using the SharePoint object model.

Getting ready

You should have a fully-functional development machine with SharePoint 2010 installed and configured. You also need Visual Studio 2010 IDE installed on the same development machine.

How to do it...

1. Launch your Visual Studio 2010 IDE as an administrator (right-click on the shortcut and select **Run as administrator.**)

2. Select **File | New | Project**. The new project wizard dialog box as shown in the following screenshot will be displayed (make sure to select **.NET Framework 3.5** in the top drop-down box):

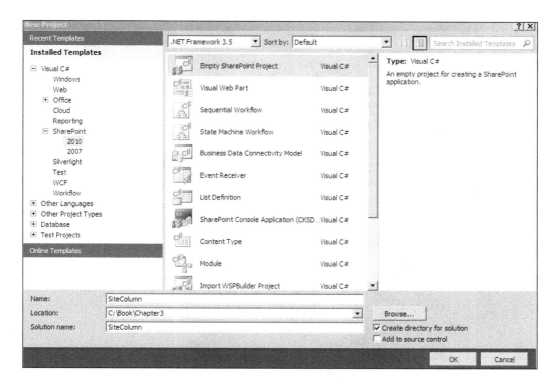

3. Select **Empty SharePoint Project** under **Visual C# | SharePoint | 2010** node from the **Installed Templates** section on the left-hand side.

4. Name the project **SiteColumn** and provide a directory location where you want to save the project and click on **OK** to proceed to the next step in the wizard.

5. By default, Visual Studio selects the SharePoint site available on the machine. Select **Deploy as Farm Solution** and click on **Next** to proceed to the next step in the wizard.

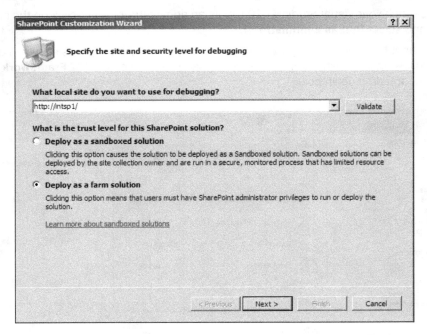

6. This should create an empty SharePoint project. To this project add a feature by right-clicking on the **Feature** folder as shown in the following screenshot:

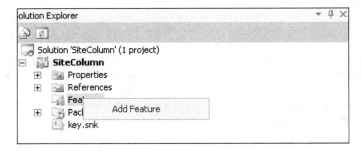

7. Add an event receiver to the new feature added by right-clicking on the feature and selecting **Add Event Receiver** as shown in the following screenshot:

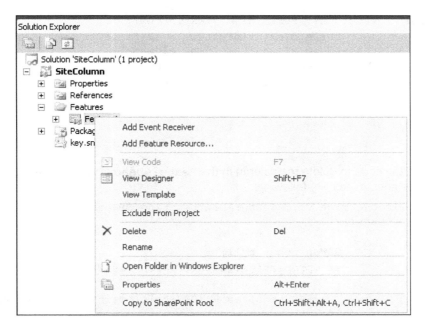

8. This should add a code file named `Feature1.EventReceiver.cs`. Uncomment `FeatureActivated` and `FeatureDeactivating` methods.

9. Add the following code to create a `TestColumn` in the `FeatureActivated` method:

```
public override void FeatureActivated(SPFeatureReceiverProperties
properties)
        {
            SPWeb web = null;
            if (properties.Feature.Parent is SPSite)
            {
                SPSite sites = (SPSite)properties.Feature.Parent;
                web = sites.RootWeb;
            }
            else
            {
                web = (SPWeb)properties.Feature.Parent;
            }
            if (web == null)
                    return;

            string columnGroup = "Chapter3 Columns";
```

```
                    // TEst Site Column
                    string sTestSiteColumnFieldName = web.Fields.
            Add("TestColumn", SPFieldType.Text, true);
                    SPFieldText fldTestCol = (SPFieldText)web.Fields.GetFi
            eldByInternalName(sTestSiteColumnFieldName);
                    fldTestCol.Group = columnGroup;
                    fldTestCol.MaxLength = 100;
                    fldTestCol.Required = true;
                    fldTestCol.Update();


                }
```

10. Add the code to delete the column in the `FeatureDeactivating` method. Your code should look like following:

```
public override void FeatureDeactivating(SPFeatureReceiverProperti
es properties)
        {
            SPWeb web = null;
            if (properties.Feature.Parent is SPSite)
            {
                SPSite sites = (SPSite)properties.Feature.Parent;
                web = sites.RootWeb;
            }
            else
            {
                web = (SPWeb)properties.Feature.Parent;
            }
            if (web == null)
                return;

            web.Fields["TestColumn"].Delete();


        }


    }
}
```

11. When you build and run this solution, you should be directed to the site that you provided in the solution creation wizard.

12. Navigate to **Site Actions | Site Settings | Galleries | Site Columns**. You should see the new site column **Test Column** created under a new group **Chapter3 Columns** as shown here:

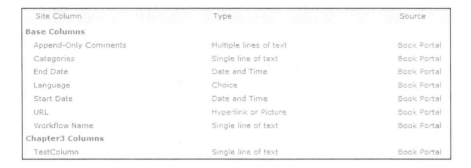

Site Column	Type	Source
Base Columns		
Append-Only Comments	Multiple lines of text	Book Portal
Categories	Single line of text	Book Portal
End Date	Date and Time	Book Portal
Language	Choice	Book Portal
Start Date	Date and Time	Book Portal
URL	Hyperlink or Picture	Book Portal
Workflow Name	Single line of text	Book Portal
Chapter3 Columns		
TestColumn	Single line of text	Book Portal

13. You can verify all the attributes like **Maximum number of characters** and **Require that is column contains information** properties by clicking on the **TestColumn** column. The following screenshot shows the attributes of our example column:

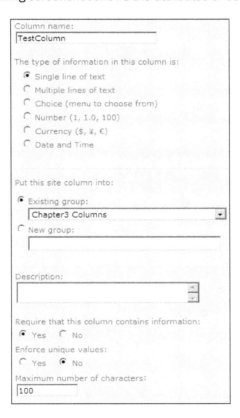

How it works...

This is a real-world example where feature receivers can come in handy.

The code is pretty simple in the sense; we add a field (the term field and column are used to refer to the same object) to the site's field collection. The add method on the field collection object is overloaded to take different parameters. We are using a method that takes in the display name of the column, the column type, and whether the column is required or not as the parameters. The method returns us the internal name of the field. This internal name is unique to a field. This way, you can use the same field in multiple lists and change the display name to suite your needs. By using this internal name, we retrieved the field object and set other additional attributes like the max length of the characters that it can hold and whether it is required or not. We also set the group name to which the field should belong. If the group does not exist, the SharePoint object model will create one and add the field to that group. When there are no fields in the group, the group is automatically deleted. So there is no exclusive code to create or delete the group.

There's more...

You can also use the site's field collection's `AddFieldAsXml` method to create a new site column. In this method, you will pass in the XML schema of the field you want to create. For our example, the following code shows the XML schema:

```
web.Fields.AddFieldAsXml("<Field DisplayName=\"TestColumn\" Type=\
"Text\" Required=\"TRUE\" Name=\"TestColumn\" Group=\"Chapter3
Columns\" MaxLength=\"100\" />");
```

Deleting the site columns on deactivation of the feature

In our recipe, we deleted the site column in the deactivating method of the feature. This is a normal way of cleaning up the site columns if they are not needed. Before deleting though make sure that it does not create any adverse effect on the content types that are already deployed and used in the site columns.

See also

- ▸ Extending an existing content type
- ▸ Creating a custom content type

Extending an existing content type

In the previous recipe, we learnt how to create a site column using the SharePoint object model. In this recipe, we will create a site column using a declarative XML and add it to the contacts content type.

Contacts content type provides a way to store the contacts in SharePoint. It provides various columns to store contact's name, phone number, fax, web page, and so on. Out of the box, it does not provide a way to categorize these contacts. We will extend this content type so we can categorize our contacts as sales lead, customer, or vendor

Getting ready

You should have completed the previous recipe successfully.

How to do it...

1. Launch your Visual Studio 2010 IDE as an administrator (right-click the shortcut and select **Run as administrator**).

2. Select **File | New | Project**. The new project wizard dialog box will be displayed (make sure to select **.NET Framework 3.5** in the top drop-down box).

3. Select **Content Type** project under **Visual C# | SharePoint | 2010** node from the **Installed Templates** section on the left-hand side.

4. Name the project **ContactsContentType** and provide a directory location where you want to save the project and click on **OK** to proceed to the next step in the wizard.

5. By default, Visual Studio selects the SharePoint site available on the machine. Select **Deploy as sandboxed Solution** and click on **Next** to proceed to the next step in the wizard.

6. In this step, make sure to select the **Contact** content type as the base content type as shown in the following screenshot and click on **Finish** to generate the project:

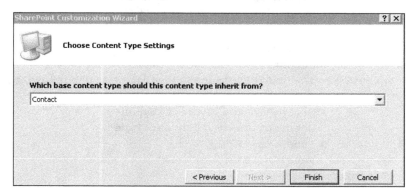

7. To this project, add a new empty element and call it **SiteColumns**. Your project structure should look like the following:

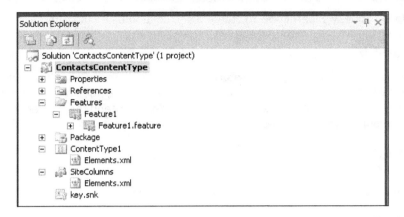

8. In the **Elements.xml** file underneath the **SiteColumns** element, add the xml to create a new site column. Your Elements.xml file should look similar to the following code:

```
<?xml version="1.0" encoding="utf-8"?>
<Elements xmlns="http://schemas.microsoft.com/sharepoint/">
  <Field ID="{CD822345-3D9D-45BC-8C7A-54198F77395C}"
Name="ContactType" Type="Choice" Required="FALSE" Group="Chapter3
Columns" DisplayName="Contact Type">
    <CHOICES>
      <CHOICE>Sales Lead</CHOICE>
      <CHOICE>Customer</CHOICE>
      <CHOICE>Vendor</CHOICE>
    </CHOICES>
  </Field>
</Elements>
```

9. We will reference this field in the content type. To do that, in the Elements.xml file underneath **ContentType1**, add the field reference to the created field in the previous step. Your Elements.xml file should look as follows:

```
<?xml version="1.0" encoding="utf-8"?>
<Elements xmlns="http://schemas.microsoft.com/sharepoint/">
  <!-- Parent ContentType: Contact (0x0106) -->
  <ContentType ID="0x01060016ac0527de4d4b989b1b9bcf8c9d2b38"
               Name="ContactsContentType - ContentType1"
               Group="Custom Content Types"
               Description="My Content Type"
               Inherits="TRUE"
               Version="0">
    <FieldRefs>
```

```
    <FieldRef ID="{CD822345-3D9D-45BC-8C7A-54198F77395C}"
Required="TRUE"/>
    </FieldRefs>
  </ContentType>
</Elements>
```

10. Run the project by pressing *F5*. This will create the content type and site column as shown in the following screenshot:

Site Content Type Information

Name:	ContactsContentType - ContentType1
Description:	My Content Type
Parent:	Contact
Group:	Custom Content Types

Settings

- Name, description, and group
- Advanced settings
- Workflow settings
- Delete this site content type
- Information management policy settings

Columns

Name	Type	Status	Source
Last Name	Single line of text	Optional	Item
Last Name Phonetic	Single line of text	Optional	Contact
First Name	Single line of text	Optional	Contact
First Name Phonetic	Single line of text	Optional	Contact
Full Name	Single line of text	Optional	Contact
E-Mail	Single line of text	Optional	Contact
Company	Single line of text	Optional	Contact
Company Phonetic	Single line of text	Optional	Contact
Job Title	Single line of text	Optional	Contact
Business Phone	Single line of text	Optional	Contact
Home Phone	Single line of text	Optional	Contact
Mobile Number	Single line of text	Optional	Contact
Fax Number	Single line of text	Optional	Contact
Address	Multiple lines of text	Optional	Contact
City	Single line of text	Optional	Contact
State/Province	Single line of text	Optional	Contact
ZIP/Postal Code	Single line of text	Optional	Contact
Country/Region	Single line of text	Optional	Contact
Web Page	Hyperlink or Picture	Optional	Contact
Comments	Multiple lines of text	Optional	Contact
Contact Type	Choice	Required	

11. Navigate to **Site Actions** | **Site Settings** | **Galleries** | **Site Columns**. You should see the new site column **Contact Type** created under a new group **Chapter3 Columns**.

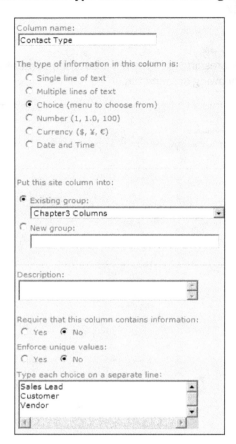

How it works...

In the strictest sense, whenever we develop a custom content type, we have to extend it from one of the available content types. In here, we extended the contacts content type. As indicated in the introduction of this chapter, the item (0x01) is the deepest we can go for inheriting the content type. We cannot inherit from the system content type (0x).

In the `Elements.xml` file underneath the **ContentType1** folder it describes the schema for the content type. It has attributes that define the name, group, description, and version. The ID attribute is GUID without any format. The ID of the content type is always prefixed with the parent content type ID and two zeros. Since we based our content type on a contact, the prefix is "0x010600". The ID attribute provides unique identification for the content type.

The `Inherits` attribute in the content type xml schema, specifies to SharePoint that all the fields from the parent content type are used in the derived child content type. So in our case, we still have all the fields defined in the contact content type, but we also added our own choice column for selecting the contact type.

When the feature is deployed, SharePoint reads the xml schema and creates the field based on the schema supplied. In our case, we created a new site column of type **Choice** and provided the choices that can be selected as well. All of this information was provided in the XML schema. Since Visual Studio does not have a specific template for creating site columns, we added a new empty element and provided the schema for creating the column in this element file. We do not have to do this. You can specify the field definitions in the content type `Elements.xml` file itself. It is a good practice though to have separate `Elements.xml` file when deploying fields and content types. In the later recipe, we will show how to include the field definitions in the content type `Elements.xml` file.

In the schema for the site column, you can see GUID for ID attribute. This is generated using the tool that Visual Studio provides. You can access this tool from the menu **Tools** | **Create GUID**. This will bring up a similar dialog box as the one follows:

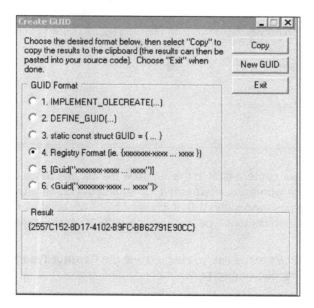

Select the registry format and copy to the ID attribute. This ID attribute is also used when referencing the field in the content type. The rest of the attributes in the field schema defines the column.

There's more...

To use the content type we created in this recipe, refer to the following steps:

1. From the SharePoint user interface, create a contacts list.

2. From the list settings page, click on the **Advanced Settings** and select **Yes** for the management of the content types. This will enable the content types section for the list.

3. Click on **Add** in the existing site content types link underneath the content types section in the list settings. Add **ContactContentType – ContentType1** as shown in the following screenshot:

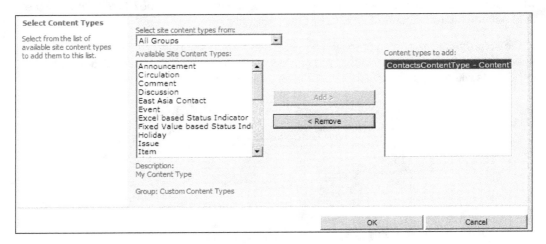

4. This will add our content type to the list. Now the list has Since list already has a default content type associated with it, by adding our content type, the list now has two content types associated with it. content types associated with it. Since we want to use our custom content type, remove the default content type associated with the list.

5. Add a new contact to the list, you should see the **Contact Type** field listed as required as shown in the following screenshot:

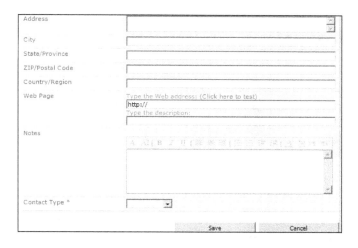

Deployment of previous solution

The previous example shows that the site column has to be deployed first in order for it to be referenced in the content type. To make sure that happens, we need to add a second feature to the project. To this feature, add the content type element and remove the same from the first feature. Also create a feature dependency such that feature 2 is dependent on the deployment of feature 1. This ensures that the site column is deployed before the content type gets deployed.

Here are steps to add feature dependency:

1. Double-click on **Feature 2** to open up the feature designer and click on the **+** next to the **Feature Activation Dependencies**.

2. Click on **Add** button to add the feature dependency as shown in the next screenshot:

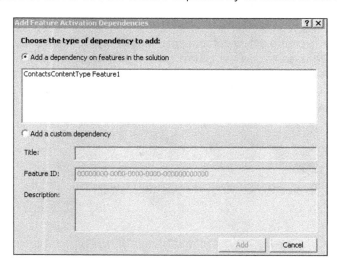

3. This will list the features that are in the project. In our case, we only have two features and hence **Feature 1** is shown in the list. Select **Feature 1** and click on **Add** to create the feature dependency.

Inherits attribute in content type

In the recipe, we learnt that the `Inherits` attribute specifies to SharePoint that all the fields from the parent content type is used in the child. If for some reason, you need to delete a column in the child that is available in the parent, make sure to set the `Inherits` attribute to false and use the `RemoveFieldRef` element as shown:

```
<RemoveFieldRef ID="ea8f7ca9-2a0e-4a89-b8bf-c51a6af62c73"/>
<RemoveFieldRef ID="fdc8216d-dabf-441d-8ac0-f6c626fbdc24"/>
```

By adding this preceding XML to content type `Elements.xml`, we will be removing the **First Name Phonetic** and the **Last Name Phonetic** columns from the content type.

See also

▶ *Creating a site column* recipe
▶ *Creating a custom content type using an object model* recipe

Creating custom content type using an object model

In the previous recipe, we extended a content type using an XML schema. This can get pretty difficult as Visual Studio does not provide ways to debug the XML schemas. Instead of using the xml schema method, you can always use object model APIs to create the content type. In this recipe we will do just that.

For this recipe, we will create a new content type called **Project Proposal** that has four custom columns **Amount**, **Department**, **Project Start Date**, and **Project End Date**. The `Department` field is a choice type where you can select the department to which the project belongs. The `Amount` field is of currency type and the `Project Start Date` and the `Project End Date` are of `DateTime` type. The content type will be inherited from the document content type.

Getting ready

You should have completed the previous recipes successfully.

How to do it...

1. Launch your Visual Studio 2010 IDE as an administrator (right-click the shortcut and select **Run as administrator**).

2. Select **File | New | Project**. The new project wizard dialog box will be displayed (make sure to select **.NET Framework 3.5** in the top drop-down box).

3. Select **Empty SharePoint Project** under **Visual C# | SharePoint | 2010** node from the **Installed Templates** section on the left-hand side.

4. Name the project **ProjectProposal** and provide a directory location where you want to save the project and click **OK** to proceed to the next step in the wizard.

5. By default, Visual Studio selects the SharePoint site available on the machine. Select **Deploy as Farm Solution** and click on **Next** to proceed to the next step in the wizard.

6. This should create an empty SharePoint project. To this project, add a feature by right-clicking on the **Feature** folder.

7. Add an event receiver to the new feature added by right-clicking on the feature and selecting **Add Event Receiver**.

8. This should add a code file named `Feature1.EventReceiver.cs`. Uncomment `FeatureActivated` and `FeatureDeactivating` methods.

9. Add the code to create a `Project Proposal` content type in the `FeatureActivated` method. The code is as follows:

```
public override void FeatureActivated
(SPFeatureReceiverProperties properties)
{
    SPWeb web = null;
    if (properties.Feature.Parent is SPSite)
    {
        SPSite sites = (SPSite)properties.Feature.Parent;
        web = sites.RootWeb;
    }
    else
    {
        web = (SPWeb)properties.Feature.Parent;
    }
    if (web == null)
        return;


    string columnGroup = "Chapter3 Project Proposal Site
    Column Group";

    // Project Amount
```

```
string sAmountFieldName = web.Fields.Add("Chapter3
Project Amount", SPFieldType.Currency, false);
SPFieldCurrency fldAmount = (SPFieldCurrency)
web.Fields.GetFieldByInternalName(sAmountFieldName);
fldAmount.Group = columnGroup;
fldAmount.DisplayFormat = SPNumberFormatTypes.
TwoDecimals;
fldAmount.MinimumValue = 0;
fldAmount.Update();
Guid fldGuid = fldAmount.Id;


// Project Start Date
string sProjectDateFieldName = web.Fields.
Add("Chapter3 Project Start Date", SPFieldType.DateTime, false);
SPFieldDateTime fldProjectStartDate =
(SPFieldDateTime)web.Fields.GetFieldByInternalName(sProjectDateFie
ldName);
fldProjectStartDate.Group = columnGroup;
fldProjectStartDate.DisplayFormat =
SPDateTimeFieldFormatType.DateOnly;
fldProjectStartDate.DefaultValue = "[today]";
fldProjectStartDate.Update();

// Project End Date
string sProjectEndDateFieldName = web.Fields.
Add("Chapter3 Project End Date", SPFieldType.DateTime, false);
SPFieldDateTime fldProjectEndDate =
(SPFieldDateTime)web.Fields.GetFieldByInternalName(sProjectEndDate
FieldName);
fldProjectEndDate.Group = columnGroup;
fldProjectEndDate.DisplayFormat =
SPDateTimeFieldFormatType.DateOnly;
fldProjectEndDate.DefaultValue = "[today]";
fldProjectEndDate.Update();

// Department
string sDepartmentFieldName = web.Fields.Add("Chapter3
Department", SPFieldType.Choice, false);
SPFieldChoice fldDepartment = (SPFieldChoice)web.
Fields.GetFieldByInternalName(sDepartmentFieldName);
fldDepartment.Choices.Add("Human Resources");
fldDepartment.Choices.Add("Information Technology");
fldDepartment.Choices.Add("Finance");
fldDepartment.Choices.Add("Research and Development");
fldDepartment.Choices.Add("Sales");
fldDepartment.Choices.Add("Marketing");
fldDepartment.Group = columnGroup;
```

```
fldDepartment.Update();


string contentTypeGroup = "Chapter3 Project Proposal
Content Type Group";

// We will use Document Content type as the parent
SPContentType documentCType = web.AvailableContentType
 s[SPBuiltInContentTypeId.Document];

// Create the Budget Proposal Content type.
SPContentType ctProjectProposal = new SPContentType
(documentCType, web.ContentTypes, "Chapter3 Project
Proposal");


ctProjectProposal = web.ContentTypes.
 Add(ctProjectProposal);
ctProjectProposal.Group = contentTypeGroup;

// Add columns created earlier
SPFieldLink projectStartDateFieldRef = new SPFieldLink
(fldProjectStartDate);
projectStartDateFieldRef.Required = true;
ctProjectProposal.FieldLinks.Add(projectStartDateField
Ref);

// Add columns created earlier
SPFieldLink projectEndDateFieldRef = new SPFieldLink
(fldProjectEndDate);
projectEndDateFieldRef.Required = true;
ctProjectProposal.FieldLinks.Add
(projectEndDateFieldRef);

SPFieldLink frAmount = new SPFieldLink(fldAmount);
ctProjectProposal.FieldLinks.Add(frAmount);

SPFieldLink frDepartment = new SPFieldLink
(fldDepartment);
ctProjectProposal.FieldLinks.Add(frDepartment);
// Commit changes.
ctProjectProposal.Update();


}
```

10. Add the code to delete the content type and columns in the `FeatureDeactivating` method. The code should be as follows:

```
public override void FeatureDeactivating(SPFeatureReceiver
Properties properties)
{
    SPWeb web = null;
    if (properties.Feature.Parent is SPSite)
    {
        SPSite sites = (SPSite)properties.Feature.Parent;
        web = sites.RootWeb;
    }
    else
    {
        web = (SPWeb)properties.Feature.Parent;
    }
    if (web == null)
        return;

    web.AllowUnsafeUpdates = true;

    web.ContentTypes["Chapter3 Project Proposal"].
    Delete();
    web.Fields.GetFieldByInternalName("Chapter3_x0020_
    Project_x0020_Amount").Delete();
    web.Fields.GetFieldByInternalName("Chapter3_x0020_
    Department").Delete();
    web.Fields.GetFieldByInternalName("Chapter3_x0020_
    Project_x0020_End_x0020_Date").Delete();
    web.Fields.GetFieldByInternalName("Chapter3_x0020_
    Project_x0020_Start_x0020_Date").Delete();
    web.Update();
    web.AllowUnsafeUpdates = false;


}
```

11. Build and run the project by pressing *F5*. Visual studio will launch the browser with the site you provided during the project creation. Navigate to **Site Actions | Site Settings | Galleries | Site Columns**. You should see the new site columns created under a new group **Chapter3 Project Proposal Site Column Group**. Similarly, navigate to **Site Actions | Site Settings | Galleries | Site Content Types** to see the **Project Proposal** content type as shown in the following screenshot:

Site Content Type	Parent	Source
Business Intelligence		
Excel based Status Indicator	Common Indicator Columns	Book Portal
Fixed Value based Status Indicator	Common Indicator Columns	Book Portal
Report	Document	Book Portal
SharePoint List based Status Indicator	Common Indicator Columns	Book Portal
SQL Server Analysis Services based Status Indicator	Common Indicator Columns	Book Portal
Web Part Page with Status List	Document	Book Portal
Chapter3 Project Proposal Content Type Group		
Chapter3 Project Proposal	Document	Book Portal
Content Organizer Content Types		
Rule	Item	Book Portal

How it works...

Instead of the schema, we made use of the object model APIs to create the site columns. This was explained in our first recipe. The addition to this recipe is to create the content type and reference the site columns that were created previously.

For this, we used the `SPContentType` constructor and passed in the parent content type and the name of the content type. We added this to our web content type collection.

To add a reference to the fields, we created an instance of `SPFieldLink` and added to the content type. The content type was updated with the reference to the fields when we called the update method on the content type.

See also

▸ *Associating a document template with the content type* recipe

Associating a document template with the content type

In the introduction to content types, we specified that a content type can include document templates and/or workflows. In this recipe, we will include a document template for our `Project Proposal` content type.

Getting ready

You should have completed the previous recipes successfully. Create a word template and name it `ProjectProposal.dotx`.

How to do it...

1. If you have closed Visual Studio IDE, launch it as an administrator.

2. Open the previously created **ProjectProposal** solution.

3. Right-click on the project and select **Add | SharePoint "Layouts" Mapped Folder** as follows:

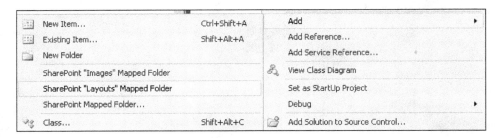

4. This will create a mapped folder to the **Layouts** folder and add a subfolder with the same name as the project underneath it. In our case it is called **ProjectProposal**.

5. Add your `ProjectProposal.dotx` file to this folder. Your project structure should be as follows:

6. Open `Feature1.EventReceiver.cs` file and add code to associate the document template before the content type update method in feature activating method. Your code should look like the following:

```
SPFieldLink frDepartment = new SPFieldLink(fldDepartment);
        ctProjectProposal.FieldLinks.Add(frDepartment);

        //Associate the document template created.
```

```
                    ctProjectProposal.DocumentTemplate = "/_layouts/
ProjectProposal/ProjectProposal.dotx";

                    // Commit changes.
                    ctProjectProposal.Update();
```

7. Build and run the project. Navigate to **Site Actions | Site Settings | Gallery | Site content types** and select **Chapter3 Project Proposal**. Click on the **Advanced settings** link and you should see the URL for the document template attached as shown here:

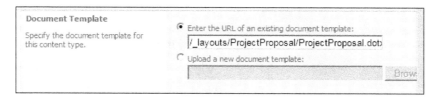

How it works...

Visual Studio always creates a subfolder underneath the mapped folder when we add a reference to the mapped folders. We added our template file to this location. The layouts mapped folder can be referenced as `_layouts` and hence we provided the URL for the document template from this location.

You can associate this content type to a library as explained in the previous recipes. When you create a new document from this library, the template will be opened from the `_layouts` folder as shown in the next screenshot:

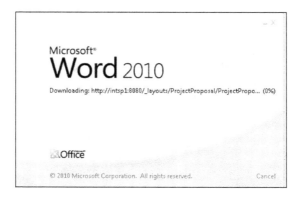

There's more...

In this recipe, we used the `_layouts` folder to deploy the document template. This will not work with sandboxed solutions. For sandboxed solutions, since you do not have access to the SharePoint root on the file system, you have to deploy the document templates to the content databases. For my example here, I have created an excel template called `BudgetProposal.xltx`. The content type is called **DocumentTemplateContentType**. Here is the step-by-step instructions on deploying the document template in a sandboxed solution:

1. Create a new content type project and make sure you select the **Sandboxed** solution in the wizard. Inherit the content type from a document content type.

2. Visual Studio creates the **ContentType1** folder and the `Elements.xml` file underneath it along with the feature to deploy the content type.

3. Add a new module item to the **ContentType1** folder and call it **Template**.

4. Delete the default `Sample.txt` and the `Elements.xml` file that Visual Studio adds. Your project structure should look like the following:

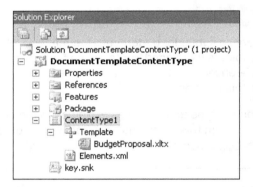

5. Edit the `Elements.xml` file of the content type and add the module information. The attribute's `Url` provides the path for clients to look for the template associated with the content type. The `Type` attribute specifies that the template is loaded into the content database. Your content type `Elements.xml` file should be as follows:

```xml
<?xml version="1.0" encoding="utf-8"?>
<Elements xmlns="http://schemas.microsoft.com/sharepoint/">

  <Module Url="_cts/DocumentTemplateContentType" Name="Template">
    <File Url="BudgetProposal.xltx" Name="BudgetProposal.xltx"
Type="Ghostable" Path="Template\BudgetProposal.xltx"/>
  </Module>

  <!-- Parent ContentType: Document (0x0101) -->
  <ContentType ID="0x010100a3c7c0095daf42ac924b1258ab88563c"
```

```
            Name="DocumentTemplateContentType"
            Group="Custom Content Types"
            Description="My Content Type"
            Inherits="TRUE"
            Version="0">
       <FieldRefs>
       </FieldRefs>
       <DocumentTemplate TargetName="BudgetProposal.xltx"/>
     </ContentType>
   </Elements>
```

 For the list of built-in content types and their IDs refer to MSDN at: `http://msdn.microsoft.com/en-us/library/ms452896.aspx`.

See also

▸ *Associating a workflow to a content type* recipe

Associating a workflow to a content type

We added metadata columns to our content type, we added a document template that provides the common format for uploading project proposals to the library, and in this recipe we will add "Approval workflow" to our content type.

Approval Workflow is out-of-the-box workflow available in the SharePoint server.

Getting ready

You should have completed the previous recipes successfully.

How to do it...

1. If you have closed Visual Studio IDE, launch it as an administrator.

2. Open the previously created `ProjectProposal` solution.

3. Open `Feature1.EventReceiver.cs` file and add code to associate the workflow before the content type update method in the feature's activating method. Your code should look like the following:

```
//Associate the document template created.
        ctProjectProposal.DocumentTemplate = "/_layouts/
```

```
ProjectProposal/ProjectProposal.dotx";

SPWorkflowTemplate approvalTemplate = null;

for (int i = 0; i < web.WorkflowTemplates.Count; ++i)
{
    if (web.WorkflowTemplates[i].Name == "Approval -
    SharePoint 2010")
        approvalTemplate = web.WorkflowTemplates[i];
}

SPList wrkHistoryList = null;
// Try to get workflow history list
try
{
    wrkHistoryList = web.Lists["Workflow History"];
}
catch (Exception)
{
    // Create workflow history list
    Guid listGuid = web.Lists.Add("Workflow History",
    "", SPListTemplateType.WorkflowHistory);
    wrkHistoryList = web.Lists[listGuid];
    wrkHistoryList.Hidden = true;
    wrkHistoryList.Update();
}


SPList wrkTasksList = null;
// Try to get workflow tasks list
try
{
    wrkTasksList = web.Lists["Tasks"];
}
catch (Exception)
{
    // Create workflow tasks list
    Guid listGuid = web.Lists.Add("Tasks", "",
    SPListTemplateType.Tasks);
    wrkTasksList = web.Lists[listGuid];
    wrkTasksList.Hidden = true;
    wrkTasksList.Update();
}
```

```
        Microsoft.SharePoint.Workflow.SPWorkflowAssociation
wrkAssoc = SPWorkflowAssociation.CreateListContentTypeAssocia
tion(approvalTemplate, "Chapter3 Project Proposal Approval",
wrkTasksList, wrkHistoryList);

        wrkAssoc.AutoStartCreate = false;
        ctProjectProposal.WorkflowAssociations.Add(wrkAssoc);

        // Commit changes.
        ctProjectProposal.Update();
```

4. Build and run the project. Navigate to **Site Actions | Site Settings | Gallery | Site Content Types** and select **Chapter3 Project Proposal**. Click on the **Workflow Settings** and you should be able to see our "Approval workflow" associated with the content type as shown in the following screenshot:

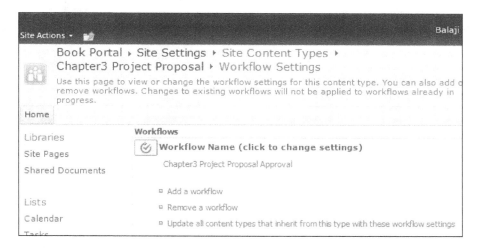

How it works...

The first step to associate a workflow to a content type is to get the workflow template that we need to associate. We loop through the Web object to get our template. In our example, we got the template for "Approval – SharePoint 2010". This is the name of the workflow. When you know the name of the workflow, you can iterate through the Web object for all the workflows that are available on that site. After this, we created the necessary supporting lists like the tasks and the workflow history list for the workflow. Based on the template, we created an association object for the content type and associated this object to our content type.

A workflow associated object represents the binding of the template to a particular content type or list. It has a static method to create the binding association. In our case, we used the `CreateListContentTypeAssociation` method to create the binding association. For more information on workflow association please refer to MSDN at: `http://msdn.microsoft.com/en-us/library/microsoft.sharepoint.workflow.spworkflowassociation.aspx`.

There's more...

You can also pass the association data to the workflow template. Association data is of the XML format and is different for each of the workflows. The following is the code to pass association data to the approval workflow that we have used. Make sure to substitute proper user IDs for your environment.

```
string sAssocData = "<dfs:myFields xmlns:xsd=\"http://www.w3.org/2001/
XMLSchema\" xmlns:dms=\"http://schemas.microsoft.com/office/2009/
documentManagement/types\" xmlns:dfs=\"http://schemas.microsoft.com/
office/infopath/2003/dataFormSolution\" xmlns:q=\"http://schemas.
microsoft.com/office/infopath/2009/WSSList/queryFields\" xmlns:
d=\"http://schemas.microsoft.com/office/infopath/2009/WSSList/
dataFields\" xmlns:ma=\"http://schemas.microsoft.com/office/2009/
metadata/properties/metaAttributes\" xmlns:pc=\"http://schemas.
microsoft.com/office/infopath/2007/PartnerControls\" xmlns:xsi=\
"http://www.w3.org/2001/XMLSchema-instance\"><dfs:queryFields></
dfs:queryFields><dfs:dataFields><d:SharePointListItem_RW><d:
Approvers><d:Assignment><d:Assignee><pc:Person><pc:DisplayName>Balaji
Kithiganahalli</pc:DisplayName><pc:AccountId>INTEGRATELLCDEV\\
balaji</pc:AccountId><pc:AccountType>User</pc:AccountType></pc:
Person><pc:Person><pc:DisplayName>SP Test1</pc:DisplayName><pc:Acco
untId>INTEGRATELLCDEV\\sptest1</pc:AccountId><pc:AccountType>User</
pc:AccountType></pc:Person></d:Assignee><d:Stage xsi:nil=\"true\"
/><d:AssignmentType>Serial</d:AssignmentType></d:Assignment><d:
Assignment><d:Assignee><pc:Person><pc:DisplayName>SP Test2</pc:
DisplayName><pc:AccountId>INTEGRATELLCDEV\\sptest2</pc:AccountId><pc:
AccountType>User</pc:AccountType></pc:Person></d:Assignee><d:Stage
xsi:nil=\"true\" xmlns:xsi=\"http://www.w3.org/2001/XMLSchema-
instance\" /><d:AssignmentType>Serial</d:AssignmentType></d:
Assignment></d:Approvers><d:ExpandGroups>true</d:ExpandGroups><d:
NotificationMessage /><d:DueDateforAllTasks xsi:nil=\"true\" /><d:
DurationforSerialTasks xsi:nil=\"true\" /><d:DurationUnits>Day</
d:DurationUnits><d:CC /><d:CancelonRejection>false</d:
CancelonRejection><d:CancelonChange>false</d:CancelonChange><d:EnableC
ontentApproval>false</d:EnableContentApproval></d:SharePointListItem_
RW></dfs:dataFields></dfs:myFields>";

approvalTemplate.AssociationData = sAssocData;
```

See also

▸ _Creating an external content type_ recipe

Creating an external content type

External content types are defined as reusable objects with metadata descriptions of connectivity information to external systems and data definitions. They could also contain the behaviors you want to apply to the external data. They are similar to the content types that we have dealt so far. The difference is that we will be managing the external data in external content types. The external data can be from relational databases like SQL server or Oracle or data coming from some web service.

For our recipe, we will use a SQL server table and create a content type based on the table data. We will use the `HumanResources.Department` table in the `AdventureWorks` database. We will create a `GetDepartments` method that will retrieve the list of all departments and a `GetDepartment` method that retrieves the single department object.

We will use LINQ to SQL to access relational data as objects. You do not have to use LINQ to SQL for data access in external content types. In this example, we are using it for the sake of simplicity of the code. If you want to learn more about LINQ to SQL, refer to MSDN at: `http://msdn.microsoft.com/en-us/library/bb425822.aspx`.

Getting ready

For this recipe, you need to have access to the `AdventureWorks` database. You can download it from: `http://msftdbprodsamples.codeplex.com/`.

How to do it...

1. Create an empty SharePoint project with the farm level deployment option.

2. Add a new item to this project and select **Business Data Connectivity Model** and name the item as **DepartmentsModel** as shown here:

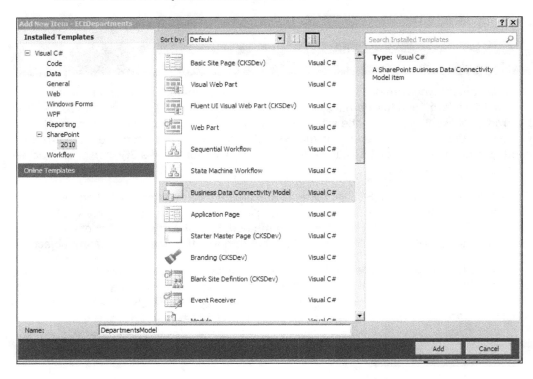

3. Visual Studio adds the necessary files and brings up the BDC designer with a default entity called **Entity1**. Delete this default entity. Also delete the files `Entity1.cs` and `Entity1Service.cs` associated with this entity.

4. From the ToolBox, add a new entity to the designer surface and rename this as **Department** in the properties window of the entity. Add a new identifier to this entity and call it **DepartmentID** and change the **Type Name** to `System.Int16`. Visual Studio will add a new service file called `DepartmentService.cs` in your solution explorer.

5. To the project, now add a new item and select **Data | LINQ to SQL Classes** and name it **Department** as shown in the following screenshot:

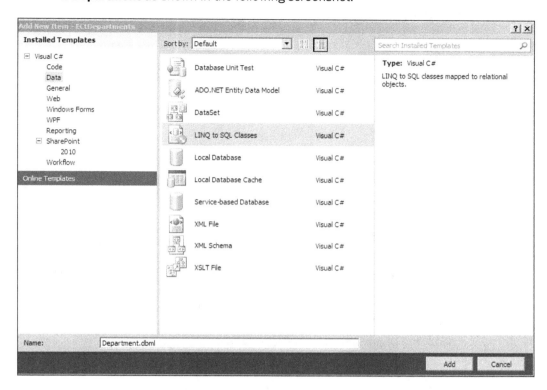

6. From the server explorer, add a new data connection to your **AdventureWorks** database. Now from your LINQ to SQL designer window, navigate through the Server Explorer to the tables node from the data connection you just added. Expand the tables node and drag the `Departments` table and it to the designer. Visual Studio will generate the necessary LINQ `DataContext` classes for the external table. You can refer to this `DataContext` class in the `Department.designer.cs` file. Close this designer surface. We will not be making any changes to this class file.

7. Now back in the **DepartmentsModel**, select the **Department Entity** created previously, and **Create a Finder Method** from the **BDC Method Details** window and name it `GetDepartmentList`. Also `Create a Finder Specific` method and name it `GetDepartment`. The final screenshot should look like the following:

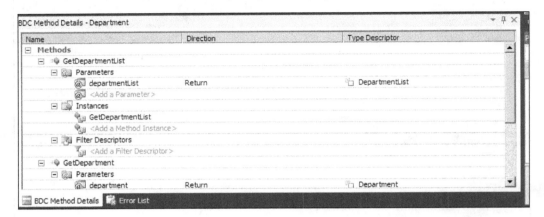

8. Select the **DepartmentList Type Descriptor** in the **BDC Method Details** window and from the drop-down select **Edit** menu option to bring up the BDC explorer window. In here, change the `Type Name` property to **Current Project | Department**. Make sure that the **Is Enumerable** checkbox is selected.

9. Underneath the **DepartmentList**, select **Department** and change the `Type Name` property to **Current Project | Department**. In this case, the **Is Enumerable** checkbox is not selected. Underneath this department, add a `Type Descriptor` and name it **DepartmentID**. The type name should be `System.Int16`. In the same manner, add three more **Type Descriptors** named **Name**, **GroupName**, and **ModifiedDate**. The **Type Name** for the **Name** and the **GroupName** is `System.String` and for **ModifiedDate** it is `System.DateTime`. The final screen should be as shown in the following screenshot:

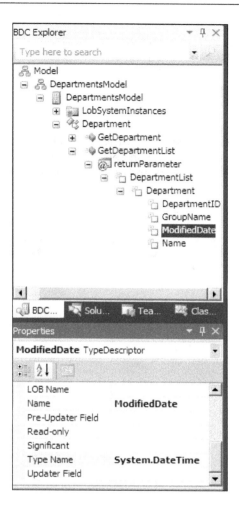

10. Open the `DepartmentService.cs` file and add code to retrieve the departments from the database to the `GetDepartmentList` method and add code to retrieve the single object to the `GetDepartment` method. Your code should be as follows. Make sure to change the database connection string to your environment:

```
public static IEnumerable<Department> GetDepartmentList()
        {
            DepartmentDataContext dx = new DepartmentData
            Context("Data Source=intsql;Initial Catalog=Adventure
            Works;Integrated Security=True");
            return dx.Departments;
        }

        public static Department GetDepartment(short id)
```

```
        {
            DepartmentDataContext dx = new DepartmentData
Context("Data Source=intsql;Initial Catalog=AdventureWorks;
Integrated Security=True");
            return dx.Departments.Single(d => d.DepartmentID ==
            id);
        }
```

11. Press *F5* to build and run the project. This should bring up the site that was provided during the project creation wizard. In here, from the site actions menu, create an external list called **Departments** and add the content type we just created as shown here:

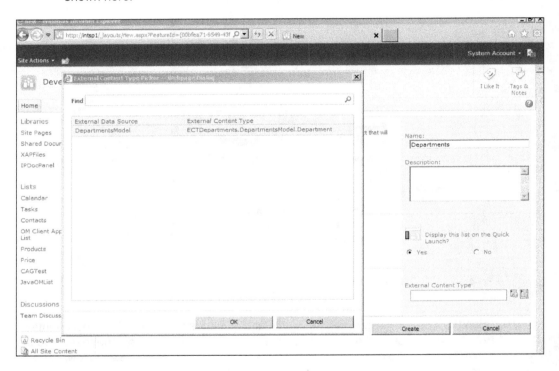

12. This should list all the departments from the `Departments` table in the `AdventureWorks` database as shown in the next screenshot:

	DepartmentID	Name	GroupName	ModifiedDate
	1	Engineering	Research and Development	6/3/2011 8:00 PM
	2	Tool Design	Research and Development	5/31/1998 8:00 PM
	3	Sales	Sales and Marketing	5/31/1998 8:00 PM
	4	Marketing	Sales and Marketing	5/31/1998 8:00 PM
	5	Purchasing	Inventory Management	5/31/1998 8:00 PM
	6	Research and Development	Research and Development	5/31/1998 8:00 PM
	7	Production	Manufacturing	5/31/1998 8:00 PM
	8	Production Control	Manufacturing	5/31/1998 8:00 PM
	9	Human Resources	Executive General and Administration	5/31/1998 8:00 PM
	10	Finance	Executive General and Administration	5/31/1998 8:00 PM
	11	Information Services	Executive General and Administration	5/31/1998 8:00 PM
	12	Document Control	Quality Assurance	5/31/1998 8:00 PM
	13	Quality Assurance	Quality Assurance	5/31/1998 8:00 PM
	14	Facilities and Maintenance	Executive General and Administration	5/31/1998 8:00 PM
	15	Shipping and Receiving	Inventory Management	5/31/1998 8:00 PM
	16	Executive	Executive General and Administration	5/31/1998 8:00 PM

How it works...

Visual Studio refers to external content types as an entity because BDC schema refers to this as entities. BDC Designer is built on top of ADO.Net Entity Designer and hence that reference. If you are familiar with ADO.Net Entity Designer, this will work the same way. In here, we can create entities and associate them with some relationship.

For our external content type to work, we need to create at least two methods of type `Finder` and `SpecificFinder` method. In our example, we created `GetDepartmentList` and `GetDepartment` that corresponds to these types. This is important because SharePoint calls these methods to render the list and display the selected item when the item is selected. There are other types of methods that can be used in external content types. Refer to MSDN at: `http://msdn.microsoft.com/en-us/library/ee557363(office.14).aspx` for more information on different method types that can be developed in the external content types.

The finder method, `GetDepartmentList` does not take any input parameters, but has one return parameter. This is defined in the **Method Details** window. In here, we provided information about the type of our parameter and direction of the parameter. The direction can be "In", "Out", "InOut", and "Return". The "In" direction is used on the parameters that are used to pass in the values to the methods. The "Out" direction, as the name refers to, is the output parameter and "InOut" is similar to "ref" parameter in C#. We also provided the type of our parameter. For this, we used the `Department` object that was created through LINQ to SQL. We set the type of the parameter through type descriptors. Type descriptors are metadata information that is used during the runtime to determine the type of the parameter passed or returned. There are other properties in type descriptors that tell SharePoint how to use this parameter. For example, the `Creator Field` property in a type descriptor tells that it is used in the form for user input. the collection property tells that the parameter is a collection. Not all of the type descriptors make sense for each of the parameters that pass in the method. It comes in handy, depending upon the type we want to retrieve or pass.

Each of the methods that we defined also has a method instance. This is because, in BCS, when we define a method, it is defined as an abstract piece of code. An instance is created during run time and executed.

There's more...

If you receive **Access denied by Business Data Connectivity** error as shown here, follow these steps:

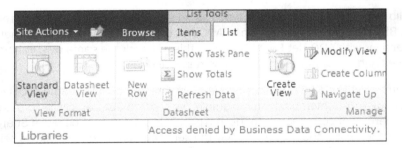

1. Open **Central Administration | Application Management | Manage Service applications** and select **Business Data Connectivity Service**. You should see the list of all external content types deployed.

2. From the drop-down menu select your content type and select **Set Permissions** as shown in the following screenshot:

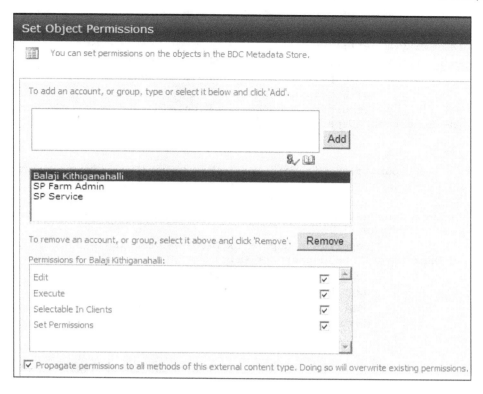

3. Add users and set appropriate permissions for the user executing the ECT.

Create, update, and delete methods

For our preceding example, to add other CRUD methods like create, update, and delete methods, follow these steps:

1. From the **BDC Method Details Window**, create **Creator Method** for creating the department. Name this method `CreateDepartment`. For updating, the method type should be `Updater Method` and for delete `Deleter Method`. Also name the updater method as `UpdateDepartment` and the deleter method as `DeleteDepartment`.

2. Visual Studio automatically wires up the necessary parameters and its type descriptors and adds method signatures in the `DepartmentService.cs`. Add the code in the `DepartmentService.cs` for create, update, and delete. Your code should look as follows:

```
        public static Department CreateDepartment(Department
newDepartment)
            {
```

```
          DepartmentDataContext dx = new DepartmentDataContext
("Data Source=intsql;Initial Catalog=AdventureWorks;Integrated
Security=True");
              newDepartment.ModifiedDate = DateTime.Today;
              dx.Departments.InsertOnSubmit(newDepartment);
              dx.SubmitChanges();
              return dx.Departments.Single(d => d.DepartmentID ==
newDepartment.DepartmentID);
        }

        public static void UpdateDepartment(Department department)
        {
          DepartmentDataContext dx = new DepartmentDataContext
("Data Source=intsql;Initial Catalog=AdventureWorks;Integrated
Security=True");
              Department dept = dx.Departments.Single(d =>
d.DepartmentID == department.DepartmentID);
              dept.GroupName = department.GroupName;
              dept.Name = department.Name;
              dept.ModifiedDate = DateTime.Today;
              dx.SubmitChanges();
        }

        public static void DeleteDepartment(short departmentID)
        {
          DepartmentDataContext dx = new DepartmentDataContext
("Data Source=intsql;Initial Catalog=AdventureWorks;Integrated
Security=True");
              dx.Departments.DeleteOnSubmit(dx.Departments.Single(d
=> d.DepartmentID == departmentID));
              dx.SubmitChanges();
        }
```

Connection strings

In our example, we have hard coded the connection string. There are several ways you can access the connection string data without hard coding it like getting the connection string from web.config or from a custom SharePoint list that is used to store the configuration information. The other approach is to use the BCS LobSystemInstance object. For our example:

1. Navigate from BCS Explorer window **Model | DepartmentsModel | DepartmentsModel | LobSystemInstances | DepartmentsModel**.

2. From the properties windows, add a custom property in the custom property collection and add your connection string as shown:

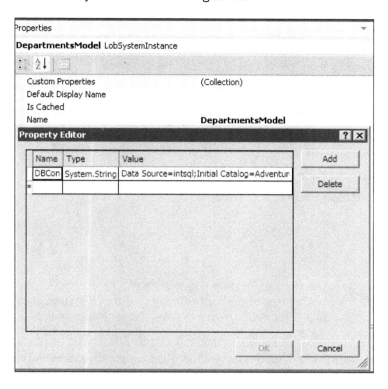

3. Add a reference to `Microsoft.BusinessData.dll` found in `\Program Files\ Common Files\Microsoft Shared\Web Server Extensions\14\ISAPI`.

4. This connection string now can be accessed from the code by making `DepartmentService` implement the `IContextProperty` interface. The following is the code for getting the DB connection string.

```
public  string GetDBCon()
      {
          Microsoft.BusinessData.MetadataModel.Collections.
INamedPropertyDictionary dic = this.LobSystemInstance.
GetProperties();
              if (dic.ContainsKey("DBCon"))
                  return dic["DBCon"].ToString();
              else
                  return "";
      }


      public  Microsoft.BusinessData.Runtime.IExecutionContext
```

```
ExecutionContext
    {
        get;
        set;
    }

    public  Microsoft.BusinessData.MetadataModel.
ILobSystemInstance LobSystemInstance
    {
        get;
        set;
    }

    public  Microsoft.BusinessData.MetadataModel.
IMethodInstance MethodInstance
    {
        get;
        set;
    }
```

The other method is to use the secure store service to store the connection string. Although it is used to store the user credentials for logging into the external system, it can be used to store the connection string. Information on configuring the secure store service can be found on MSDN at `http://technet.microsoft.com/en-us/library/ee806866.aspx`.

For our example, create a new secure store application called **AdventureWorks** with one field of type **Generic**. Call that field **Connection String** as shown here:

Follow the next steps to get credentials from the secure store programmatically.

1. Add a new class to the project and call it `SecureStoreUtilities.cs`.
2. Add a reference to `Microsoft.BusinessData.dll` from the ISAPI folder.
3. Add a reference to `Microsoft.Office.SecureStoreService.dll` from `\Windows\assembly\GAC_MSIL\Microsoft.Office.SecureStoreService\14.0.0.0__71e9bce111e9429c\`.

4. Add the following code to `SecureStoreUtilities.cs` to retrieve and decrypt the string:

```
public static Dictionary<string, string> GetSSCreds(string
applicationID)
        {
            var credKVP = new Dictionary<string, string>(); //Key
Value pair
            using (SPSite site = new SPSite("http://intsp1/"))
            {
               //  Console.WriteLine(site.RootWeb.CurrentUser.
Name);
                SPServiceContext serviceContext =
SPServiceContext.GetContext(site);

                var secureStoreProvider = new SecureStoreProvider
{ Context = serviceContext };

                using (var creds = secureStoreProvider.
                GetCredentials(applicationID))
                {
                    var taFields = secureStoreProvider.GetTarget
                     ApplicationFields(applicationID);
                    for (var i = 0; i < taFields.Count; i++)
                    {
                        var field = taFields[i];
                        var credential = creds[i];
                       var decryptedCredential = DecryptCredential
(credential.Credential);

                        credKVP.Add(field.Name,
decryptedCredential);
                    }
                }
            }

            return credKVP;
        }

        public static string DecryptCredential(this SecureString
        encryptedString)
        {
            var ssBSTR = Marshal.SecureStringToBSTR
            (encryptedString);

            try
```

```
        {
            return Marshal.PtrToStringBSTR(ssBSTR);
        }
        finally
        {
            Marshal.FreeBSTR(ssBSTR);
        }
    }
```

5. Create a following utility method in your `DepartmentService.cs` called `GetDBConnectionString` and pass the return value from this method to the `DepartmentDataContext` constructor:

```
public static string GetDBConnectionString()
        {
            string sDbCon = "";
            Dictionary<string, string> ssList =
SecureStoreUtilities.GetSSCreds("AdventureWorks");
            foreach (KeyValuePair<string, string> kvp in ssList)
            {
                if (kvp.Key == "Connection String")
                {
                    sDbCon = kvp.Value;
                    break;
                }
            }

            return sDbCon;
        }
```

You can use this approach to dynamically construct a LOB connection string by storing the credentials in the secure store.

See also

▶ *Creating a list definition* recipe

Creating a list definition

In all the previous recipes, when we deployed the content type, we had to manually create a list based on the content type using the SharePoint UI. We can create list instances based on the content type using Visual Studio without going through the SharePoint UI.

In this recipe, we will create a custom content type called an `Expense` content type and based on that content type, we will create a list `Definition` and list `Instance`.

Our Expense content type will be based on an Item content type and will have three fields named Title, Amount, and Expense category which is a choice field.

Getting ready

You should have completed the previous recipes successfully.

How to do it...

1. Launch your Visual Studio 2010 IDE as an administrator (right-click the shortcut and select **Run as administrator**).

2. Select **File | New | Project**. The new project wizard dialog box will be displayed. (Make sure to select **.NET Framework 3.5** in the top drop-down box).

3. Select **List Definition** project under **Visual C# | SharePoint | 2010** node from **Installed Templates** section on the left-hand side.

4. Name the project **Chapter3ListDefinition** and provide the location to save the project.

5. Select **Deploy** as a farm solution and move to the next step in the wizard.

6. In the **Choose List Definition Settings** dialog box, provide the name for your list definition and select **Custom List** for **What is the type of the list definition?** and make sure to check **Add a list instance for this list definition** as shown here:

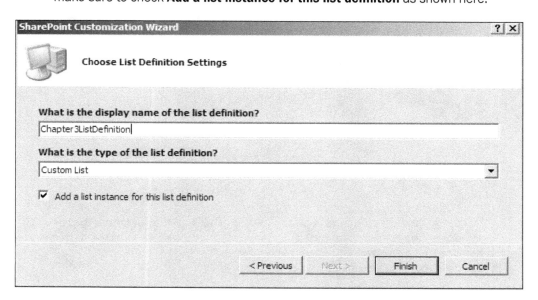

7. This creates a folder names **ListDefinition1** with two XML files named `Elements.xml` and `Schema.xml`. This folder also contains a subfolder named **ListInstance1**. This folder too has an XML file named `Elements.xml`. By default, Visual Studio opens the `Elements.xml` file from the folder `ListDefinition1`.

8. To this add the XML definition that creates the required fields, content type, and the list definition. Your `Elements.xml` file inside the **ListDefinition1** folder should be as follows:

```xml
<?xml version="1.0" encoding="utf-8"?>
<Elements xmlns="http://schemas.microsoft.com/sharepoint/">

    <Field ID="{ACFCD9F9-56D4-42B0-91E7-702511A41E0D}"
Name="Chap3Amt" Description="Chap3 Expense Amount" Type="Currency"
DisplayName="Chap3 Expense Amount" Required="TRUE" LCID="1033"></
Field>
    <Field ID="{1C9A5A95-12EA-4FED-8D2B-419C0E883DAF}"
Name="Chap3Cat" Description="Chap3 Expense Category" Type="Choice"
DisplayName="Chap3 Expense Category" Required="TRUE">
        <CHOICES>
          <CHOICE>Books</CHOICE>
          <CHOICE>Food</CHOICE>
          <CHOICE>Rent</CHOICE>
          <CHOICE>Entertainment</CHOICE>
          <CHOICE>ISP</CHOICE>
          <CHOICE>Cable</CHOICE>
        </CHOICES>
    </Field>

    <ContentType ID="0x0100794FFBC7EB4A4441AFC07DA551BB610E"
                 Name="Chap3ExpenseCT"
                 Group="Custom Content Types"
                 Description="Expense Content Type -
                 Chapter 3 example"
                 Version="0">
        <FieldRefs>

          <FieldRef ID="{ACFCD9F9-56D4-42B0-91E7-702511A41E0D}"/>
          <FieldRef ID="{1C9A5A95-12EA-4FED-8D2B-419C0E883DAF}"/>
        </FieldRefs>
    </ContentType>
    <!-- Do not change the value of the Name attribute below. If
it does not match the folder name of the List Definition project
item, an error will occur when the project is run. -->
    <ListTemplate
        Name="Chapter3ListDef"
```

```
                Type="10999"
                BaseType="0"
                OnQuickLaunch="TRUE"
                DisallowContentTypes="FALSE"
                SecurityBits="11"
                Sequence="410"
                DisplayName="Chapter3ListDefinition"
                Description="My List Definition"
                Image="/_layouts/images/itgen.png"/>
    </Elements>
```

9. In the `Elements.xml` file inside the `ListInstance1` folder, change the `TemplateType` attribute to the same number as the one provided in the `ListDefinition` `Elements.xml` file for the attribute type. Also add a default row to the list instance that gets populated when the list instance gets created. Your `Elements.xml` in the `ListInstance1` folder should look as follows:

```
<?xml version="1.0" encoding="utf-8"?>
<Elements xmlns="http://schemas.microsoft.com/sharepoint/">
    <ListInstance Title="Chapter3ListDefinition - Chapter3ListInst"
                  OnQuickLaunch="TRUE"
                  TemplateType="10999"
                  Url="Lists/Chapter3ListInst"
                  Description="My List Instance">
        <Data>
          <Rows>
            <Row>
              <Field Name="Title">Movie</Field>
              <Field Name="Chap3Amt">10.00</Field>
              <Field Name="Chap3Cat">Entertainment</Field>
            </Row>
          </Rows>
        </Data>
    </ListInstance>
</Elements>
```

10. In the `Schema.xml` file underneath the `ListDefinition1` folder, add a new attribute `EnableContentTypes="True"` to the list node. Part of the list node is provided as follows:

```
<List xmlns:ows="Microsoft SharePoint" Title="Chapter3ListDefiniti
on" EnableContentTypes="TRUE"
```

11. Add the field definitions that we added to the `Elements.xml` file under the `ListDefinition1` folder to the `<Fields>` section in `Schema.xml`. The following is the `Fields` section in `Schema.xml`:

```
<Fields>
        <Field ID="{ACFCD9F9-56D4-42B0-91E7-702511A41E0D}"
Name="Chap3Amt" Description="Chap3 Expense Amount" Type="Currency"
```

```
DisplayName="Chap3 Expense Amount" Required="TRUE" LCID="1033"></
Field>
        <Field ID="{1C9A5A95-12EA-4FED-8D2B-419C0E883DAF}"
Name="Chap3Cat" Description="Chap3 Expense Category" Type="Choice"
DisplayName="Chap3 Expense Category" Required="TRUE">
            <CHOICES>
                <CHOICE>Books</CHOICE>
                <CHOICE>Food</CHOICE>
                <CHOICE>Rent</CHOICE>
                <CHOICE>Entertainment</CHOICE>
                <CHOICE>ISP</CHOICE>
                <CHOICE>Cable</CHOICE>
            </CHOICES>
        </Field>
    </Fields>
```

12. Add a `ContentTypeRef` node to the `<ContentTypes>` section in `Schema.xml`. The ID attribute for this element should be the same as the one defined in the `Elements.xml` underneath the `ListDefinition1` folder. The `ContentRef` node is as follows:

```
<ContentTypeRef ID="0x0100794FFBC7EB4A4441AFC07DA551BB610E"></
ContentTypeRef>
```

13. Add the `FieldRef` elements to the default view in the section `<ViewFields>`. The following code shows the listing of `ViewFields` section:

```
<ViewFields>
        <FieldRef Name="Attachments"></FieldRef>
        <FieldRef Name="LinkTitle"></FieldRef>
        <FieldRef Name="Chap3Amt"></FieldRef>
        <FieldRef Name="Chap3Cat"></FieldRef>
    </ViewFields>
```

14. Press *F5* to build and run the application. This will bring up the site that was provided during the project creation wizard. Your list is created with a row already populated as follows:

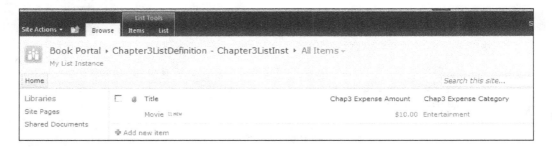

How it works...

In the previous recipes, we have explained how the XML schema is used by the SharePoint to create the necessary fields and content types. In this recipe, the added item is a list definition. A list definition, also referred to as a list template provides the information on what the list contains. It is like an architectural diagram for a building. You can use it to build many buildings of the same type. Similarly, a list definition provides information on whether we allow management of content types, if so, what content type the list uses, whether we need to allow it on the quick launch toolbar and so on. The main attributes of a list template are as follows:

Attribute Name	Description
AllowDeletion	A Boolean flag to indicate whether the list can be deleted or not. When set to false, you do not get the menu item delete in this list in the settings page.
Name	Provides the unique name for the list template.
Type	Not to conflict with the default list types provided, always use number above 10000.
DisallowContentTypes	When set to false, it allows the management of the content types.
SecurityBits	Item level security on the list.

More information on the attributes that can be passed in the ListTemplate can be found on MSDN at: http://msdn.microsoft.com/en-us/library/ms439434.aspx.

Using this list definition, we created a list instance and provided a default row. A list instance can override some of the properties like VersioningEnabled, OnQuickLaunch, and Hidden that are set on list definition. The properties on the list instance will always prevail over the properties set on list definition. More information on all the attributes that can be set on list instance can found on MSDN at: http://msdn.microsoft.com/en-us/library/ms476062.aspx.

See also

▶   *Working with Web Parts* recipe

7
Workflows

This chapter is taken from *Microsoft SharePoint 2010 Development with Visual Studio 2010 Expert Cookbook* (Chapter 2) by Balaji Kithiganahalli.

In this chapter, we will cover:

- ► Creating a sequential workflow
- ► Creating a site workflow with initiation form
- ► Deploying an InfoPath form with a workflow
- ► Creating a task from the workflow
- ► Creating a custom task form

Introduction

According to **Workflow Management Coalition** (http://www.WFMC.org) a standards organization that solely concentrates on processes, defines a workflow as follows:

> *The automation of a business process, in whole or part, during which documents, information or tasks are passed from one participant to another for action, according to a set of procedural rules.*

In simple terms, it means a workflow is a system that manages the execution of a business process. Organizations implement workflows for many different reasons such as:

- ► Auditing and tracking
- ► Better efficiency

- ▸ Consistency
- ▸ Better customer support

Whatever may be the reason for workflow implementation; it is implemented by breaking up the business processes into small activities and executed in a logical order.

An activity in a workflow is the smallest piece or item that you execute. Take for instance a business process that manages employee time and expense reporting (T&E). In here, when employee submits the T&E, a notification is sent to the manager to make a decision regarding approval or rejection and when once that is complete, a notification is sent back to the employee. Each of these steps that happen in the business process is considered an activity. There are three types of activities:

1. Standard activities.
2. Control flow activities.
3. Container activities.

Standard activities are those that perform some tasks like sending an e-mail or executing a .NET code or creating a task and so on. **Control flow activities** are those that are used as decision points. Examples of control flow activities are if-else, while loop, and so on. These activities require you to provide rules for decision-making purposes. These rules can be defined declaratively or code based. The declarative rules are stored in an XML file with .rules extension. **Container activities** are those that can host other activities and create a composite activity. Examples of container activities are sequence activity, conditioned activities groups, and so on. Remember some control flow activities are container activities too.

SharePoint 2010 workflows are based on **Windows Workflow Foundation (WF)**. WF is part of .NET 3.5 Framework. Using WF you can build many workflow enabled applications that do not need to interact with SharePoint at all. Your applications can also host other workflows and execute them. In this scenario, your application has to manage the lifecycle of the hosted workflows. Since workflows can be long running processes, and a system reboot or reset should not terminate the workflow process, hosts can persist the status of the workflow instance as it sees fit like may be in a database or in XML storage. The applications that host workflows are called **host applications**. Host applications can provide custom communication and other services that can make your hosted workflows interact with external applications in an efficient manner. Hosts have workflow runtime engines and some runtime services that help the workflow activities to perform their function.

SharePoint is a host application. It provides a runtime engine for workflows to execute. It has runtime services like persistence service, which stores the status of the workflow instance to a content database. There is a communication service that manages the communication of tasks on a SharePoint workflow. Tasks are the way SharePoint communicates with the users. There is a transaction service as well that manages the transactional scenarios in the workflow like rolling back to a previous state in case of an exception.

SharePoint also provides a timer service and a tracking service that store the history of the workflow instance in a history list. The timer service helps in automatically rehydrating the workflow from idle state after some lapse of time. In our example, of T&E if a manager does not respond to a task within five business days, we can code a delay activity that wakes up after the inactivity and sends an alert to the manager of the impending task.

WF supports two types of workflows—state machine, and sequential workflows. SharePoint based on WF supports both of these types. In sequential workflows, the activities are placed in a logical order with an explicit start and an explicit end. The activities are executed sequentially one after the other like a flow chart. There is no going back to the previous step in a sequential workflow. Sequential workflows are better suited to automated processes that do not need human interaction like moving documents from one library to another or in an order entry process after the user submits the order, the system can automatically do the credit check, inventory check and send a notification to the fulfillment department. They can also be used in a situation where you want the users to follow a certain pattern. Visual Studio 2010 provides templates to develop both state machine and sequential workflows for SharePoint 2010. To define a workflow, we create a project and add activities to the workflow designer surface to construct our logical flow.

In SharePoint, the workflow definitions can be associated with lists or document libraries, content types, and sites. When associated with lists or document libraries, the workflow acts on the item in it. You can manually start the workflow, or start automatically when a new item is created or modified. Since site workflows do not have any items to act upon, it has to be started by an external event like clicking on the link to start the workflow or an external application starting it via code.

When workflows are associated with a content type, workflows can be started on any item that contains this content type irrespective of the list or libraries that the item belongs to.

Site workflows are new to SharePoint 2010. There are no dependencies on lists or libraries in these kinds of workflows. These exists at the site level and can act on all the lists and libraries associated in the site. These types of workflows are usually used in scheduling maintenance tasks or where workflows needs to interact with multiple items located in different lists of the same site.

Both state machine and sequential workflows can be associated with all three categories listed previously. Your business requirements will be the driving factor on what type of workflow that needs to be created and whether it needs to be site or list workflow. When associating, you can ask the user associating the workflow to provide information for the workflow. This can be configuration information like approval groups or database connection string and so on that are specific to the site or list to which the workflow is associated. This is done by providing a form so that users associating the workflow can input this information. This is called an **Association Form**. You can also present a form for user input on every instance of the workflow started. This form is called an **Initiation Form**.

Initiation forms are generally used to get the input from users. This can also be used for overriding associated data for specific instances of the workflow. **Task Forms** are those that are presented to the users when the user is assigned a task. As stated before, tasks are the way SharePoint interacts with the user for the activities to progress.

Apart from providing a framework for developing custom workflows, SharePoint also provides many **out of the box** (**OOB**) workflows like the approval workflow, the three-state workflow, the collect feedback workflow, the disposition workflow, and others. The number of OOB workflows enabled depends on the version of SharePoint that is deployed. For more information on the OOB workflows, please refer to MSDN at: `http://office.microsoft.com/en-us/ sharepoint-server-help/about-the-workflows-included-with-sharepoint-HA102420739.aspx`.

Creating a sequential workflow

In this recipe, we will learn how to create a sequential workflow. For this recipe, we will model a credit approval process. When a user adds an item to a list, we will let the workflow instantiate automatically on the inserted item and flow through the process of checking the user's requested credit line and approving it based on user's employment and credit history.

Getting ready

You should have a fully functional development machine with SharePoint 2010 installed and configured. You also need Visual Studio 2010 IDE installed on the same development machine. We are using a team site template for our examples.

Use the custom list template and create a list from the SharePoint user interface called **Credit Approval**. The following table provides information on fields and its properties:

Field Name	Data Type	Required
Credit Requested	Currency	Yes
Employment History	Choice (Choices - Good, Bad, and None Exists)	Yes
Credit History	Choice (Choices - Good, Bad, and None Exists)	Yes

The following screenshot shows the end result:

How to do it...

1. Launch your Visual Studio 2010 IDE as an administrator (right-click on the shortcut and select **Run as administrator**).

2. Select **File | New | Project**. The new project wizard dialog box as shown will be displayed (make sure to select **.NET Framework 3.5** in the top drop-down box).

3. Select **Sequential Workflow** under **Visual C# | SharePoint | 2010** node from the **Installed Templates** section on the left-hand side.

4. Name the project **SequentialWF** and provide a directory location where you want to save the project and click on **OK** to proceed to the next step in the wizard.

5. By default, Visual Studio selects the SharePoint site available on the machine. Select **Deploy as Farm Solution** and click on **Next** to proceed to the next step in the wizard.

6. In here, provide a name for your workflow and make sure to select **List Workflow** for the workflow template type as shown in the following screenshot:

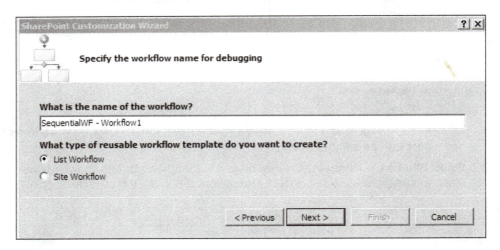

7. Click on **Next** and move on to select the list association and task list and history list selection window. Select **Credit Approval** list from the drop-down for **The library or list to associate your workflow with** and take default selections for the rest as shown in the following screenshot:

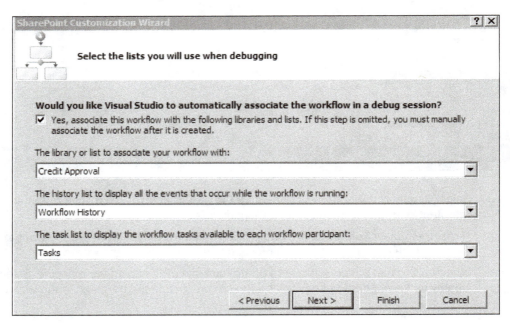

8. In the next window, keep the defaults for **How do you want the workflow to start?** as shown in the following screenshot:

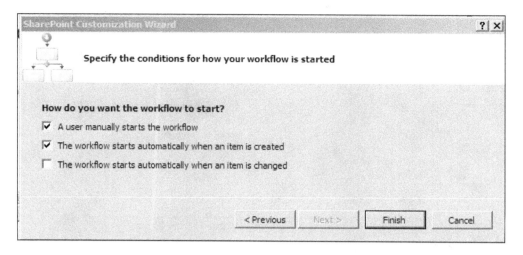

9. By selecting **Finish** the wizard and Visual Studio will generate the necessary files and by default they will open up the workflow designer surface with workflow start and workflow terminator. In between these two items, you should also see the `onWorkflowActivated` activity added.

10. We will build our workflow flowchart by starting off with **LogToHistoryListActivity**. The **LogToHistoryListActivity** is a SharePoint specific activity that can be found in the **Toolbox** under the **SharePoint Workflow** section as shown in the following screenshot:

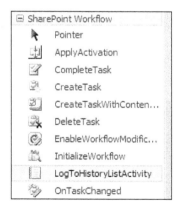

11. Add this activity below the `onWorkflowActivate` activity and change the name to **logWorkflowStarted** from the properties window. Also set the **HistoryDescription** property to **Workflow Started** as shown in the following screenshot:

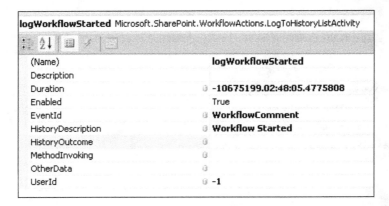

12. Drag an **IfElse** activity and drop it on the designer just below the **logWorkflowStarted** and name it **CheckEmploymentHistoryActivity**. The **IfElse** activity by default adds two branches. One of the branches follows when the condition evaluates to true and the other to false.

- Add **LogToHistoryListActivities** on both of these branches and name the one in the left as **GoodEmploymentHistoryBranch** and the one in the right as **BadEmploymentHistoryBranch**.

- Also change the names of the **LogToHistoryListActivities** underneath these branches. The one under **GoodEmploymentHistoryBranch** is called **logGoodEmploymentHistory** and other as **logBadEmploymentHistory**.

- Set the **HistoryDescription** property for **logGoodEmploymentHistory** to **Employment History is good** and for the other **Employment History is bad**.

The following screenshot shows the finished screen:

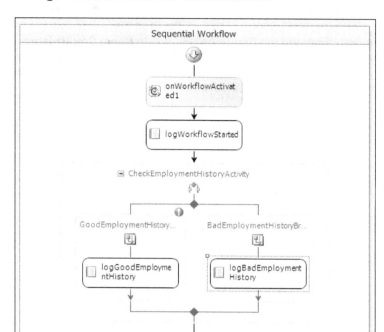

13. The exclamation mark on the branch is indicating that the condition evaluation to execute the branch is not set. This is a required action for an **IfElse** activity. Without this the **IfElse,** activity does not know which branch to execute. From the properties window of the branch, select the **Code Condition** and set the **Condition** property to **CheckEmploymentHistory** as shown in the following screenshot:

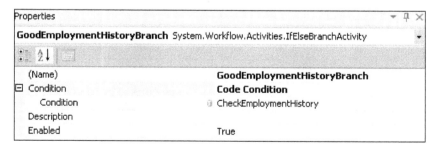

14. Follow the same routine and add another **IfElse** activity under the
GoodEmploymentHistoryBranch and name it **CheckCreditHistoryActivity** and
add **LogToHistoryListActivity** on both of the branches. Here too, set the condition
to **Code Condition** and the **Condition** property to **CheckCreditHistory**. The
HistoryDescription property on **GoodCreditHistoryBranch** should be set to **Credit
History is good** and for the other property set it to **Credit History is bad**. The
completed workflow flowchart should look as follows:

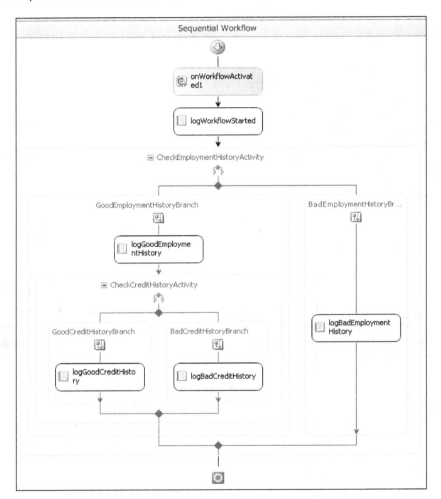

15. From the code view, add the code to verify the employment history. Since the workflow acts on the item that is inserted into the list, you can verify the item values in the workflow. Your code for `CheckEmploymentHistory` method should look like the following:

```
   private void CheckEmploymentHistory(object sender,
ConditionalEventArgs e)
        {
            string sEmpHistory = "";
            sEmpHistory = workflowProperties.Item["Employment
History"].ToString();

            if (sEmpHistory.Trim().ToLower() == "good")
                e.Result = true;
            else
                e.Result = false;
        }
```

16. Similarly, add the code to verify the credit history as well. Your code in the `CheckCreditHistory` method should be as follows:

```
private void CheckCreditHistory(object sender,
ConditionalEventArgs e)
        {
            string sCrdHistory = "";
            sCrdHistory = workflowProperties.Item["Credit
History"].ToString();

            if (sCrdHistory.Trim().ToLower() == "good")
                e.Result = true;
            else
                e.Result = false;
        }
```

17. Build and run the project by pressing *F5*. This should bring up the site that you provided during the project creation. The workflow is already associated with the list that we provided during the project creation. Add a new item to the list with all fields filled in as follows:

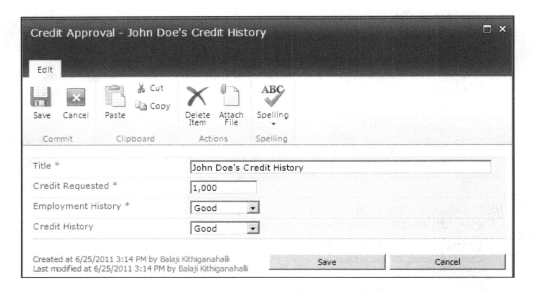

18. As soon as you save the item to the list, the workflow will get initiated and start an instance of it. Since there is no user interaction, the workflow completes and shows the status as shown in the following screenshot:

19. Click on the **Completed** status of the workflow to see the history list associated with the workflow. This should list all the history that we logged during the workflow process. The following screenshot shows the history list:

	Date Occurred	Event Type	User ID	Description	Outcome
	6/25/2011 3:14 PM	Comment	System Account	Workflow Started	
	6/25/2011 3:14 PM	Comment	System Account	Employment History is Good	
	6/25/2011 3:14 PM	Comment	System Account	Credit History is Good	Credit is approved

Workflow History

⊡ View workflow reports

The following events have occurred in this workflow.

20. Add more items to the list with different conditions of employment history and credit history to verify the other conditions of the workflow.

How it works...

Every SharePoint workflow project starts with an `onWorkflowActivated` activity. This activity is a mandatory activity and hence Visual Studio added it to the designer automatically. By default, this activity is bound to a variable called `workflowProperties` of type `SPWorkflowActivationProperties`. The `workflowProperties` provides information about the current workflow context, the item that initiated the workflow, the list to which this workflow belongs to, the originator user, and other information. SharePoint workflow runtime fills in all these values for us to make use of. For all the items that `workflowProperties` provide, refer to: `http://msdn.microsoft.com/en-us/library/microsoft.sharepoint.workflow.spworkflowactivationproperties.aspx`.

Using the `workflowProperties` we were able to get access to the list item that initiated the workflow and from this, we were able to access the item information in the code and create the conditions for the `IfElse` activities. The code is pretty simple such that it checks the values that were put in and makes decision on them.

The `logToHistoryListActivity` is a SharePoint specific activity that logs information to the history list. This activity behind the scenes calls the method `LogToHistoryList` from the `ISharePointService` interface, which is implemented in the assembly `Microsoft.SharePoint.Workflow.dll`. The following code shows the method signature for this method:

```
void LogToHistoryList(
   Guid workflowId,
   SPWorkflowHistoryEventType eventId,
   int userId,
   TimeSpan duration,
   string outcome,
   string description,
   string otherData
)
```

In this method, you can specify an event type like the one workflow started, a workflow comment, and others to group your comments to a specific category. For more information on event types that can be passed to this method, refer to MSDN at: `http://msdn.microsoft.com/en-us/library/microsoft.sharepoint.workflow.spworkflowhistoryeventtype.aspx`.

The `ISharePointService` interface enables activities to exchange data outside of the workflow instance. In this case, writing to the history list. There are other methods like `SendEmail`, `SetState` that are part of this interface as well. Refer to MSDN for more information at: `http://msdn.microsoft.com/en-us/library/microsoft.sharepoint.workflow.isharepointservice_members.aspx`.

In Visual Studio 2010, all the SharePoint project items like Event Receivers, workflow projects, or content types will have a similar structure such as having a feature, a folder for the project item, and so on. When our workflow project was created, Visual Studio added a feature folder with `Feature.xml` file and a `Workflow1` folder that contains the `Elements.xml`, `Workflow1.cs`, and `Worlflow1.designer.cs`. The last two files make up the activities of the workflow and the code associated with these activities. Like with Event Receivers, the `Elements.xml` file provides metadata information about the workflow to the SharePoint. You can name this file anything you want. But Visual Studio, always names it `Elements.xml` for all of the SharePoint templates when you first create the project. In here you set the attributes like the workflow name, the class file, and assembly that contains the code and so on. You can also set the association form, the initiation form, and the task form that are associated with the workflow. Since our workflow did not have any of these resources, we did not make any changes. All the attributes of the `Elements.xml` are as follows:

```
<Workflow
  Title="Text"
  Name="Text"
  CodeBesideAssembly="Text"
  CodeBesideClass="Text"
  Description="Text"
  Id="Text"
  EngineClass="Text"
  EngineAssembly="Text"
  AssociationUrl="Text"
  InstantiationUrl="Text"
  ModificationUrl="Text"
  StatusUrl="Text"
  TaskListContentTypeId="Text" >
</Workflow>
```

For more information on the descriptions of all the elements of the workflow `Elements.xml` file, refer to MSDN at: `http://msdn.microsoft.com/en-us/library/aa543564.aspx`.

In the project creation wizard, we set our sequential workflow as a list workflow. This information can be found in the `.spdata` file located in the `Workflow1` folder. By default this file is hidden. To list this file in the project explorer, toggle the **Show All Files** menu item from **Project** menu. The `.spdata` file is a SharePoint project metadata information file. This is of XML format. You should not manually change this file as it may get overwritten by Visual Studio when you make changes to the project structure like adding and removing items to and from the project. This file is used during the packaging process. It contains information about the SharePoint project item that is in the solution. You can also verify that property from the properties window of the `Workflow1` folder. The other items that we set during the project creation wizard can also be verified in the properties window. You can see the history list and task list associated with the workflow. The target list property specifies the list that the workflow is associated with. This is only for debugging purposes. You can always associate the workflows to different lists after it is built and deployed. You do the association with the target list via SharePoint user interface or through object model code using Feature receivers. You can also associate it to a content type and deploy it.

There's more...

When we build and deploy a workflow to a production environment, you have a couple of ways to associate the workflow with the content type, the list or with the site:

- Manually by using SharePoint user interface
- During activation of the feature via feature receiver

Here is the manual way to associate a workflow to a list.

1. Navigate to **List Settings | Workflow Settings** of the list to which you need to associate a workflow as shown in the following screenshot:

2. Click on the **Add Workflow** link to add a new workflow. The following screenshot shows the **Add Workflow** page:

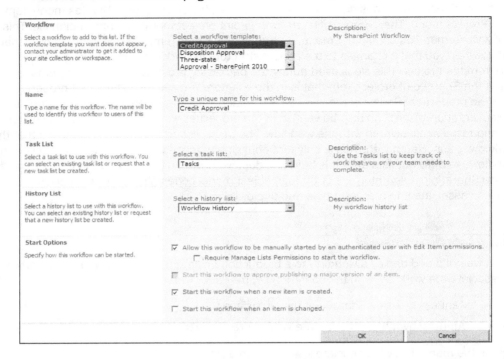

3. Provide a unique name to your workflow and select the supporting task list and history list. Start options provide the way to initiate the workflow.

See also

▶   *Creating a site workflow with an initiation form recipe*

Creating a site workflow with an initiation form

The previous recipe is a good example of a sequential workflow where there is no human interaction. If it were really dealing with a credit approval process on a credit application, this could have gone through the external applications to verify the credit history and employment history and made the decision. So to take advantage of this automation, let us create our own credit application approval system. In this recipe, we will create a site workflow to enact our credit application approval process. Since site workflows are not associated with any lists, there is no form that we can get out of the box for a user to input data and start the workflow. For this purpose, we will also incorporate an initiation form that upon submission will start the workflow.

To keep the workflow simple, the workflow will base its decision on the credit amount requested. If the credit amount is less than $1000.00 it will be automatically approved or if it is greater than that amount, it is rejected.

Getting ready

Since this recipe incorporates ideas from the previous recipe, you should have successfully completed the previous recipe.

How to do it...

1. Launch your Visual Studio 2010 IDE as an administrator (right-click the shortcut and select **Run as administrator**).

2. Select **File | New | Project** and select **Sequential Workflow** under **Visual C# | SharePoint | 2010** node from the **Installed Templates** section on the left-hand side.

3. Name the project **SiteWF** and provide a directory location where you want to save the project and click **OK** to proceed to the next step in the wizard.

4. By default, Visual Studio selects the SharePoint site available on the machine. Select **Deploy as Farm Solution** and click **Next** to proceed to the next step in the wizard.

5. In here, provide a name for your workflow and make sure to select **Site Workflow** for the workflow template type as shown in the following screenshot:

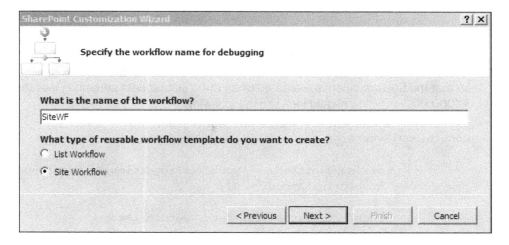

6. Click on **Next** and move on to select the task list and history list selection window. Take the defaults and proceed to the next step.

7. The only option for the site workflows will be to start the workflow manually. Select the default option provided and finish the wizard to create the project.

8. Similar to the *Creating the sequential workflow* recipe, place **LogToHistoryListActivity** and the **IfElse** activity and build our workflow flowchart. Name the code condition for the **IfElse** activity as `CheckCreditAmount`. The final result should be as shown in the following screenshot:

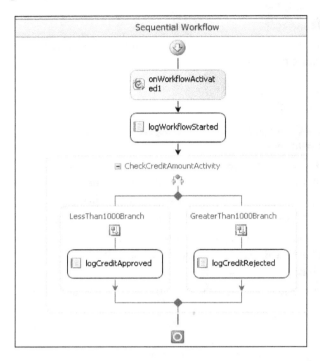

9. In the code file of the workflow, add the code for the method `CheckCreditAmount` so that the true condition is evaluated when the credit request amount is less than $1000.00. Your code should look like the following:

```
private void CheckCreditAmount(object sender,
ConditionalEventArgs e)
        {
            string sInitData =  workflowProperties.InitiationData;
            double initAmount = 0;

            double.TryParse(sInitData, out initAmount);

            if (initAmount <= 1000)
                e.Result = true;
            else
                e.Result = false;
        }
```

10. Right-click on the **Workflow1** folder and from the context menu, **Add** | **New Item** and select **Workflow Initiation Form** and name it `CreditApplication.aspx` as shown in the following screenshot:

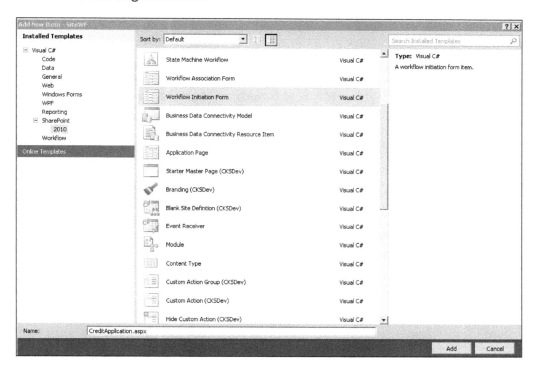

11. Visual Studio adds the code behind file along with the `.aspx` page. There is no designer support for building the user interface. Visual Studio by default also adds a couple of buttons for the **Start Workflow** and **Cancel** in the main content placeholder. Just before these buttons, add a label control and have the text property set to **Credit Amount Requested:** Add a textbox control and name it **txtCreditRequested**. Your `.aspx` markup should look like the following:

```
<asp:Content ID="Main" ContentPlaceHolderID="PlaceHolderMain"
runat="server">


<asp:Label ID="lblEnterCreditAmount" runat="server" Text="Credit
Amount Requested:"></asp:Label>
<asp:TextBox ID="txtCreditAmount" runat="server"></asp:TextBox>
<br />
    <asp:RequiredFieldValidator ID="rfCreditAmount" runat="server"
ErrorMessage="Credit Amount is Required" ControlToValidate="txtCre
ditAmount"></asp:RequiredFieldValidator>


<br />
```

```
        <asp:Button ID="StartWorkflow" runat="server"
OnClick="StartWorkflow_Click" Text="Submit" />
             
        <asp:Button ID="Cancel" runat="server" OnClick="Cancel_Click"
Text="Cancel" />
</asp:Content>
```

12. Open the code behind file of the ASPX page and find the method
`GetInitiationData` and return the contents of `txtCreditAmount`
textbox from this method. Your code in the method should look as follows:

```
private string GetInitiationData()
        {
                return this.txtCreditAmount.Text;
        }
```

13. Build and run the project by pressing *F5*. This should bring up the site that was
provided in the project wizard. As there is no list associated with the workflow, the
main page of the site provided will be displayed. Navigate to **All Site Content | Site
Workflows | Start a New Workflow** and start the workflow by clicking on the name
of the workflow as shown in the following screenshot:

14. This will bring up the initiation form as shown in the following screenshot:

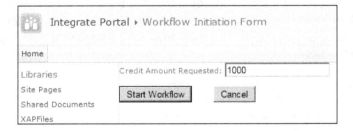

15. Enter the amount **1000** in the textbox and click on the **Start Workflow** button to kick
start the workflow. This will start the workflow. You should see the complete status
and you should be able to verify the history list for the statuses that the workflow
added during the execution.

How it works...

The workflow code and process flow is similar to the recipe *Creating a sequential workflow*. An initiation form provided the data that was needed to do the condition check. An initiation form is an ASPX page which is presented to the user to input the data necessary for the workflow. This form is presented for every instance of the workflow that is started. You can also provide an association form that is common to all the workflow instances. Adding an association form to a workflow is similar to initiation form. An `InfoPath` form can also be added. The deployment procedure for the InfoPath form is different compared to an ASPX page. Since an initiation form is an ASPX page, you can do all the things like adding validation controls, writing business logic in the code behind file, and so on. Designing the ASPX page using the designer is not supported. Since designing a properly formatted ASPX page without designer support is hard, InfoPath forms have taken a special role in creating workflow-related forms. We will learn about deploying InfoPath forms with workflows later in this chapter. In our recipe, we utilized the ASPX page due to the fact that Visual Studio provides the template to create it. InfoPath forms cannot be created with Visual Studio. Previous versions of Visual Studio provided that capability but it was removed from the current 2010 version.

Initiation forms are not just for site workflows. They are equally applicable to list workflows. In fact, they can be presented to all kinds of SharePoint workflows. Workflow manager manages these forms. Whenever an initiation form or association form is submitted, Workflow Manager passes the information from these forms to each instance of the workflow that is created and can be accessed from the Workflow properties collection. Workflow manager is responsible for filling in the property collection of the workflow instance. If there is no initiation data, then it passes an empty string.

Similar to application pages, initiation pages are also stored in the root layouts folder. Visual Studio deployment creates a folder in the same name as the project and a subfolder underneath it with the workflow folder name. In our recipe, this is `SiteWF` and `Workflow1` respectively. If you deploy this workflow, you can navigate to the root layouts folder to verify the initiation page. As stated in the previous recipe, `InstantiationUrl` is one of the attributes of the workflow element in the `Elements.xml` file. Visual Studio automatically updates this attribute with the proper URL of the initiation form. In case you want to change the name of the initiation page, this is the place to verify and make changes if needed.

The Initiation form template in Visual Studio also adds a default code that starts workflow. Workflow is started based on the workflow template ID which is passed to the form as a query string parameter to the initiation form from the workflow runtime. Since ours is a site workflow, only the workflow template ID is passed in the query string. If it were a list workflow, List ID and Item ID that initiated the workflow would have been passed to the initiation form.

On submission of the form, workflow is started programmatically by calling the `SPWorkflowManager` object's `StartWorkflow` method. `SPWorkflowManager` is at the site collection level and is the object responsible for managing the workflow templates and instances across the site collection. The `StartWorkflow` is an overloaded method and takes initiation data as one of the parameters. It is of `string` type. Here is where we passed in our Textbox contents. If you have multiple values to pass, construct a XML string and pass it to this parameter. For more information on `SPWorkflowManager` and `StartWorkflow` refer to MSDN at: `http://msdn.microsoft.com/en-us/library/microsoft.sharepoint.workflow.spworkflowmanager_members.aspx`.

There's more...

As we stated previously, InfoPath forms have become a preferred method for developing initiation, association, or task forms in SharePoint workflows. This is because InfoPath designer provides easier development and designer support to develop custom forms. InfoPath forms when used with SharePoint workflows, opens the form in a browser window. This is controlled by InfoPath form services in SharePoint. This is not available with the SharePoint foundation.

See also

▶ *Creating a sequential workflow recipe*

▶ *Deploying an InfoPath form with the workflow recipe*

Deploying an InfoPath form with the workflow

In this recipe, we will recreate the previous recipe to use InfoPath forms for initiation form.

Getting ready

This recipe assumes that you are familiar with creating InfoPath forms using InfoPath designer 2010. Your SharePoint server should be configured to use form services. Refer to MSDN at: `http://technet.microsoft.com/en-us/library/cc262263.aspx` for more information on configuring the form services.

How to do it...

1. Using InfoPath designer, create a browser compatible form template.
2. Add a textbox control and name it **txtCreditRequested**. Also add a **Submit** button.

3. Go to the Submit Options of the button and add a new data connection to submit to the **Hosting environment** as shown in the following screenshot:

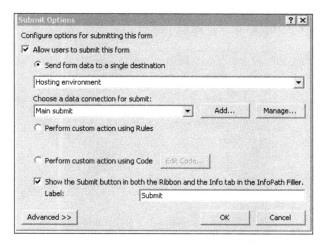

4. From the **File** tab, click on the **Form options** button to open the options dialog box.

5. Uncheck the **Automatically determine security level (recommended)** and select **Domain (the form can access content from the domain in which it is located)** security as shown in the following screenshot:

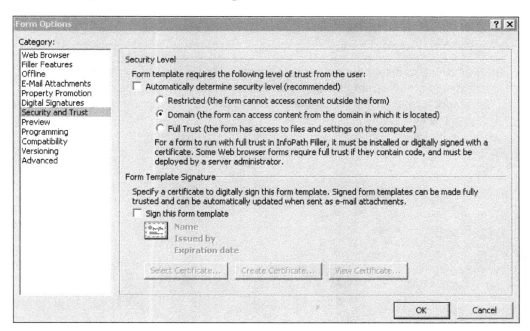

6. From the **File** tab, select **Publish** menu and click on **Network Location** to start the publishing wizard.

7. Provide the path and name of the template for the published form in the wizard's first step as shown in the following screenshot:

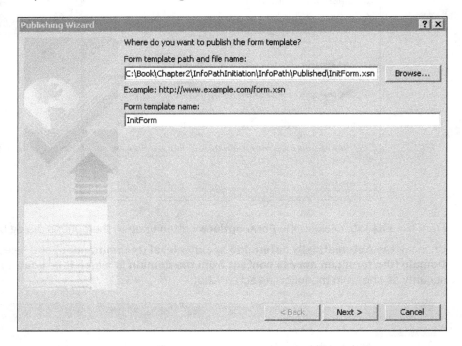

8. Make sure to delete the access path that is added by default by the designer in the next step of the wizard as it only applies to the forms that can be opened from a network location using the InfoPath client application. Ignore the warning and move on to the next step.

9. The final step of the wizard shows the summary of your selection in the previous steps as shown in the following screenshot:

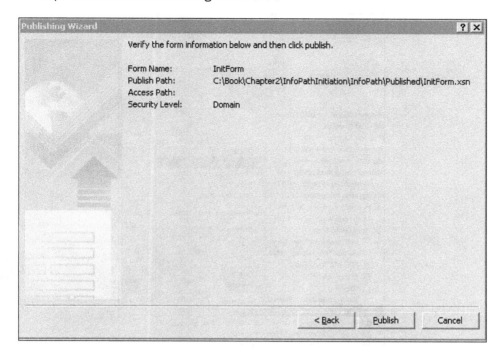

10. After we are done with publishing, from the **File** tab, select **Publish** and select the **Export Source files** option. Provide a location to store the source files of the InfoPath form. This will also save the **XSD** (**XML Schema Definition**) of the form. By default this is always named myschema.xsd. There are situations when you use controls like people picker on the form, the export option may also create another XSD file named BuiltInActiveXControls.xsd.

11. Open **Visual Studio Command Prompt (2010)** from **Start | All Programs | Microsoft Visual Studio 2010 | Visual Studio Tools** as an administrator as shown in the following screenshot:

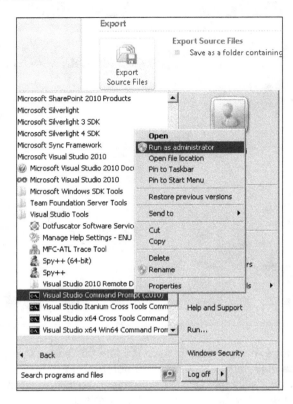

12. From the command prompt, navigate to the location where you saved the source files and type in the following command to generate the class file from the schema file using XSD tool:

    ```
    Xsd.exe myschema.xsd /c /l:cs
    ```

13. This will generate the C# class file of the InfoPath form. By default this is named `myschema.cs`. To generate the VB.Net class file, change the switch `/l:cs` to `/l:vb`. In case you had `BuiltInActiveXControls.xsd` file, provide that too in the preceding command. The command in this case would be as follows:

    ```
    Xsd.exe myschema.xsd BuiltInActiveXControls.xsd /c /l:cs
    ```

14. Add this C# class file to your workflow project. Also add a new module and name it IPForms to your workflow project. This module is used to upload the InfoPath forms that are associated with the workflow to the server.

15. Module is just a folder with two files `Sample.txt` and `Elements.xml`. The `Elements.xml` is used by the project feature to deploy the contents of the module. Delete the `Samples.txt` file as it is just a placeholder to show that files can be deployed using modules. Visual Studio automatically makes the necessary changes to `Elements.xml` whenever you add and delete files from the module.

16. Add the published InfoPath form to this module and Visual Studio automatically updates the `Elements.xml` file in the module. The following code shows the `Elements.xml` file contents:

```xml
<?xml version="1.0" encoding="utf-8"?>
<Elements xmlns="http://schemas.microsoft.com/sharepoint/">
  <Module Name="IPForms">
  <File Path="IPForms\InitForm.xsn" Url="IPForms/InitForm.xsn" />
</Module>
</Elements>
```

17. Open the feature that deploys the module and click the **Manifest** link as shown in the following screenshot:

18. Click the **Edit Options** link to open the manifest editor as shown in the following screenshot:

19. Open the manifest editor and add a new property `RegisterForms` and provide the path of your module that contains the InfoPath forms for the value of the property. This will register the forms in the module when the feature is activated. Your end result of the manifest changes should be similar to the following code:

```xml
<?xml version="1.0" encoding="utf-8" ?>
<Feature xmlns="http://schemas.microsoft.com/sharepoint/">
  <Properties>
    <Property Key="GloballyAvailable" Value="true" />
    <Property Key="RegisterForms" Value="IPForms\*.xsn" />
  </Properties>
</Feature>
```

20. From the feature's property window, set the `Receiver Assembly` and `Receiver Class` properties to the following values:

```
Receiver Assembly = Microsoft.Office.Workflow.Feature,
Version=14.0.0.0, Culture=neutral, PublicKeyToken=71e9bce111e9429c
Receiver Class = Microsoft.Office.Workflow.Feature.
WorkflowFeatureReceiver
```

21. The `WorkflowFeatureReceiver` class processes the manifest file changes that we did in the previous step. This class will manage the registration of the InfoPath files for use with `Workflow`. Until now we created the form and we created the necessary source files that can be used in the workflow and also we made changes to the feature to register the forms for workflow. The last step is to associate this form with the workflow. To do this, we will open the `Elements.xml` file of the workflow and add the **URN (Uniform Resource Name)** of the InfoPath form.

22. To get the URN of the InfoPath Form, go to **File** tab in the **InfoPath Designer** of your form and click the button **Form template properties**. This should bring up the form properties as shown in the following screenshot. From this window, copy the ID element of the form. The URN may be different for you than what is shown:

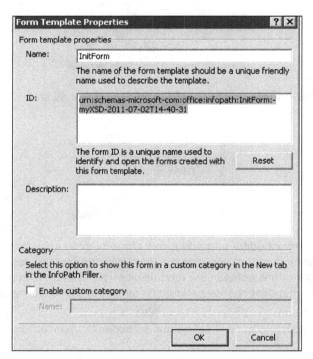

23. Open the `Elements.xml` file of the workflow and add the `Instantiation_FormURN` property under `MetaData` element and also make changes to `InstantiationUrl` property. `InstantiationUrl` refers to an ASPX page that hosts the InfoPath form. Your `elements.xml` file should look like following:

```
<?xml version="1.0" encoding="utf-8" ?>
<Elements xmlns="http://schemas.microsoft.com/sharepoint/">
  <Workflow
      Name="InfoPathInitiation - Workflow1"
      Description="My SharePoint Workflow"
      Id="d1b973a0-9f8b-4abd-befa-0113641cfb34"
      CodeBesideClass="InfoPathInitiation.Workflow1.Workflow1"
      CodeBesideAssembly="$assemblyname$"
      InstantiationUrl="_layouts/IniWrkflIP.aspx">
    <Categories/>
    <MetaData>
      <AssociationCategories>Site</AssociationCategories>
      <Instantiation_FormURN>urn:schemas-microsoft-com:office:
infopath:InitForm:-myXSD-2011-07-02T14-40-31</Instantiation_
FormURN>
      <StatusPageUrl>_layouts/WrkStat.aspx</StatusPageUrl>
    </MetaData>
  </Workflow>
</Elements>
```

24. Now on to the workflow code, where we will use the `XmlSerializer` to deserialize the string initiation data (in the XML format) from our form to `.NET` object. The `myFields` object is in the `myschema.cs` file that we created via the XSD tool. Make changes to the `CheckCreditAmount` method as follows:

```
private void CheckCreditAmount(object sender,
ConditionalEventArgs e)
        {

                string sInitData = workflowProperties.InitiationData;

                XmlSerializer ser = new XmlSerializer(typeof(myFields)
);
                XmlTextReader reader = new XmlTextReader(
                  new System.IO.StringReader(sInitData));
                myFields ipInitForm =
                  (myFields)ser.Deserialize(reader);

                string sCreditRequested = ipInitForm.
txtCreditRequested;
                double initAmount = 0;
```

```
                    double.TryParse(sCreditRequested, out initAmount);

                    if (initAmount <= 1000)
                        e.Result = true;
                    else
                        e.Result = false;
            }
```

25. Build and run the project and when you manually invoke the site workflow, you should see the InfoPath form as shown in the following screenshot:

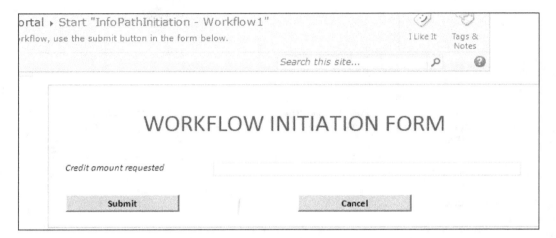

How it works...

As usual, we get the initiation data from the `WorkflowProperties` object like we did in the previous recipe. The difference in here is that we get XML string for the initiation data as InfoPath forms are XML files. To read values from this XML string, we cast the string into a `.NET` class that was generated from the form's schema definition file. This is the reason why we used the XSD generator to create the `.NET` class for our initiation form. The XSD generator when created the `.NET` class from the schema file, each of the control in the form is mapped to a property. Hence we can just use the dot notation to read the values of the form's controls. The `XmlSerializer` is used in the `CheckCreditAmount` method to cast the XML string to the `.NET` class.

To make use of the InfoPath forms in the workflow, we need to deploy it to the form server of the SharePoint and make it workflow enabled. This is the reason, why we used a feature to deploy our InfoPath form. Just using feature would not deploy it to the forms server. We need to instruct the feature to do that task, for this purpose, we made use of the event receiver. We made use of the built-in event receiver `Microsoft.Office.Workflow.Feature.WorkflowFeatureReceiver` for this task.

Apart from deploying InfoPath forms to the form server, we need to hook this form to the workflow so it opens it at the initiation stage. Since InfoPath forms are XML files, it needs to be hosted on some page. SharePoint provides `IniWrkflIP.aspx` that resides in the `_layout` root directory in the SharePoint server. This ASPX page can host InfoPath forms. Apart from that we need to notify the workflow what form to open. This is done providing the form's URN (Uniform Resource Name). We made these changes to the workflow's `Elements.xml` file.

 If you have managed code with your InfoPath forms, the procedure is exactly the same. Just add the compiled DLL with the published InfoPath form to the module and proceed with the rest of the steps.

See also

▸ *Creating a sequential workflow recipe*

▸ *Creating a site workflow with an initiation form recipe*

▸ *Creating a task from the workflow recipe*

Creating a task from the workflow

So far we created workflows that run automatically without stopping for user input in the middle of the process. Initiation or association data come before the workflow is started. There are many situations where in the middle of the workflow process you may want input from a user to proceed further. To do this, we will create tasks in SharePoint.

In this recipe, we will create an **Employee Suggestion Program** (**ESP**) workflow, where employees of a company can provide suggestions on the betterment of the business processes that are in place in the company. For this, when an employee suggests a process improvement, a task is assigned to the department director to take a look at and decide on the value of the suggestion.

Getting ready

Create a custom list from the SharePoint UI called ESP. The following table lists all the attributes of the fields in the list:

Field Name	Data Type	Required
Title	Single line of text	Yes
Department Director	Person or group	Yes
Suggestion	Multiple lines of text	Yes

How to do it...

1. Create a sequential list workflow project named **ESPWF** and associate the workflow to ESP list created using Visual Studio 2010 new project wizard.

2. On the workflow designer surface, add **CreateTask** activity from the toolbox under the section SharePoint workflow below the **onWorkflowActivated1** activity as shown in the following screenshot:

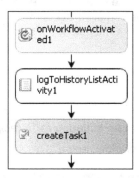

3. Set the **CorrelationToken** of this activity to **taskToken** and **OwnerActivityName** to **Workflow1**. The properties window of **CreateTask** activity is shown in the following screenshot:

Properties	
createTask1 Microsoft.SharePoint.WorkflowActions.CreateTask	
(Name)	**createTask1**
☐ CorrelationToken	**taskToken**
OwnerActivityName	**Workflow1**

4. Next, we need to set a binding variable to the **TaskId** property. We will bind this property to a new field named **taskId**. In order to do this, click on the yellow cylinder icon next to the property, as shown in the following screenshot:

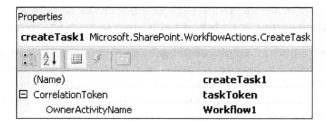

5. This will bring up the variable binding window and select the tab **Bind to a new member** as shown in the following screenshot:

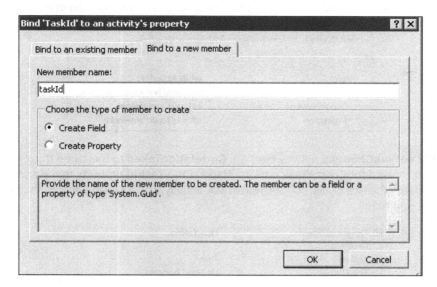

6. Repeat the process for **TaskProperties** as well. Name the variable as **taskProps**.

7. Right-click on the **CreateTask** activity and generate an event handler method as shown in the following screenshot:

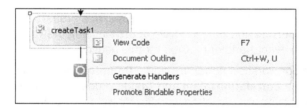

8 Visual Studio will add an event handler in the `Workflow1.cs` file. While in the code file, declare a new variable of type `bool` called `isTaskComplete` and set the default value to false.

9. From the workflow designer, add a `while` activity below the **CreateTask** activity and inside this `while` loop add an **onTaskChanged** activity.

10. Set the `while` loop condition property to `Declarative Rule Condition` and set the **ConditionName** and expression to **IsTaskCompleted** and the **!this. isTaskComplete** respectively. The following screenshot shows the end result:

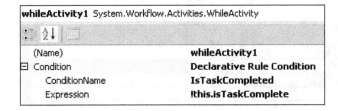

11. For **onTaskChanged** activity bind the **CorrelationToken** to the same thing as the one created for **CreateTask** activity. Also set the **TaskId** property to the same bind variable that we declared for **CreateTask** activity. The following screenshot shows the end result:

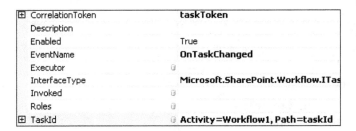

12. Bind the **AfterProperties** and the **BeforeProperties** property to new variables named **taskAfterProperties** and **taskBeforeProperties** using the variable binding window. Also create an event handler method for this activity.

13. To complete our workflow flowchart, add a **CompleteTask** below the `while loop` activity. Set the **CorrelationToken** and **TaskId** properties to the same ones as the **CreateTask** activity. Your finished workflow flowchart should look as shown in the following screenshot:

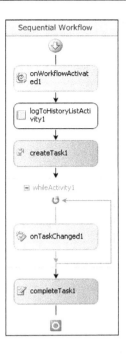

14. In the code file `Workflow1.cs`, add the following code to the `createTask1_ MethodInvoking` and `onTaskChanged1_Invoked` methods.

```
private void createTask1_MethodInvoking(object sender,
EventArgs e)
        {
            taskId = Guid.NewGuid();
            string sDepartmentDirector = workflowProperties.
Item["Department Director"].ToString();
            SPFieldLookupValue fld = new SPFieldLookupValue
(sDepartmentDirector);
            taskProps.AssignedTo = fld.LookupValue;
            taskProps.Title = "Review Employee Suggestion";
            taskProps.DueDate = DateTime.Today.AddDays(7);
            taskProps.SendEmailNotification = true;
        }
private void onTaskChanged1_Invoked(object sender,
ExternalDataEventArgs e)
        {
            Guid statusFieldID = workflowProperties.TaskList.
Fields["Status"].Id;
            string taskStatus = taskAfterProperties.Extended
            Properties[statusFieldID].ToString();
```

```
                    if (!string.IsNullOrEmpty(taskStatus) &&
                    taskStatus == "Completed")
                    {
                        // If so, let the While Loop Activity know
                        that we are done!
                        this.isTaskComplete = true;
                    }


                }
```

15. Build and run the application and this will open the site and list that the workflow is associated. Add a new item to the ESP list and the workflow should start automatically with a task created to the person provided in the list item. The following screenshot shows the task list of the workflow with task created:

16. Click on the **Review Employee Suggestion** title in the task list to open the task item. Edit this item to bring up the task edit form as shown in the following screenshot:

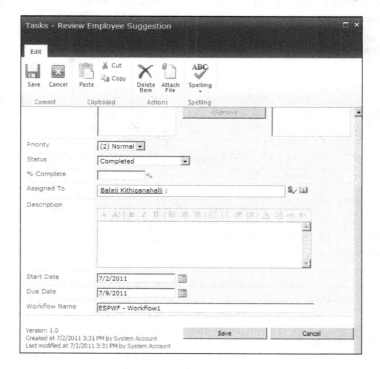

17. Set the **Status** field to **Completed** and save the form. This will complete the workflow as shown in the following screenshot:

Workflow Information			
Initiator: System Account		**Item:**	Use SharePoint
Started: 7/2/2011 3:31 PM		**Status:**	Completed
Last run: 7/2/2011 3:47 PM			

How it works...

Tasks are the way SharePoint workflows interact with the users. So if your workflows need input from users in the middle of the workflow process, you will create a task for that user and ask them to provide input through the task forms. This is exactly what we achieved in this recipe.

Since SharePoint workflows only interact via the tasks, Visual Studio provides a `CreateTask` activity which can be conveniently used to create a task for any person available on SharePoint. The `CreateTask` activity implements the `ITaskService` to create a task item in the task list associated with the workflow.

For every `CreateTask` activity it is necessary to create a correlation token. This should be unique for each task you reference in the workflow. Correlation tokens are unique string identifiers that are used by the workflow to map the items in the workflow to the hosting environment and workflow runtime. Workflows to maximize the resource usage will reuse objects in multiple instances of the workflow. That is, when SharePoint workflow is initiated, it verifies to see if any other instance is already running. Then if so, it tries to reuse some of the objects that were created during that instance. This helps in resource usage and also in performance. To correctly identify an instance to which any received messages need to be passed, the runtime environment needs to have a unique key to identify the workflow instance. This is accomplished by the correlation tokens.

Any other activities like `OnTaskChanged` and `CompleteTask` that refer to the same task should also set their `CorrelationToken` properties to the same as the one used in the `CreateTask` activity.

The `CreateTask` activity also has the task properties object of type `SPWorkflowTaskProperties`. This object is used to specify the task properties such as `AssignedTo`, `DueDate`, `Title`, and whether to send an e-mail notification to the assigned user when the task is created. For more information on `SPWorkflowTaskProperties` refer to MSDN at `http://msdn.microsoft.com/en-us/library/microsoft.sharepoint.workflow.spworkflowtaskproperties_members.aspx`.

We can always associate custom task forms in the workflow. If no custom forms are provided, a default task form is presented to the user to complete the task. This is what we did in this recipe and in the `OnTaskChanged` activity—we referred to this default form field to check the status set by the user to determine whether the task is completed or not. The information from the task form is available through the `AfterTaskProperties` object. The extended properties in this object stores key value pair of information based on the task form used. The `BeforeTaskProperties` is used to pass the information from the workflow to the task form.

There's more...

We made use of the `IfElse` activity and while activity from the general activities list. Out of 30 activities that are listed in the general activity list, not all of them can be used in the SharePoint workflow. The following table provides the activities that cannot be used in the SharePoint workflows:

Activity Name	Description
Compensate	This is used to undo in case of an error. None of the compensating activities can be used in SharePoint.
CompenstableSequence	This is used to execute a group of activities and is capable of compensating in case of an error.
CompenstableTransactionScope	Executes activities inside this sequentially under a transaction and compensates in case of an error.
InvokeWebService	Invokes a web service from the workflow.
InvokeWorkflow	Invokes another workflow from inside of the workflow.
Policy	A group of IfElse statements that make up a policy and are applied to a workflow item.
ReceiveActivity	Implements **Windows Communication Foundation** (**WCF**) service interfaces. This way a workflow can be exposed as a web service.
SendActivity	Implements WCF client side operations.
Suspend	Suspends the workflow execution.
Throw	Throws an exception.
TransactionScope	Groups the activities to work inside a transaction.
WebServiceInput	Used in enabling workflow to act as a web service.
WebServiceOutput	Used in enabling workflow to act as a web service.
WebServiceFault	Throws an exception to a web service

See also

▸   *Creating a custom task form* recipe

Creating a custom task form

In the previous recipe, when the department director completes the task, we cannot determine whether he wants the suggestion implemented or rejected. We may have to find out using the comments field as there is no other field that provides a way for him to convey that information. If the workflow has to take action based on this input, the default form provided will not fit the situation. We may have to create a custom form and present it to the user to perform their tasks. You can use either the ASPX page or InfoPath form to create the custom task form. In this recipe, we will create a custom InfoPath task form.

Getting ready

This recipe is an extension of the previous recipe. Hence, a successful completion of the previous recipe will provide a good foundation for understanding this. This recipe also assumes that you have working knowledge of designing InfoPath forms.

How to do it...

1. Using InfoPath designer, create a form named `TaskEditForm.xsn` with a drop-down list control for status with values "Approved", "Rejected", and "Working". Add some textbox controls for the department director to enter comments on the suggestion and to show the title and suggestion information entered by the employee. The end result of the InfoPath screen is shown in the following screenshot:

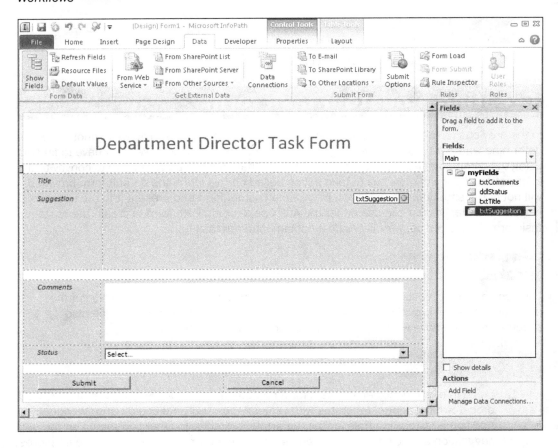

2. Create a new XML file called `ItemMetadata.xml`. The file name is case-sensitive and should be named `ItemMetadata.xml`. Add the following content to this file:

```
<?xml version="1.0" encoding="utf-8"?>
<z:row xmlns:z="#RowsetSchema"
ows_Title=""
ows_Suggestion=""
/>
```

3. Add a receive data connection to the InfoPath form with the previously created XML file and associate the `txtTitle` and `txtSuggestion` with `ows_Title` and `ows_Suggestion`.

4. Also create a submit data connection that submits the form to the hosting environment.

5. Follow the same procedure outlined in the recipe for creating the InfoPath initiation form to publish this form. Follow all the steps in that recipe from 3 to 9. For task forms there is no need to save the InfoPath source files and create the class file using `XSD.exe` as indicated in that recipe.

6. Open the **ESPWF** solution file that we created in the previous recipe. Add a new module to this project and name the module **IPForms**.

7. Remove the added `Sample.txt` file from the **IPForms** module and add the published InfoPath form. Visual Studio will automatically update the `Elements.xml` file under **IPForms**.

8. Add the property key **RegisterForms** to the feature manifest file and set the value to the path of **IPForms** module. Also set the feature's receiver assembly and class properties to the following values:

```
Receiver Assembly = Microsoft.Office.Workflow.Feature,
Version=14.0.0.0, Culture=neutral, PublicKeyToken=71e9bce111e9429c
 Receiver Class = Microsoft.Office.Workflow.Feature.
WorkflowFeatureReceiver
```

9. Modify the workflow `Elements.xml` file and add a new attribute `TaskListContentTypeId` to the workflow element and set the value to "0x010801 00C9C9515DE4E24001905074F980F93160".

10. Add a new element under the **MetaData** element to define the task types. Add the URN of your InfoPath form as the element's value. You can get the URN from the InfoPath form's template properties section. The following code shows the end result:

```
<Task0_FormURN>urn:schemas-microsoft-com:office:infopath:
TaskEditForm:-myXSD-2011-07-03T12-10-50</Task0_FormURN>
```

11. Make modification to the `createTask1_MethodInvoking` method in the workflow code to associate this form to the task. Your resulting code should be as follows:

```
private void createTask1_MethodInvoking(object sender,
EventArgs e)
        {
                taskId = Guid.NewGuid();
                string sDepartmentDirector = workflowProperties.
                Item["Department Director"].ToString();
                SPFieldLookupValue fld = new SPFieldLookupValue
                (sDepartmentDirector);
                taskProps.AssignedTo = fld.LookupValue;
                taskProps.Title = "Review Employee Suggestion";
                taskProps.DueDate = DateTime.Today.AddDays(7);
                taskProps.EmailBody = "An employee suggestion is
                 received. Please review this";
                taskProps.SendEmailNotification = true;
                taskProps.ExtendedProperties["ows_Title"] =
                workflowProperties.Item["Title"].ToString();
```

```
        taskProps.ExtendedProperties["ows_Suggestion"] =
        workflowProperties.Item["Suggestion"].ToString();
        taskProps.TaskType = 0;
    }
```

12. Also make changes to the `onTaskChanged1_Invoked` method to check the status from the drop-down field from the InfoPath form. Your resulting code should be as follows:

```
private void onTaskChanged1_Invoked(object sender,
ExternalDataEventArgs e)
        {
            string taskStatus = taskAfterProperties.Extended
            Properties["ddlStatus"].ToString();
            if (!string.IsNullOrEmpty(taskStatus) &&
        (taskStatus == "Approved" || taskStatus =="Rejected"))
            {
                // If so, let the While Loop Activity know that
                we are done!
                this.isTaskComplete = true;
            }

        }
```

13. Build and run the project. Create a new item in your list and the workflow should automatically start on the insert of the new item and create a task for the person specified in the list item. When you click the task item, you should see the InfoPath form associated with the task edit as shown in the following screenshot:

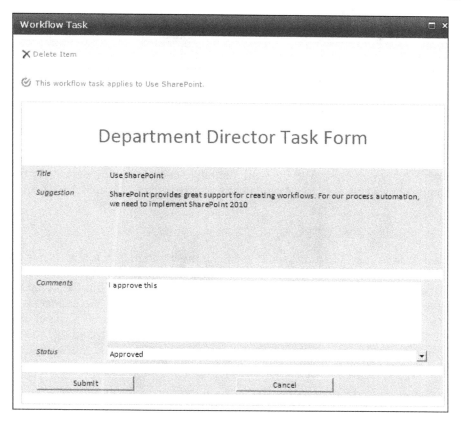

How it works...

The workflow is exactly the same as the previous recipe except for the fact that we are using the custom task edit form instead of the default form. Task edit forms can be created by either using ASPX pages or by using InfoPath forms. For using ASPX pages, you have to create a custom content type and associate the ASPX page with the content type. Instead of `CreateTask` activity, you will be using `CreateTaskWithContentType` activity for this purpose. This activity will create a task based on a specific content type. All the other procedures will remain the same. In case all the tasks in the workflow use the same form, you will only need to create one content type and can reuse it in all task creation activities. If your workflow is creating many types of tasks then using the ASPX page approach will end up creating many different content types. Managing all these content types in a huge workflow will become a daunting task. But if you are not running form services, then this is the only way to create custom task forms. You cannot use InfoPath forms as it depends on the form services in the SharePoint.

InfoPath forms provide a better alternative to task forms even though the deployment procedure is a little convoluted. You do not have to create all the content types for deploying InfoPath forms as task edit forms. This is due to the fact that InfoPath forms are hosted from an ASPX page. This page (`WrkTaskIP.aspx`) is located in the root `_layouts` folder. This page is also associated with a content type but is capable of hosting the InfoPath forms. Hence, we provide the default content type ID in the workflow `Elements.xml` file.

To associate different task forms for the tasks that we create in the workflow, we create task type elements in the `Elements.xml` file of the workflow. This stores the URN information of the form. We can use as many number here of these as we need. All we need to do is increment the number in the task type element. In the code during the creation of the task, we set the `TaskType` property with the right number to show the corresponding form. The following code shows how we can define multiple task types in `Elements.xml` file.

```
<Task0_FormURN>URN of form 1</Task0_FormURN>
<Task1_FormURN>URN of form 2</Task1_FormURN>
```

The `ItemMetadata.xml` file is a mandatory file for the InfoPath task forms. This is the way SharePoint workflow passes data to the task form. Since during the form load event, SharePoint always passes the data to the task form, it expects to see this file associated with the InfoPath task forms. If this is not provided, an exception is thrown. We can use this file and pass in any necessary information that we need to display on the task form. In our example we passed title and suggestion from the workflow item. This is done, by setting those values in the `TaskProperties ExtendedProperties` object. This `ExtendedProperties` object is a hashtable that contains key-value pairs of the data that needs to be passed.

Similar to how we pass the data to the task form via the `ExtendedProperties` object, SharePoint stores all the InfoPath elements data in the `ExtendedProperties` of the task `AfterProperties` object when the task form is submitted. We can use the name of the field defined in the InfoPath form to access the value of the field. This is the reason why we do not have to create the class file of the InfoPath form using the XSD tool.

Do not use group elements in your schema when you are designing InfoPath task forms. The reason is SharePoint cannot associate these to the `ExtendedProperties` object. Always use flat structure in designing InfoPath task forms.

There's more...

When you create a task using the preceding method, any person with sufficient permission on the task list will be able to edit the task and complete the task. Tasks are not restricted to the person associated to the task via the `AssignedTo` property. This may not work in real-world workflows as you may need to audit the task completion time and the users for whatever reasons. If you need to restrict that only `AssignedTo` person be able to edit the task you have to set `SpecialPermissions` property on `CreateTask` activity.

The `SpecialPermissions` object is of `HybridDictionary` type and takes in username and permission type to be set. So in the `CreateTask` method invoking adds the following code to restrict the task edit by a `AssignedTo` user.

```
createTask1_TaskProperties1.AssignedTo = "domain\\user";
System.Collections.Specialized.HybridDictionary specialPermissions =
new System.Collections.Specialized.HybridDictionary();
specialPermissions.Add(createTask1_TaskProperties1.AssignedTo,
SPRoleType.Contributor);
createTask1.SpecialPermissions = specialPermissions;
```

Task delete

The person who can edit the task can also delete it. If you are not handling the deleted task event, your workflow can go haywire if the user deletes the task. There is no straightforward way to restrict the deletion of the task. One method to restrict deletion is to write an event handler on the task list and throw an error message whenever someone tries to delete the task.

The other method is to add a listening activity to your workflow and listen to multiple events like the task changed and the task deleted events. Depending on your business requirements, you can send an e-mail or stop the workflow completely or just continue to the next step. The following screenshot shows how to add a listening activity and handle the `delete` event of the task:

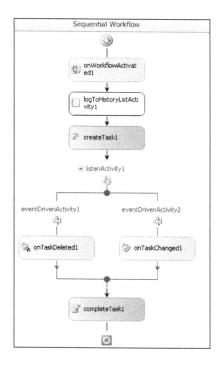

8

Introduction to Programming Windows Phone 7 with the SharePoint Client Services

 This chapter is taken from *Microsoft SharePoint 2010 Enterprise Applications on Windows Phone 7* (Chapter 6) by Todd Spatafore.

This chapter will introduce programming Windows Phone 7 applications. We will use RSS feeds that are provided from lists in SharePoint to display information to the Windows Phone 7 user. Throughout the chapter, we will build a simple RSS Reader application for Windows Phone 7 and add complexity to it as we go along. In this chapter, we will cover the following:

- Security in SharePoint 2010
- Using WebClient to get data from the Web
- RSS feeds available from SharePoint
- Parsing XML in Windows Phone 7
- Simple page navigation
- Using the WebBrowser control to display detail

So, let's begin this chapter with a brief discussion on security in SharePoint 2010.

Security in SharePoint 2010

We begin this chapter with a discussion on security for a very simple reason: security in SharePoint is tricky. In addition to that one very simple reason, authenticating users against SharePoint from within a Windows Phone 7 client application is even trickier.

That is to say, it is not impossible. In this chapter, the example RSS reader that we develop will only use anonymous access to the RSS feeds in SharePoint. Setting up anonymous access is very simple and we'll walk through the steps here.

When writing this chapter, I came across a lot of errors on my testing server, but not my development server. After a couple of days of unsuccessful web searches and reinstalling different components, I discovered the root of my problem was due to the fact that the SharePoint 2010 Prerequisites install a non-final version of ADO. NET Data Services 1.5. Make sure the final version is installed from Microsoft. More information is available at the following URL:

```
http://blogs.msdn.com/b/astoriateam/
archive/2010/01/27/data-services-update-for-net-3-
5-sp1-available-for-download.aspx
```

There are two places where we need to make changes to our SharePoint site to enable anonymous access:

- Central Administration
- Site Permissions

Central Administration

Classic mode authentication is more or less just classic Windows authentication using NTLM or Kerberos.

Although Internet Explorer Mobile in Windows Phone 7 can do the NTLM authentication, as we've been doing up to now to view SharePoint sites in the browser, the version of Silverlight that is included in Windows Phone 7 cannot currently use this authentication mechanism.

Converting our classic mode authenticated site into a **Claims Based Authenticated** site allows us to use forms based authentication along with a more bare metal approach to web connections to gain access to secure content.

For now, let us continue with our path to anonymous access. Carry out the following steps to configure Central Administration for anonymous access:

1. From the **Start** menu, select **All Programs**.

2. Find the folder named `Microsoft SharePoint 2010 Products` in the list of programs and click on it.

3. Click on **SharePoint 2010 Central Administration**.

4. You need to select the **Yes** option on the User Account Control dialog that may appear.

At this point, the home page for SharePoint 2010 Central Administration should appear as displayed in the following screenshot:

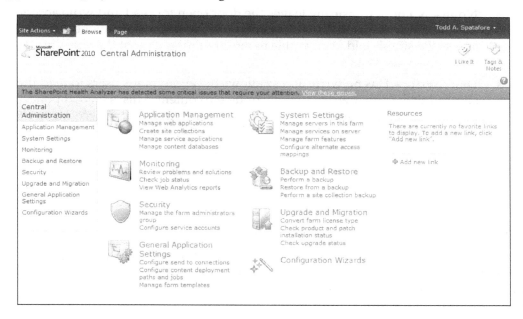

Next, click on **Manage web applications**. The page that appears lists out all of the Web applications in the SharePoint site. There should be two items listed here, but it is possible there are more. Select the main website by clicking on its name. This main website is usually titled **SharePoint – 80**. Once selected, the ribbon bar across the top should light up, as all the icons become active.

Carry out the following steps to enable anonymous access:

1. Click on the **Authentication Providers** icon.

2. In the **Authentication Providers** dialog that appears, select the **Default** link.

3. The **Edit Authentication** dialog box will appear. In the third section, down under a heading of **Anonymous Access** there is a check box listed as **Enable anonymous access**. Check that box.

4. Scroll all the way to the bottom of the dialog box and select the **Save** button.

5. SharePoint 2010 will process the request. Then, return to the **Authentication Providers** dialog box and close it.

There is one more section that may need tweaking and if this is a production environment, it should be considered. That section is **Anonymous Policy**. Click on the icon for it in the ribbon and a dialog box will appear. From here, we can customize the anonymous policy for the site.

- **None – No policy** basically leaves the door open for read and write access from anonymous users. This is a good policy to use when anyone who can access the site should also be able to modify the content of the site. This is a good policy for Wiki's.

- **Deny Write – Has no write access** allows the anonymous users to read the site, but they cannot write, update, or delete content. This is a good policy to use for sites that we want to specify particular authenticated accounts write access, but allow everyone the ability to read the content. Some Wiki's use this policy and a lot of blogs use this policy.

- **Deny All – Has no access** selecting this removes all permissions to the anonymous user. Secure content should always use this policy.

Site Permissions

Once we have updated the Web application to allow anonymous access, we have to give anonymous users access to the site collection. To do this, we close Central Administration and open our SharePoint site. Once on the site, select **Site Permissions** from the **Site Actions** menu.

This will open the **Permissions** home page. In the ribbon at the top, there is an icon named **Anonymous Access**. Click on that button and the **Anonymous Access** dialog will appear, as shown in the following screenshot:

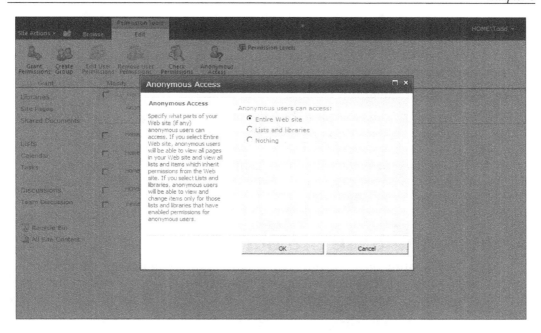

This dialog has three radio buttons to fine tune the access that anonymous users have. The key point to remember here is that although we are really opening up the site for everyone to see, we can break the inherit permissions model on a child page at any time if we need to remove anonymous access.

Now that we have opened up our SharePoint site to anonymous users, we can begin to write applications for Windows Phone 7. In a production environment, we may not have the privilege of opening a SharePoint site this wide, but remember that we are only doing it for demonstration purposes here. We have to walk before we can run. Now, let's get started on the RSS reader.

Using WebClient to get data from the Web

As was stated in the introduction to this chapter, we are going to build a really simple RSS reader for Windows Phone 7. We are going to keep everything really simple. What that means is that we are going to focus on the pieces of code that actually do something.

This is what we are going to do:

- Create our base project
- Add a text block to display the WebClient results
- Create a WebClient
- Use the WebClient to request the contents of our SharePoint home page
- Display the raw HTML that is returned in the text block on the page

First, a quick word about WebClient. WebClient isn't the most robust method of making requests over a network, but it's really simple and works for simple cases, such as the one we are working with.

Creating the base project

We can start by creating our base project. This RSS reader will use the Visual Studio `Silverlight for Windows Phone Windows Phone Application` template. Carry out the following steps to start the project:

1. Open Visual Studio 2010.
2. Select **File** from the main menu and then select **New Project...**.
3. In the **New Project** dialog box that appears, select **Silverlight for Windows Phone**.
4. Then select **Windows Phone Application** from the list of templates for Windows Phone.
5. Give the project a name, for example **SimpleRSSReader**.
6. Give the **Solution** a name, for example **Chapter06.**
7. Change the **Location** as desired and click on the **OK** button.

At this point, Visual Studio will go off and create the solution and project. When it has finished, **MainPage.xaml** will appear on the screen in split screen mode, as shown in the following screenshot:

Displaying WebClient results by adding a text block

The first thing we are going to do here is add a text block to the content panel. Add the following code to the Grid that has a name of `ContentPanel`.

```
<TextBlock x:Name="webClientResults" />
```

This creates a text block named `webClientResults` and puts it in `ContentPanel`. We could spruce this up a bit by providing a font size, or padding, but we are going to keep this really simple and only show the code needed to get things done.

Save the progress.

Creating a WebClient

Open up the code behind by either clicking on it in the top tab bar, double-clicking the file name in **Solution Explorer**, or press *F7* while in the XAML code.

In the code behind, create a private member variable, outside the constructor, named `client` of type `WebClient` and a private member variable, also outside the constructor, named `siteUrl` of type `string`. The `siteUrl` should have a value that is the URL to your SharePoint home page.

```
private WebClient client = new WebClient();
private string siteUrl = "http://ssps2010/";
```

These are the variables that we'll be using in just a minute. The first is the `WebClient` that makes the requests on the network. The second is the `Url` for our SharePoint home page. This is the address that the WebClient will use to request a web page.

Requesting the contents of our SharePoint home page

Now that we have a WebClient, let us do something with it. Add the following code to the Main Page constructor:

```
client.DownloadStringCompleted += new DownloadStringCompletedEventHand
ler(client_DownloadStringCompleted);
client.DownloadStringAsync(new Uri(siteUrl));
```

The first line adds a new event handler to the `DownloadStringCompleted` event. This event handler is called `client_DownloadStringCompleted` and we will write it shortly. The second line is what starts an asynchronous request to our SharePoint home page to get the HTML content.

Displaying the raw HTML that is returned

Until now, we've created a place in the content panel to display our results. We've created a couple of variables. We've added a new event handler for when the WebClient finishes and we've made the Web request for our SharePoint home page. Next, we are going to receive the result from the WebClient.

Earlier, when we added a new event handler to the WebClient, we told WebClient that when it finishes downloading the string, it should call our method named `client_DownloadStringCompleted`. The following is the code for that method:

```
void client_DownloadStringCompleted(object sender,
DownloadStringCompletedEventArgs e) {
    if(e.Error == null) {
        webClientResults.Text = e.Result;
    }
}
```

First, we check to see if there is an error. To make this as simple as possible, we are not handling the situation where there is an error. We only care if there are no errors. Always check that errors are null. If there is an exception in the WebClient request, the `DownloadStringCompletedEventArgs` Error property will contain an object of type `Exception`. These exceptions can range from network connections being down, which is common for cell phones, to invalid URLs.

We then take the result of the Web request and put it in the text block we created earlier. Save the progress and press *F5* to see the application run on the Windows Phone 7 Emulator.

In the preceding screenshot, `ApplicationTitle` and `PageTitle` have also been updated. Both of these text blocks are found in the XAML in `TitlePanel`.

We have successfully used WebClient to read data from the Web and display it on the screen. It is still in a raw format though, and it isn't much of an RSS reader, especially since this page isn't even RSS. We will get there, but first let's find some RSS in SharePoint.

RSS feeds available from SharePoint

One of the really cool things in SharePoint is that almost every list in it has an RSS feed associated with it. Unless specifically set to not emit an RSS feed, all lists have a feed associated with them.

Carry out the following steps to ensure RSS is enabled on a site collection:

1. From the site's home page, select **Site Settings** from the **Site Actions** menu.
2. On the **Site Settings** page, under the **Site Administration** section, select the **RSS** link.
3. This opens up the page that allows us to enable or disable RSS feeds. Ensure that the **Site Collection RSS** and **Enable RSS** section check boxes are checked.
4. Add in any of the **Advanced Settings** information that may be required. We won't be using it in our demos, but in production these might be needed.
5. Finally, click on the **OK** button and SharePoint will save the settings.

The basic question of how to customize the feed from each list comes up a bit and that procedure is actually quite simple.

1. Navigate to the list that we want to customize.
2. At the top, click on **List** in the **List Tools** section.
3. In the list ribbon, click on the **List Settings** icon. If the icon is disabled, you may be viewing the site anonymously and will need to login from the link at the top left.
4. Under **Communications** is a link for **RSS settings**. Click on that link.

The **Modify RSS Settings** page has a lot of information that can be customized, from the ability to turn off RSS altogether, down to what columns from the list should be included in the RSS description. The following example is a screenshot of this page:

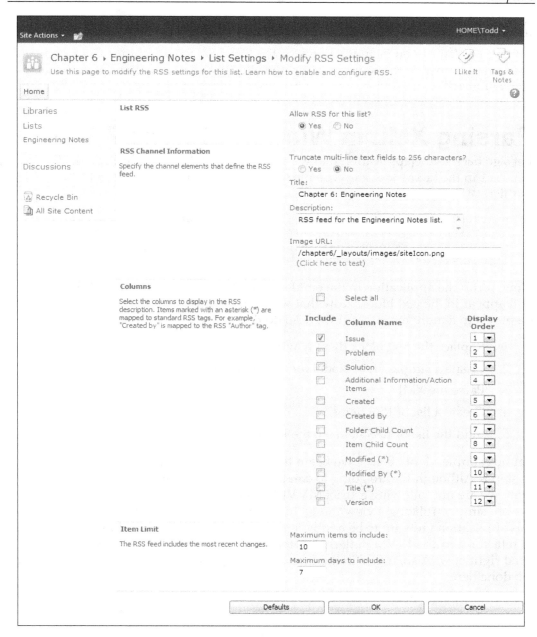

After customizing the content, click on the **OK** button to save changes.

Now that we have the feed customized, where's the link? Good question. Back on the default view for the list, click on **List** in the **List Tools** menu to display the list ribbon. The list ribbon includes a link for the RSS Feed in the middle. Click on it and the feed will open in the browser. Copy the URL because we will use it in the next step of our RSS reader.

Parsing XML in Windows Phone 7

Let's go back to the application that we are building in Visual Studio. First, change `siteUrl` in the `MainPage.xaml.cs` file to the RSS Feed URL that we got from our list.

```
private string siteUrl = "http://ssps2010/chapter6/_layouts/listfeed.
aspx?List=%7BD45848A1%2D12E8%2D4722%2DAB5B%2D511BF802F8D8%7D&Source=h
ttp%3A%2F%2Fssps2010%2Fchapter6%2FLists%2FEngineering%2520Notes%2FAll
Items%2Easpx";
```

Now, rerun the application in the emulator and the raw XML from the RSS feed will appear in the text block. Now that we have the XML feed in a string, we should display it in a more meaningful way. To do that, let's do the following:

1. Replace the text block display with a listbox

2. Create a simple view model for an RSS Item

3. Parse the XML

4. Create a list of RSS Items

5. Bind the list of RSS Items to the listbox

Sounds simple, right? Before we begin though, a quick word about a term we used in step 2. Although we are going to create a view model that will hold each RSS item, we are not following a strict **MVVM (Model View ViewModel)** pattern here. We are simply utilizing a view model to assist in binding the data to the view. If this application grew up to be a fully featured RSS reader, we would probably want to refactor it to an MVVM pattern, but that is an optimization that we simply don't need right now. Also, it flies in the face of attaining the simplest code that will get the job done here.

Replacing the text block display with a listbox

The first step here is to replace the text block that we were using to dump the string output with a listbox, where we can display each individual RSS item. To do that, open `MainPage.xaml` and delete the TextBlock with a name of `webClientResults`. In its place, enter the following XAML:

```
<ListBox x:Name="feedListBox">
  <ListBox.ItemTemplate>
    <DataTemplate>
      <StackPanel HorizontalAlignment="Stretch">
        <TextBlock Text="{Binding Title}" TextWrapping="Wrap" />
        <TextBlock Text="{Binding Date}" />
      </StackPanel>
    </DataTemplate>
  </ListBox.ItemTemplate>
</ListBox>
```

Working from the inside out, we are going to display each RSS item's title and date. We do this with text blocks and bind the text property to the data for the particular listbox item. As the titles can get long, we've included text wrapping on the title.

These text blocks are placed inside a stack panel. This means that the title will be stacked on top of the date. We have also set the width of the stack panel. Without this width, the title text block won't wrap properly.

This stack panel is placed inside the data template for the listbox item template. This listbox item template is a property of the listbox that we've replaced our text block with.

The name of this listbox is `feedListBox`. In the code behind, we will bind the RSS item list to the items source for this listbox. Save the progress.

Creating a simple view model for an RSS Item

Before we can bind the RSS items list to the listbox, we need to have a list of RSS items. Before we can have a list of RSS items, we need to define what an RSS item is. This is where the view model comes in. Carry out the following steps to create a class that will house our view model:

1. Right click on the **SimpleRSSReader** project in **Solution Explorer**.

2. In the context menu that appears, select **Add** and then select the **Class...** option.

3. This will open the **Add New Item** dialog with the **Class** template already selected.

4. In the **Name** field, name the new class as **RSSItem.cs**.

5. Click on the **Add** button and Visual Studio will create the class and open it in the main IDE window.

In the class, add the following code:

```
public string Title { get; set; }
public string Date { get; set; }
public string PostUrl { get; set; }
```

This creates three public properties that we will use for our RSS feeds. Although RSS items have more fields associated with them, these are the only three that we will need for this exercise.

Something of note in these properties is the `Date` field. The publish date of a post is `DateTime`, but we are using it as a string here for the simple fact that we don't really need a DateTime. When we parse the XML in the next step, it will save us from having to convert from string to DateTime and then back to string when we data bind it to the text block. Save the progress.

Parsing the XML

We've replaced the text block with a listbox and created a simple view model for our RSS items. Next, we will parse the XML string that was returned from the WebClient.

1. In **Solution Explorer**, right click on **References** for the **SimpleRSSReader** project.

2. In the **Add Reference** dialog box, find **System.Xml.Linq** and add it to the project.

3. Open the Main Page code behind.

4. Add this using statement to the top of the page: `using System.Xml.Linq;`

5. Locate the `client_DownloadStringCompleted` event handler.

6. Delete this line of code: `webClientResults.Text = e.Result;`

7. Add the following code where the preceding line of code was:

```
var result = e.Result;
var rssElement = XElement.Parse(result);
```

8. Save the file.

The first thing we did here was to add a reference to Windows Phone 7's LINQ to XML namespace. This contains classes, such as XElement that we use to parse the XML string, as well as the LINQ engine that we will use in the next step to create the list of RSS items.

 Language-Integrated Query, LINQ, was introduced into the .NET Framework in Version 3.5. It provides a general purpose syntax that allows for powerful data processing in .NET. More information on LINQ is available at the following URL:

http://msdn.microsoft.com/en-us/library/bb308959.aspx

Next, let's create a list of RSS Items.

Creating a list of RSS Items

Now we have a place to put the RSS items, we have a model of what an RSS item looks like, and we have an XElement with our RSS feed stuffed in it. The next thing to do is take the XElement and perform a LINQ statement to get a list of RSS Items.

In the previous step, we parsed the XML into a variable named rssElement. Immediately after that, add the following statement:

```
var items = from item in rssElement.Descendants("item")
        select new RSSItem
        {
          Title = item.Element("title").Value,
          Date = item.Element("pubDate").Value,
          PostUrl = item.Element("link").Value
        };
```

Wow, that is one statement. What we are doing here is searching through the XElement for all item elements. Once we have an item element, we call it an item and use it to create a new RSSItem. Lines 4, 5, and 6 parse the item element further to get the string values for specific elements in the item element.

Again at this point, you'll notice in line 5 that we could have parsed the publish date as a DateTime, but since we will only ever use it as a string, it's easier to just grab the value as a string.

Once the RSSItem has been created, it is added to the list of RSS items in the variable items. We will use this variable to bind to our listbox.

Binding the list of RSS Items to the listbox

We've come to the point where we take the list of RSS items and actually bind that data to the listbox we created earlier. This is done in a single line of code, as follows:

```
feedListBox.ItemsSource = items;
```

Save the file, build, and then run the application in the Windows Phone 7 Emulator. You will see something similar to the following screenshot:

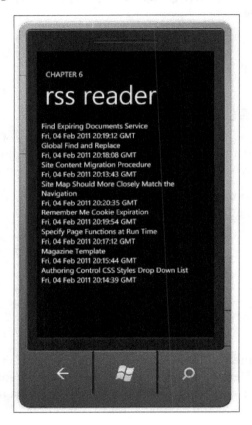

It's a bit hard to read, so let's go back to the XAML and make some changes to the text blocks.

First, change the `Title` text block as follows:

```
<TextBlock Text="{Binding Title}" TextWrapping="Wrap"
    Style="{StaticResource PhoneTextTitle2Style}" />
```

This adds a style from the static resources included with the phone that is more fitting a title.

Next, change the `Date` text block as follows:

```
<TextBlock Text="{Binding Date}"
    Style="{StaticResource PhoneTextAccentStyle}" />
```

This adds the accent color from the phone to the date to make it stand out a bit, as shown in the following screenshot:

Windows Phone 7 has customization available to the end user, which allows them to select between 10 different accent colors and an overall theme of dark or light. The advantage of using the built-in Static Resources for Windows Phone 7's styles is that when the end user changes the theme color from dark to light or the accent color to one of the 10 options on the phone, your application will pick it up and look like it's more of a part of the phone.

This works well if that is the goal of your application. If we want to maintain a certain corporate branding though, we should create a custom resource file which contains all of our corporate color schemes and use that resource data. This, of course, is beyond the scope of this book.

Simple page navigation

Up to now, we've learned how to create a WebClient to request data from the network. We have used that to get an RSS feed and parse the data into a list of RSS items. We then bound that data to a listbox where we displayed the title and the date of the posts. An RSS post is more than just a title and a date though. The user needs some way to read the entire post. In this section, we will perform simple page navigation with the following steps:

- Build a details view page
- Set up a new event handler to listen for selected item changes on the listbox
- When the event handler is triggered, build an URI for navigation
- Navigate to the details view page
- Handle the loaded event on the details view page

Building multiple page applications in Windows Phone 7 is a lot like building web applications. Each view has a different page associated with it. Navigating between pages happens with an URI and a query string in which we will pass the URL for the post link. We will then display that URL link in a message box on the screen.

Building a details view page

The first thing we do to display the post is create a new page for details. Carry out the following steps to create the details view page:

1. In **Solution Explorer**, right click on the **SimpleRSSReader** project.
2. In the context menu that appears, select **Add** and then select **New Item...**.
3. In the **Add New Item** dialog that appears, select the **Windows Phone Portrait Page** template.
4. Name the new page **DetailsView.xaml**, as shown in the following screenshot:

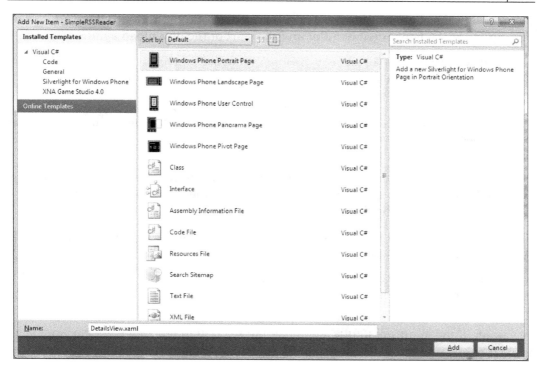

5. Click on the **Add** button and Visual Studio will create the new page.

That's all there is to creating the new details view page. There isn't anything in the page yet. Later in this section, we will listen for the page loaded event and display a message box with the link that was passed in, and in the next section we will add a WebBrowser to the page to display the RSS post. For now, save the page and reopen the `MainPage.xaml.cs` file.

Setting up a new event handler

Back in the code behind the main page, find the page constructor. We are going to refactor this constructor a bit and add in a page loaded event. Change the constructor to the following code with the highlighted line as the new line. Notice that we've also removed the client event handler and the start for the download. We will add that back in just a second.

```
public MainPage() {
  InitializeComponent();
  this.Loaded += new RoutedEventHandler(MainPage_Loaded);
}
```

Next, add in the code for this new event handler as follows; notice that we are adding the WebClient event handler and the start of the download again:

```
void MainPage_Loaded(object sender, RoutedEventArgs e) {
  client.DownloadStringCompleted += new DownloadStringCompletedEventHa
ndler(client_DownloadStringCompleted);
  client.DownloadStringAsync(new Uri(siteUrl));
  feedListBox.SelectionChanged += new SelectionChangedEventHandler(fee
dListBox_SelectionChanged);
}
```

Notice the highlighted line of code. This is the new event handler that we are adding to listen for the listbox's selection changed event handler. This event is fired when the user selects one of the listbox items on the screen.

Finally, we need to build up the base event handler for this selection changed event. Add the following code to the class:

```
void feedListBox_SelectionChanged(object sender,
SelectionChangedEventArgs e) {
}
```

We aren't doing anything in this event yet, but we will in the next part. For now just leave it blank.

Building the URI for navigation

Up to now, we created a details view page and added an event handler on the main page's listbox that listens for the selection changed event. Now, we are going to use that event to get the information needed to build the URI needed for navigation.

In the `feedListBox_SelectionChanged` event handler, add the following lines of code:

```
if(feedListBox.SelectedIndex == -1)
  return;
var selectedItem = (RSSItem)feedListBox.SelectedItem;
var navigationUri = new Uri("/DetailsView.xaml?selectedItem=" +
selectedItem.PostUrl, UriKind.Relative);
```

To start this off, we first check that an item in the list is selected. If the selected index is -1, then we know that the selected index was just reset. We can ignore this and just return the control of the app to the user.

However, if the selected index is not -1, then something is selected. We next take the selected item cast it into an `RSSItem` and save the result in a variable named `selectedItem`.

The last line does the following three things.

1. It builds up a string containing the URI for the details view page we created earlier, and it adds a query string containing the link to the post.

2. It uses this string to create a new URI.

3. It specifies that the kind of URI that we are building is a relative path. This means it will look within the XAP for the resource requested. We will use this URI in the next step to navigate to the details view page.

Navigating to the details view page

In the last section, we built up an URI to use to navigate to the details page. In this section, we will use `NavigationService` to open the details view page. Finally, we will reset the selected index of the listbox back to `-1` for when the user navigates back to the main page.

Add the following two lines of code below the line where we created the URI:

```
NavigationService.Navigate(navigationUri);
feedListBox.SelectedIndex = -1;
```

With the preceding two lines of code, the control of the application will transfer to the navigation system to transition from the main page to the details view page. Finally, the details view page will load and a loaded event will fire. We will take advantage of that event next.

Handling loaded events on the details page

In the last section, we navigated to the details page and reset the selected index of the feed listbox. In this section, we will return our attention to the details page and display the selected item query string parameter that was passed into the page.

First, we need to hook up an event handler to the loaded event. This is similar to what we did in the main page. Add the following highlighted line to the constructor of the details page:

```
public DetailsView() {
  InitializeComponent();
  this.Loaded += new RoutedEventHandler(DetailsView_Loaded);
}
```

This is exactly the same as what we saw for the main page, only the name of the event handler has changed.

Add the following code below the constructor to handle the event:

```
void DetailsView_Loaded(object sender, RoutedEventArgs e) {
  var selectedItem = string.Empty;
  if(NavigationContext.QueryString.TryGetValue("selectedItem",
    out selectedItem)) {
    MessageBox.Show(selectedItem, "SELECTED ITEM",
    MessageBoxButton.OK);
    NavigationService.GoBack();
  } else {
    MessageBox.Show("There was a problem", "ERROR",
    MessageBoxButton.OK);
    NavigationService.GoBack();
  }
}
```

This code block does a lot of things. So, let us go through it line by line. First, we create a variable to hold the value of the `selectedItem`. In our case, this will be a string that is the URL for the post we want to view.

Next, we begin the conditional statement by trying to get the query string value for `selectedItem`. This will return a Boolean and if the value is there, we display it in a message box.

If the query string value is not there, we display a simple error message. Both message boxes have an **OK** button and when the user clicks on the button, the navigation service returns us to the main page.

We are at a point now where we can compile the app and run it. The following screenshot shows what it looks like when navigated to the details view page:

Using the WebBrowser control to display the post

We have come a long way, but we aren't quite finished yet. There's one little thing left to do. The details view page is a bit bland. What we want to do next is open the post in a web browser, so that we can view the real details. To do this, we need to do the following two things:

- Add a WebBrowser to the details view
- Navigate the WebBrowser to the post's URL

Adding a WebBrowser to the details view

Open the file `DetailsView.xaml` and find `ContentPanel`. Within this grid, add the following XAML:

```
<phone:WebBrowser x:Name="browser" HorizontalAlignment="Stretch" />
```

This adds a WebBrowser control named `browser` to the content panel. It is important to give the Web browser a width by either directly specifying a width or setting `HorizontalAlignment` to stretch, as we've done here. If we don't give the browser a width, the details page will appear blank.

While we are in the XAML, let's change **ApplicationTitle** and **PageTitle** to CHAPTER 6 and `details view` respectively. It's a minor thing, and not required for the app to work, but it's a good practice to get into. Save the changes and open the code behind for the details view.

Navigating to the post's URL

Open the file `DetailsView.xaml.cs` and look for the message box that displays the success message. Replace the following two lines of code (close to line 29 and 30):

```
MessageBox.Show(selectedItem, "SELECTED ITEM", MessageBoxButton.OK);
NavigationService.GoBack();
```

with the following line of code:

```
Browser.Navigate(new Uri(selectedItem));
```

This navigates the Web browser to the location we passed in earlier. Save the file and compile. Then run the application in the Windows Phone 7 Emulator.

Summary

In this chapter, we took the first steps towards building Windows Phone 7 applications. We first briefly looked at SharePoint security and how to enable anonymous access. Next, we started our simple RSS reader by creating a WebClient to read data from the network and display it on the screen.

Next, we investigated the RSS options available in SharePoint and looked at how to customize those feeds. From those RSS feeds, we used our WebClient to load that data and then parse the XML into a list of RSS items. This was by no means the only way to parse RSS, but it was the simplest way.

Next, we had a brief introduction to page navigation, where we took a selected item and navigated to a details view page. Finally, we used the information we passed to the details view page to navigate a web browser control to the post.

9

Building SharePoint Pages for Windows Phone 7

This chapter is taken from *Microsoft SharePoint 2010 Enterprise Applications on Windows Phone 7* (Chapter 4) by Todd Spatafore.

This chapter will dive deeper into lists, libraries, and list view templates. It may come as a surprise to many that all the data in SharePoint is just content in a list. This is an important thing to know because once we realize that SharePoint is really only a data management tool, we can begin to imagine all of the amazing things that can be done with SharePoint. This book focuses on building SharePoint experiences for Windows Phone 7. It is really important that we do this right because we want our end users to be free to get the information they need and get on with their work. That is the power of SharePoint and Windows Phone 7. It is our job to see that it is done properly. With this in mind, how we display that data to the end user ultimately determines the success of the SharePoint installation.

In this chapter, we will create a custom list view using the Web editor, as well as Visual Studio 2010. To be more specific, in this chapter, we will look at the following topics:

- The difference between lists and libraries
- Adding columns to a list
- Customizing the list item output
- Replacing the mobile home page

The difference between lists and libraries

This may seem like a strange place to begin this chapter, but there is usually a lot of confusion around this topic. In the introduction, we mentioned that in SharePoint, ultimately everything is data in a list. This means that there really isn't a difference between lists and libraries except for where that data lives.

In a list, the data lives in various fields of the column. Although a list usually has meta-data associated with it, the bulk of the information is stored in those fields. Usually, when we search for data that is stored in a list, we find the search results in the data itself.

In a library, the data lives inside a file that is stored in a field of the column. Although we can search through the data in a library using various **iFilters**, for some file types the metadata associated with the file usually has more pertinent information that can be searched.

Searching content with iFilters

The content within the files in a library can be indexed and searched when an appropriate **iFilter** is installed. An iFilter gives the search index the ability to read the content or metadata contained within the file. By default, Microsoft Office files can be indexed, but other common files such as Adobe PDF and Tagged Image File Format (TIFF) files need to have an iFilter installed.

Installing and configuring the iFilter for Adobe PDF is a common request and should be done automatically. As it isn't done for us when we install SharePoint, there are several good walkthroughs. One can be found at the following URL:

`http://support.microsoft.com/kb/2293357/`

Adding columns to a list

When you click on **Site Actions** and select the **More Options** link, the **Create** dialog will appear. Anything in this list that is not a site or a page is a list.

The following is the screenshot of the **Create** dialog showing a selection of lists that we can create:

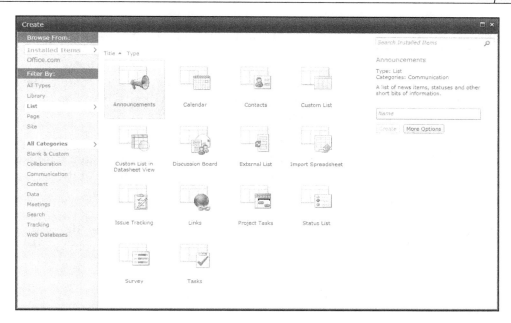

The following screenshot shows the **Create** dialog displaying a selection of the libraries which we can create:

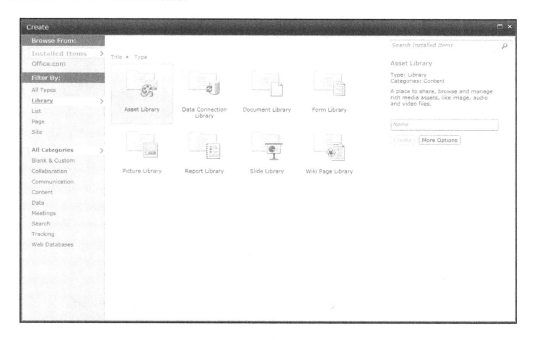

As can be seen in the preceding screenshot, there are quite a few pre-defined lists and libraries. If there isn't one that meets our needs, then the **Custom List** is there to help.

Many of these lists provide more than just a list. They also provide a custom view to display the data for that list. For example, if we create a library based on the **Picture Viewer**, the display provided is very different to the display for a **Wiki Page Library**.

Later in this chapter, we will customize the display of a list using custom templates, which is the recommended way for altering the list display in SharePoint.

Carry out the following steps to create a blank site for this chapter:

1. Open your SharePoint development site and click on the **New Site** option from the **Site Actions** drop-down list at the top left of the screen, as shown in the following screenshot:

2. Select the **Blank Site** template.
3. Give the site a title, for example Chapter4.
4. Give the site a URL similar to Chapter4.
5. Finally, click on the **Create** button.

At this point, SharePoint will create the new site and then load the new site for us. If we are successful, the following screenshot shows what we will see:

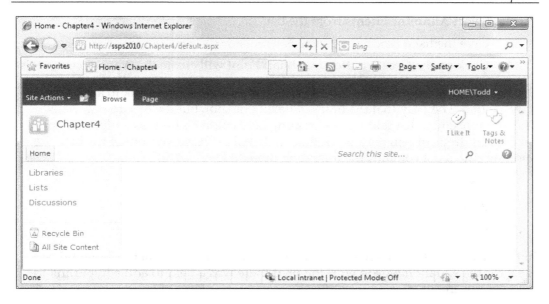

Next, let us create an announcement list that we will customize. Carry out the following steps to add an announcement list to this blank site:

1. From the **Site Actions** menu, select the **More Options...** option, as shown in the following screenshot:

2. Select **Announcements** from the list.

3. Give the list a new name, such as `Pertinent Blog Announcements`.

4. Click on the **Create** button and SharePoint will create the Announcement list.

Every day we get e-mails from co-workers that contain a hyperlink to a blog or a web video. They say that the link is amazing or cool, but it clogs up our inbox. The announcement list that we are creating here could be used as a replacement for the hundreds of e-mails a week that are like that. However, out of the box, the announcement list contains the following three fields:

1. **Title**

2. **Body**

3. **Expires**

In the background, there are also **created by** and **modified by** fields. It would be ideal for the situation we are working on if there was a field to add a hyperlink to the announcement.

To add a hyperlink column to the announcement list, carry out the following steps:

1. In the Quick Launch bar, select the announcement list that we just created.

2. From the top navigation bar, select **List** from the **List Tools** section.

3. In the list ribbon that appears, select the **List Settings** button on the right.

4. Under the **Columns** heading, there is a link named **Create column**. Click on this link.

5. Give the column a name such as `Interesting Link` or something descriptive.

6. Select **Hyperlink or Picture** for **The type of information in this column is**: option.

7. Leave the default values for the **Additional Column Settings** and select the **OK** button to create the column, as shown in the following screenshot:

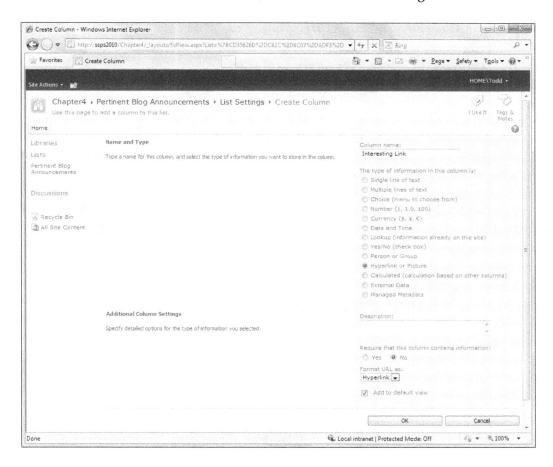

After having saved the new column to the list, go back to the list by clicking on **Pertinent Blog Announcements** in the breadcrumb at the top of the page (see the preceding screenshot). Now when we create a new item in the list, there are two additional form fields to add in the hyperlink, as shown in the following screenshot:

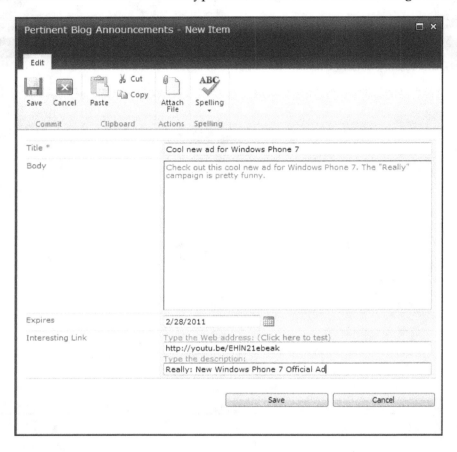

Once we have done all of that we can see what this looks like on the phone by navigating to our Announcement List on the phone, as seen in the following screenshot:

Wow, that is almost useful, isn't it? In the middle in the smallest possible font is the hyperlink that we added. In fact, all of the information for the announcement is in what can only be described as the smallest font possible.

Customizing the list item output

We can customize how the list item output looks and increase the font size by creating a custom control template. Out of the box, the announcement list does not have a customized mobile view. Even if it did, we would be able to override it with our own. Customizing a control template is fairly easy. Control templates are `aspx` files that live in the SharePoint root. We will use Visual Studio to create custom control templates.

Creating a project for our custom template

The first thing we need to do is create a project that will contain our custom control. Carry out the following steps to create a project:

1. Open Visual Studio 2010 as Administrator by right clicking on the icon and selecting **Run as administrator** on the context menu.

2. Select **Yes** in the UAC (User Authentication Control) dialog.

3. Once Visual Studio has opened, select **File | New Project**.

4. In the **2010** node of the **SharePoint** templates, select **Empty SharePoint Project**.

5. Give the project a name similar to `CustomAnnouncementForm`. 6.   Give the solution a name, such as `Chapter04`.

 We will be reusing this solution for two more projects in this chapter. That is why we are giving the solution a more generic name to encompass all three projects.

7. Select the **OK** button, as shown in the following screenshot:

This **New Project** screen may look different depending on what applications are installed and which options are selected when installing Visual Studio 2010.

8. Next, Visual Studio will ask you to **Specify the site and security level for debugging**. Enter the URL for your SharePoint server and select the trust level of **Deploy as a farm solution**.

 When we build these sites, we need to have full permission on the SharePoint site, as well as full permission to the server. As we need to restart IIS, as well as make modifications to SharePoint that only an administrator can perform, administrator rights to both the development server, as well as administrator rights in SharePoint are required.

9. Click on the **Finish** button and Visual Studio will create the empty SharePoint project for us, as seen in the following screenshot:

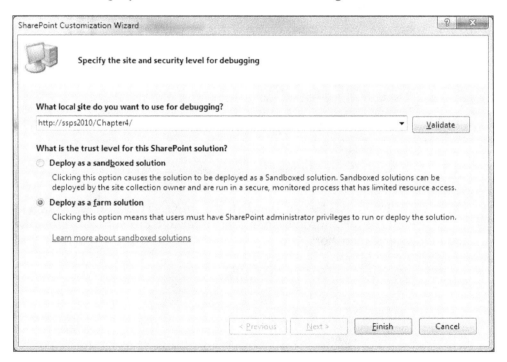

Adding a mapped folder for the custom control template

Now that we have a project to work with, we need to add a SharePoint mapped folder to the control templates. The mapped folder allows us to develop our custom control template in the appropriate folder under the SharePoint root. It allows Visual Studio 2010 to keep track of the files and even allows us to use source control for these files. Then, when we deploy the project, the files will be placed in the correct folder. SharePoint does a lot of rendering based on file convention over configuration. In this case, when the announcement is rendered, SharePoint will only look for templates within this mapped folder. Even if our control is in a subfolder, SharePoint won't find it. So, when we add this mapped folder, don't create a subfolder. Carry out the following steps to add a mapped folder to the project:

1. Right click on the **CustomAnnounementForm** project in the **Solution Explorer**.

2. In the context menu that appears, select **Add | SharePoint Mapped Folder**, as shown in the following screenshot:

3. In the **Add SharePoint Mapped Folder** tree view that appears, select the arrow to expand **TEMPLATE**.

4. Once **TEMPLATE** has been expanded, select **CONTROLTEMPLATES** and then click on the **OK** button to map this folder into our solution, as shown in the following screenshot:

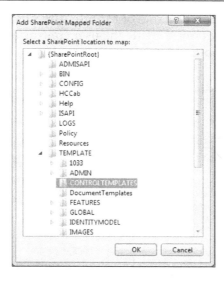

Now that we have added a mapped folder to our project, we can focus on the custom control template.

Creating the custom template

Now that we have our Visual Studio project created and we have mapped the control templates folder to our project, the next step is to create the user control that will house our custom template. Carry out the following steps to create the user control:

1. In **Solution Explorer**, right click on **CONTROLTEMPLATES**.

2. Select **Add | New Item...**

3. In the **Add New Item** dialog that appears, select **User Control** from the **SharePoint 2010** installed templates.

4. Give the user control the name of **Mobile_104_DispForm_Contents.ascx** and click on the **Add** button to create the user control, as shown in the following screenshot:

At this point, Visual Studio will create a baseline user control for us to use. We will be customizing this quite a bit next, but first let's review what we have just accomplished.

In ASP.NET programming, User Controls (ASCX files) are used in ASP.NET Pages (ASPX files) to consolidate common functionality. In SharePoint, they are used in a similar manner.

When a page is rendered for mobile browsers, the following three separate sections make up the page:

1. Header
2. Content
3. Footer

In this case, we are interested in customizing the contents of the page. The page we are customizing in this example is the display form for the contents. The name we've given to our user control specifies this in the last two parts DispForm_Contents. The first two parts specify that we are modifying the mobile web experience and the **104** is the ListTypeID for the Announcements list.

The list of **SPListTemplateType** enumerations can be found at the following URL:

`http://msdn.microsoft.com/en-us/library/microsoft.`
`sharepoint.splisttemplatetype.aspx`

Combining all this together gives us the file name `Mobile_104_DispForm_Contents.aspx`. SharePoint does not require that the file name uses this pattern. In fact, this pattern is only needed in the template itself. It is being used here because it helps when looking at the control templates folder to see when something has already been overridden.

Customizing the template

Up to this point, we've done the following:

- Created a project in Visual Studio to hold our custom template.
- Mapped a folder to the control templates. This is where our custom template will live.
- Created a blank user control within the control templates folder to house our custom template.

Now, we will write the code required for the custom template. The code we are writing for this template will be purely visual code. There won't be any need for compiled C# code. As such, the code behind files isn't needed. Delete the following two files, as they are not needed for this template:

1. `Mobile_104_DispForm_Contents.ascx.cs`
2. `Mobile_104_DispForm_Contents.ascx.designer.cs`

Finally, let's create the custom template by carrying out the following steps:

1. Open the file `Mobile_104_DispForm_Contents.ascx` and ensure that the **Source** view is enabled.
2. Delete all the contents of this file.
3. Add the following code to the file to define the user control and assemblies.

```
<%@ Control Language="C#"%>
<%@ Assembly Name="Microsoft.SharePoint, Version=14.0.0.0,
   Culture=neutral, PublicKeyToken=71e9bce111e9429c" %>
```

4. Add the following code to register the XML tag prefixes that will be used in the page:

```
<%@ Register TagPrefix="mobile" Namespace="System.
Web.UI.MobileControls" Assembly="System.Web.Mobile,
Version=1.0.3300.0, Culture=neutral, PublicKeyToken=b03f5f7f11d50a
3a" %>
<%@ Register TagPrefix="SharePoint" Namespace="Microsoft.
SharePoint.WebControls" Assembly="Microsoft.SharePoint,
Version=14.0.0.0, Culture=neutral, PublicKeyToken=71e9bce111e942
9c" %>
<%@ Register TagPrefix="SPMobile" Namespace="Microsoft.SharePoint.
MobileControls" Assembly="Microsoft.SharePoint, Version=14.0.0.0,
Culture=neutral, PublicKeyToken=71e9bce111e9429c" %>
```

5. To start the actual template code for the page, add the following code. Although we've named the file for this user control the same as the ID listed here, it is in fact the ID here that lets SharePoint know that this template should be used for rendering the announcements display form contents:

```
<SharePoint:RenderingTemplate runat="server"
  ID="Mobile_104_DispForm_Contents">
...
</SharePoint:RenderingTemplate>
```

6. Next, inside the Rendering Template element that we just added, we add an element that tells the Rendering Template that we are going to specify our own template.

```
<Template>
...
</Template>
```

7. This next element nested within the `Template` element is a `div` with an inline style attribute to let the browser know that we don't want the default font size, but instead we want a font size of `13` points, as follows:

```
<div style=="font-size: 13pt;">
...
</div>
```

8. The first element we put inside the `div` is a mobile list field, `Iterator`. Think of this like a `foreach` loop on the fields inside the current list item. For each field in the list item it will display the field name in bold and the field value followed by a line break.

```
<SPMobile:SPMobileListFieldIterator RunAt="Server" />
```

9. Next, we add the control container that we will insert with the change history inside.

```
<SPMobile:SPMobileControlContainer ID="SPMobileControlContainer1"
RunAt="Server">

...

</SPMobile:SPMobileControlContainer>
```

10. Finally, add this code inside the mobile control container. This displays the creation date and the last modified date for the announcement followed by a line break (the line break isn't required, but it does give a little extra room before the page footer).

```
<SPMobile:SPMobileCreatedModifiedPanel ID="SPMobileCreatedModified
Panel1" RunAt="Server" TemplateName="MobileCreatedModifiedInfo" />
<mobile:Label ID="Label1" RunAt="Server" BreakAfter="true" />
```

Steps 3 and 4 are fairly straightforward user control header elements. We are registering three tag prefixes that we'll be using in the custom template. They are `mobile`, `SharePoint`, and `SPMobile`.

`Mobile` contains all of the standard web UI mobile controls. These are not SharePoint specific, but we use a label to output a line break after the last modified date.

The `SharePoint` prefix will encapsulate the SharePoint web controls. This is really the big one, as it is what allows us to override the rendering template for the Announcement form.

Finally, `SPMobile` contains all of the SharePoint specific mobile controls.

Step 5 is where the actual template is created. The first thing we have is a directive to let SharePoint know that we are a rendering template: `SharePoint:RenderingTemplate`. The ID here is the same as what we have for the file name, `Mobile_104_DispForm_Contents`. In this situation, it is required that the ID is as specified with the exception that you can replace the `104` with `Announcements` if you want to.

When the SharePoint Application in IIS starts, it reads all of the user controls in the control templates folder. This lets SharePoint know what templates to use in any given situation. We could add more than one rendering template in this file and SharePoint would load each one for the intended purpose.

As an example of having multiple rendering templates in one file, `MobileDefaultTemplates.ascx` contains all of the default settings for all of the mobile templates in SharePoint.

Do not modify the file `MobileDefaultTemplates.ascx`. Although it may work for a while, this file may get overwritten during a service pack or other SharePoint update. The best way to update a template is through the methods listed in this chapter.

These rendering templates are read in from the control templates folder at application start, we don't actually need to use Visual Studio to create these templates. Visual Studio gives us the flexibility of the **deploy** option. The deploy option automatically copies the file to the correct location and restarts the SharePoint application for us. Also with Visual Studio, we could debug the template if we had custom code running. Last, but not least, Visual Studio also has great ties into source control systems allowing our application lifecycle management to be managed in the same place we are writing code.

Putting all of this together, the final code for this control looks like the following:

```
<%@ Control Language="C#"%>
<%@ Assembly Name="Microsoft.SharePoint, Version=14.0.0.0,
Culture=neutral, PublicKeyToken=71e9bce111e9429c" %>


<%@ Register TagPrefix="mobile" Namespace="System.Web.
UI.MobileControls" Assembly="System.Web.Mobile, Version=1.0.3300.0,
Culture=neutral, PublicKeyToken=b03f5f7f11d50a3a" %>

<%@ Register TagPrefix="SharePoint" Namespace="Microsoft.SharePoint.
WebControls" Assembly="Microsoft.SharePoint, Version=14.0.0.0,
Culture=neutral, PublicKeyToken=71e9bce111e9429c" %>

<%@ Register TagPrefix="SPMobile" Namespace="Microsoft.SharePoint.
MobileControls" Assembly="Microsoft.SharePoint, Version=14.0.0.0,
Culture=neutral, PublicKeyToken=71e9bce111e9429c" %>

<SharePoint:RenderingTemplate runat="server" ID="Mobile_104_DispForm_
Contents">

    <Template>
        <div style="font-size: 13pt;">
        <SPMobile:SPMobileListFieldIterator RunAt="Server" />
      <SPMobile:SPMobileControlContainer
ID="SPMobileControlContainer1"  RunAt="Server">
        <SPMobile:SPMobileCreatedModifiedPanel ID="SPMobileCreatedMo
difiedPanel1" RunAt="Server" TemplateName="MobileCreatedModifiedInfo"
/>
        <mobile:Label ID="Label1" RunAt="Server" BreakAfter="true" />
      </SPMobile:SPMobileControlContainer>
        </div>
```

```
      </Template>
  </SharePoint:RenderingTemplate>
```

Save this file and select the **Deploy** option from the **Build** menu in Visual Studio. When Visual Studio completes the deployment, open our list in Windows Phone 7, select the list item we created previously, and it should look like the following screenshot:

Replacing the mobile home page

In the last section, we learned how to customize the view for a list item on a mobile device. This works well for the list item, but what about the entire home page? We could follow the same instructions to customize the home page. All we would have to do is change the ID for the `SharePoint:RenderingTemplate` to reflect that of the site we are working with. For example, the following screenshot shows a customized home page (yes, we have used the Webdings font):

The following is the code that changed the title:

```
<%@ Control Language="C#"%>
<%@ Assembly Name="Microsoft.SharePoint, Version=14.0.0.0,
Culture=neutral, PublicKeyToken=71e9bce111e9429c" %>
<%@ Register TagPrefix="mobile" Namespace="System.Web.
UI.MobileControls" Assembly="System.Web.Mobile, Version=1.0.3300.0,
Culture=neutral, PublicKeyToken=b03f5f7f11d50a3a" %>
<%@ Register TagPrefix="SharePoint" Namespace="Microsoft.SharePoint.
WebControls" Assembly="Microsoft.SharePoint, Version=14.0.0.0,
Culture=neutral, PublicKeyToken=71e9bce111e9429c" %>
```

```
<%@ Register TagPrefix="SPMobile" Namespace="Microsoft.SharePoint.
MobileControls" Assembly="Microsoft.SharePoint, Version=14.0.0.0,
Culture=neutral, PublicKeyToken=71e9bce111e9429c" %>

<%@ Register TagPrefix="WPMobile" Namespace="Microsoft.SharePoint.
WebPartPages" Assembly="Microsoft.SharePoint, Version=14.0.0.0,
Culture=neutral, PublicKeyToken=71e9bce111e9429c" %>


<SharePoint:RenderingTemplate runat="server" ID="WebPartMobile_1_
HomePage_Title">
    <Template>
        <SPMobile:SPMobilePaddedPanel runat="server"
ForeColor="#FFFFFF" BackColor="#009933" Font-Bold="true" Font-
Size="13pt" Font-Names="Webdings">
            <WPMobile:WebPartMobilePageTitle RunAt="server" />
        </SPMobile:SPMobilePaddedPanel>
    </Template>
</SharePoint:RenderingTemplate>
```

This is almost the same as what we had before. We've changed the ID of the rendering template to target site ID type 1, which is a Blank Site. We could have also used **STS** instead of ID 1. That would have made the rendering template's ID `WebPartMobile_STS_HomePage_Title`.

Besides that, we've also added a new tag prefix for SharePoint Web Part Pages, `WPMobile`. This tag is used for the page title element in the template `<WPMobile:Web PartMobilePageTitle runat="server" />`.

Again, there's nothing here that's too different from what we did in the previous section. However, what if we wanted something completely different here? What if our designers came to us and asked for something that just isn't possible with the templates as they are right now? That is where the redirection system comes into play.

Carry out the following steps to add in a mobile home page redirect:

1. Create a new empty SharePoint project by right clicking on the **Chapter04** solution and select **Add | New Project...**.

2. On the **New Project** dialog, select **SharePoint | 2010** and then select **Empty SharePoint Project.**

3. Name the new project `HomePageRedirect`.

 As an alternative, we could reuse the existing project created for the custom announcement form, but this will keep our different projects separate.

4. Create a mapped folder to **{SharePointRoot}/TEMPLATE/LAYOUTS/MOBILE**. This can be accomplished by right clicking on the project name and selecting **Add | SharePoint Mapped Folder...** and navigating the tree to the Mobile folder.

5. Right click on this new folder in **Solution Explorer** and create a blank ASPX page by selecting **Add | New Item...** and then in the **Add New Item** dialog, select **Visual C# | Web | HTML Page**.

6. Name the page `CustomHomePage.aspx`. Notice that we are using the ASPX file extension instead of the HTML extension. This is so we get a nice clean `ASP.NET` file without the hooks that Visual Studio would put into a SharePoint Application Page.

7. Add the following HTML:

```
<!DOCTYPE HTML PUBLIC "-//W3C//DTD HTML 4.0 Transitional//EN">
<html>
  <head>
    <title>Custom Home page</title>
    <meta name="viewport" content="width=480px" />
  </head>
  <body>
    <h1>Hello World from my custom home page!</h1>
  </body>
</html>
```

8. Next, add a mapped folder to **{SharePointRoot}/TEMPLATE/CONTROLTEMPLATES**. This can be accomplished by right clicking on the project name and selecting **Add | SharePoint Mapped Folder...** and navigating the tree to the **CONTROLTEMPLATES** folder.

9. Right click on this folder and select **Add | New Item...**

10. Select a **User Control** from the **Add New Item** dialog and name it `Mobile_1_HomePage.ascx`.

11. In this file, add the following code:

```
<%@ Control Language="C#"%>
<%@ Assembly Name="Microsoft.SharePoint, Version=14.0.0.0,
Culture=neutral, PublicKeyToken=71e9bce111e9429c" %>

<%@ Register TagPrefix="SharePoint" Namespace="Microsoft.
SharePoint.WebControls" Assembly="Microsoft.SharePoint,
Version=14.0.0.0, Culture=neutral, PublicKeyToken=71e9bce111e942
9c" %>
<%@ Register TagPrefix="SPMobile" Namespace="Microsoft.SharePoint.
MobileControls" Assembly="Microsoft.SharePoint, Version=14.0.0.0,
Culture=neutral, PublicKeyToken=71e9bce111e9429c" %>
```

```
<SharePoint:RenderingTemplate runat="server" ID="WebPartMobile_1_
HomePage_Title">
    <Template>
      <SPMobile:SPMobileHomePageRedirection runat="server"
         PageFileName="CustomHomePage.aspx" />
    </Template>

</SharePoint:RenderingTemplate>
```

12. Save all files and select the **Deploy** option from the **Build** menu.

13. Load the home page on your Windows Phone and it should look like the following screenshot:

This is a very simple home page, but since we only used HTML, we can begin to see the power associated with building custom home page experiences.

The interesting part of this code is in step 11. Notice the difference highlighted in the code. This template has a home page redirection in it. This is what tells SharePoint to stop rendering the current page and instead restart on the value of the `PageFileName` attribute. In this case, the `PageFileName` attribute is `CustomHomePage.aspx`. This custom home page is very simple, as it only has a single line of text output for the user. However, from within this page, we have access to the full context and power of SharePoint.

Summary

This chapter contained a brief overview of the differences between lists and libraries. Once we understood the differences between lists and libraries, we looked closer at a particular list type named the Announcements list. We customized the Announcements list with an additional column. When we opened up the list item view for the Announcement list, we noticed that the default rendering on the Windows Phone was unreadable by default. From there, we created a project in Visual Studio to help us customize the list item rendering template. Next, we looked at how list item rendering templates were related to the home page and customized the home page in a similar manner. Finally, we took the home page customization all the way along the spectrum and replaced the entire page with a custom HTML page.

10

Building a Windows Phone 7 Dashboard Application with SharePoint Data

 This chapter is taken from *Microsoft SharePoint 2010 Enterprise Applications on Windows Phone 7* (Chapter 7) by Todd Spatafore.

This chapter will demonstrate many of the custom application paradigms that we encounter as we build enterprise applications for SharePoint 2010 and Windows Phone 7. We will build a simple dashboard that will demonstrate the display of important data and a graph to present information about key performance indicators for a fake company. To get to the data, we will introduce programming against SharePoint 2010 using the client-side API's. This includes using REST and WCF Data Services. We begin this chapter, with a brief look at security. This chapter will cover the following topics:

- Forms-based authentication
- Managed Client Object Model on the desktop
- WCF Data Services to the rescue
- Dashboard

Earlier in this book, we set up our development environment with SharePoint, Visual Studio, and all the Windows Phone 7 development tools all on one Windows 7 machine. It is at this point in the book where we should leave that behind and move to the more recommended approach of development. That is to say, we should have a SharePoint server separate from our development Windows 7 machine.

Let's start by taking a look at forms-based authentication.

Forms-based authentication

Earlier we opened our SharePoint site up for anonymous access. We did that so that we could look at the programming of an RSS feed reader against feeds found in SharePoint without having to discuss authentication. In the real world, this isn't a practical solution because our IT administrators would panic at the thought of having corporate data exposed without any authentication.

When building applications for Windows Phone 7 that use data from a SharePoint server, some form of authentication is required. Though, NTLM or Kerberos authentication are not supported in the current version of the phone. Another mechanism must be employed to authenticate to SharePoint.

This is where we will use **forms-based authentication (FBA)** using **claims-based authentication**. Back in SharePoint 2003, setting up a site for forms-based authentication was a difficult job, and the end result was a very fragile site. This got better in 2007 and with 2010 the steps required for enabling forms-based authentication are very well documented. You can read the instructions here:

```
http://blogs.msdn.com/b/sridhara/archive/2010/01/07/setting-up-fba-
claims-in-sharepoint-2010-with-active-directory-membership-provider.
aspx
```

These instructions do the following:

- Create a new site using claims-based authentication
- Configure the central administration site's `web.config` file for both an LDAP connection string and a membership provider
- Configure the Web application's `web.config` file for both an LDAP connection string and a membership provider
- Configure the **Security Token Service** Application's **(STS)** `web.config` file for both an LDAP connection and a membership provider
- Configure the Web application to use the specified membership provider

The trickiest thing in this whole exercise is getting the LDAP URI correct for the Active Directory domain that we need to authenticate against.

These instructions work great if we are just setting up a site for the first time. However, if a site already exists that we want to continue using, we'll need some way to convert an existing web application from classic mode to claims mode.

Obviously, the first step in doing this type of thing is to backup the SharePoint environment. Next, follow the instructions from the TechNet website:

```
http://technet.microsoft.com/en-us/library/gg251985.aspx
```

The decision of what mode we use for authentication should ideally be made before creating the Web application. Earlier in this book, it didn't matter because we were using a web interface and our browser could authenticate using NTLM. At this point in our development of Windows Phone 7 applications that get data from SharePoint, we must use the forms-based mode of authentication.

Connecting with forms based authentication

Windows Phone 7 doesn't exactly make it easy for us to connect to SharePoint using forms-based authentication. We have to build all the plumbing ourselves. We also have to leave behind the comfort of the WebClient. In .NET and in Silverlight, the WebClient has the mechanisms needed to pass authentication information along with the requests. Windows Phone 7's implementation of WebClient does not provide that luxury. Instead, we have to build up the authentication requests manually using **HttpWebRequest**.

HttpWebRequest allows us to have a fine grained control over our request to the server. This allows us to add in whatever headers and cookies we want. This means that we can build a request to the authentication web service for SharePoint and send it off. SharePoint will authenticate the user using forms-based authentication and then provide an authorization cookie that we can pass back to SharePoint on every request. With this authorization cookie, we can access SharePoint securely and our IT teams can sleep at night.

Accessing the RSS feeds securely

In simple RSS example instead of communicating to the RSS feed using an anonymous connection, let's connect to the RSS feed that is protected by forms-based authentication.

We will be doing a couple of examples in this chapter, so a generic solution to contain all of these samples will be good.

1. Open Visual Studio 2010.
2. From the **File** menu, select **New Project...**.
3. In the **Installed Templates** list, select **Other Project Types**.

4. Under **Other Project Types**, select **Visual Studio Solutions**, as shown in the following screenshot:

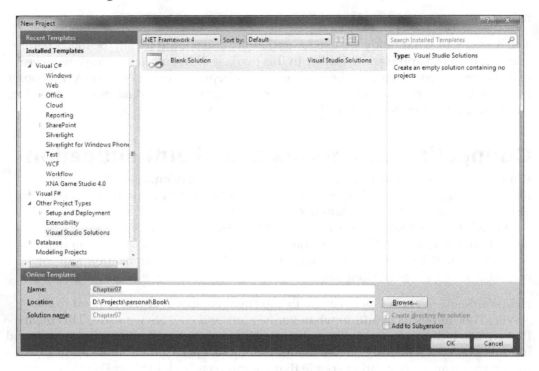

5. Give the solution the name **Chapter07**
6. Click on the **OK** button and Visual Studio will create an empty solution for us.

Next, we'll need a project in this solution. The following steps show how to add the copy of this project into this solution:

1. In **Solution Explorer** in Visual Studio, right click on the solution name.
2. In the context menu that appears, select **Add** and then **Existing Project...**.
3. Navigate to the location of the **SimpleRSSReader** folder.
4. Select the **SimpleRSSReader.csproj** file and click on the **Open** button.

The WebClient way of getting the RSS feed involved an event handler that was added to our client to listen for the `DownloadStringCompleted` event. Once the string was downloaded, we parsed the result into an XElement and then used LINQ to XML to get a list of RSSItem that we then data bound to the feedListBox.

We can reuse the part of the event handler that parses the RSS feed and does the data binding by pulling that part out into its own method:

```
private void ResultsToListBox(string result)
{
    var rssElement = XElement.Parse(result);
    var items = from item in rssElement.Descendants("item")
                select new RSSItem
                {
                    Title = item.Element("title").Value,
                    Date = item.Element("pubDate").Value,
                    PostUrl = item.Element("link").Value
                };
    feedListBox.ItemsSource = items;
}
```

Now, we could update the `client_DownloadStringCompleted` event handler to use this method, but we aren't going to be using the WebClient anymore. Instead, delete the rest of the `client_DownloadStringCompleted` event handler method.

As we aren't using the WebClient in this version, remove the client parameter at the top of the class and replace it with a new HttpWebRequest parameter:

```
private HttpWebRequest webRequest;
```

Next, remove the initialization code for the WebClient from the `MainPage_Loaded` event handler. That is to say, remove the following two lines of code:

```
client.DownloadStringCompleted += new
  DownloadStringCompletedEventHandler(client_DownloadStringCompleted);
client.DownloadStringAsync(new Uri(siteUrl));
```

In its place, add the new initialization code for the HttpWebRequest. This is what the `MainPage_Loaded` event handler should look like with the new lines highlighted:

```
private void MainPage_Loaded(object sender, RoutedEventArgs e)
{
    webRequest = (HttpWebRequest)HttpWebRequest.Create(new
    Uri(siteUrl));
    webRequest.BeginGetResponse(new AsyncCallback(BlogCallBack),
    webRequest);
```

```
feedListBox.SelectionChanged += new SelectionChangedEventHandler(f
eedListBox_SelectionChanged);
}
```

HttpWebRequest handles calls backs a little different to WebClient. They are both asynchronous, which is good because we don't want to block the UI thread, but the HttpWebRequest uses a dependency injection to tell it explicitly what to do when the response comes back. The WebClient doesn't need an event handler. We could just call `DownloadStringAsync` and the call would go through. With HttpWebRequest, we must pass in a method for it to call when the request goes through.

In this case, we have called that method `BlogCallBack`. The following is the code for that method:

```
private void BlogCallBack(IAsyncResult asyncResult)
{
    var request = (HttpWebRequest)asyncResult.AsyncState;
    var response = (HttpWebResponse)request.
    EndGetResponse(asyncResult);
    using (var sr = new StreamReader(response.GetResponseStream()))
    {
        var result = sr.ReadToEnd();
        Dispatcher.BeginInvoke(() => ResultsToListBox(result));
    }
}
```

This code speaks for itself to a certain extent. First, we get the request object from the result. From the request we can get the response from the server. This will come in the form of a stream, so we'll have to add the following line to the top of our file:

```
using System.IO;
```

Next, by framing our `StreamReader` inside a using statement we are assured that dispose will be called on it, thus freeing up the memory allocation that comes along with a stream.

We read the result and pass that result into the `ResultsToListBox` method that we extracted earlier. In order to do that though we need to think about one very important thing: At this point in the code, we are not working on the UI thread. The background processor thread cannot interrupt the UI thread. To get around this, we call `Dispatcher.BeginInvoke`.

Nice and tidy.

Next, let's turn off anonymous access to our SharePoint site. Make sure you've configured it for forms authentication and setup a user account because we'll need it when we try to get access to the RSS feed.

Removing anonymous access

Before we can make a request to our RSS feed that is protected by forms authentication, we need to authenticate against SharePoint. This will return an authorization cookie that we must return with every request to the server. To get this authorization cookie, we make a request to the authentication web service on SharePoint. Its address is: `http://<your server>/_vti_bin/authentication.asmx`. Looking at this path in a browser shows that the `authentication.asmx` web service request needs to be a SOAP POST with a specific format:

```
POST /_vti_bin/authentication.asmx HTTP/1.1
Host: SharePointServer
Content-Type: text/xml; charset=utf-8
Content-Length: length
SOAPAction: "http://schemas.microsoft.com/sharepoint/soap/Login"
```

```
<?xml version="1.0" encoding="utf-8"?>
<soap:Envelope xmlns:xsi="http://www.w3.org/2001/XMLSchema-instance"
xmlns:xsd="http://www.w3.org/2001/XMLSchema" xmlns:soap="http://
schemas.xmlsoap.org/soap/envelope/">
  <soap:Body>
    <Login xmlns="http://schemas.microsoft.com/sharepoint/soap/">
      <username>string</username>
      <password>string</password>
    </Login>
  </soap:Body>
</soap:Envelope>
```

This is a very basic SOAP message. SOAP messages are XML documents sent in the body of a POST to the server. The message itself is contained within an envelope that describes the schema of the message. The message body is contained within a SOAP body. The element name within the body describes the action that we want to take. In this case, we want to login. This element has a payload of the username and password.

In this SOAP message header, we need to specify the Content-Length based on the actual length of the message body that we are sending to the server. That length really depends on the length of the username and password string that we need to supply. Thankfully, HttpWebRequest will add in the Content-Length header for us. We will also add our CookieContainer to the headers for our requests for data. This is how SharePoint will know that we are authenticated.

The response to this web service call will be in the following form:

```
HTTP/1.1 200 OK
Content-Type: text/xml; charset=utf-8
Content-Length: length

<?xml version="1.0" encoding="utf-8"?>
<soap:Envelope xmlns:xsi="http://www.w3.org/2001/XMLSchema-instance"
xmlns:xsd="http://www.w3.org/2001/XMLSchema" xmlns:soap="http://
schemas.xmlsoap.org/soap/envelope/">
  <soap:Body>
    <LoginResponse xmlns="http://schemas.microsoft.com/sharepoint/
    soap/">
      <LoginResult>
        <CookieName>string</CookieName>
        <ErrorCode>NoError or NotInFormsAuthenticationMode or
        PasswordNotMatch</ErrorCode>
        <TimeoutSeconds>int</TimeoutSeconds>
      </LoginResult>
    </LoginResponse>
```

```
        </soap:Body>
    </soap:Envelope>
```

With this result, we first need to check the `ErrorCode`. If the `ErrorCode` is `NoError` then we know that the `cookieJar` has been populated with our authentication token.

Enough theory, let's look at an example. We know that we really can't do anything in our application until we authenticate against SharePoint. So, let's open our `MainPage.xaml.cs` file and rewrite the `MainPage_Loaded` method.

First though let's hardcode our username and password into class member variables. In a real application, we would have a settings page where the user would enter their credentials, but hardcoding this information for now will demonstrate the concepts that we need to learn. Add the following code inside the class outside of any methods:

```
private string mUsername = "JQP";

private string mPassword = "P@ssw0rd";
```

We will also need a variable to hold our cookie when we get it from SharePoint. Add the following class member variable right after the username and password variables:

```
private CookieContainer cookieJar = new CookieContainer();
```

So all of the code that we previously had in our `MainPage_Loaded` method is still important, we just can't run it until we have an authentication token. Let's change the name of this method to `LoadFeed`:

```
private void LoadFeed()
{
    webRequest = (HttpWebRequest)HttpWebRequest.Create(new
    Uri(siteUrl));
    webRequest.BeginGetResponse(new AsyncCallback(BlogCallBack),
    webRequest);

    feedListBox.SelectionChanged += new SelectionChangedEventHandler(f
    eedListBox_SelectionChanged);
}
```

Now once we have our authentication token set, we can make a call to this method. Next, make a new blank `MainPage_Loaded` event handler. This is where we will start our call to the authentication service. Let's make a call to a new method that we'll call `Authenticate`. Then create a new method called `Authenticate`.

```
private void MainPage_Loaded(object sender, RoutedEventArgs e)
{
    Authenticate();
}

private void Authenticate()
{
}
```

The `Authenticate` method will create an HttpWebRequest, set the Web request headers, and then make a call to the asynchronous `BeginGetRequestStream` method FBA:BeginGetRequestStream method. Add code to the `Authenticate` method to appear like this:

```
private void Authenticate()
{
    var authWebService = "http://ssps2010/_vti_bin/authentication.
    asmx";
    var authWebRequest = (HttpWebRequest)HttpWebRequest.
    Create(authWebService);
    authWebRequest.Method = "POST";
    authWebRequest.ContentType = "text/xml; charset=utf-8";
    authWebRequest.Headers["SOAPAction"] = "http://schemas.microsoft.
    com/sharepoint/soap/Login";
    authWebRequest.CookieContainer = cookieJar;

    authWebRequest.BeginGetRequestStream(new AsyncCallback(Authenticat
    ionRequestCallback), authWebRequest);
}
```

Let's look at this code line by line. In the First line we instantiate a string that contains the URL for the authentication web service. Be sure to update the URL to point to the appropriate server.

The second line uses a factory to create an HttpWebRequest object for us taking in the authentication web service string we initialized in the first line. Next, we explicitly set the request method to POST. After we set the request method, we set the `ContentType` header to `text/xml; charset=utf-8` to let the Web Service know that what we are sending should be treated as xml encoded in UTF-8.

The next header we add isn't a typical request header, so we have to specify the key explicitly as `SOAPAction`. This lets the Web Service know that we are sending an action inside of a SOAP envelope. The value for this header specifies which SOAP action should be called. In this case, it's the Login action at the Web Service endpoint that we are calling.

Next, we add the empty cookie container to the request. Upon success, this container will be filled with our authentication token. Finally, we tell the Web request to begin an asynchronous stream and call the method `AuthenticationRequestCallback`, so that we can fill the body of the request. Let's look at that code now:

```
private void AuthenticationRequestCallback(IAsyncResult asyncResult)
{
    var request = (HttpWebRequest)asyncResult.AsyncState;
    var soapEnvelope = string.Format(@"<?xml version=""1.0""
encoding=""utf-8""?>
                        <soap:Envelope xmlns:xsi=""http://www.
w3.org/2001/XMLSchema-instance""
                            xmlns:xsd=""http://www.w3.org/2001/
XMLSchema""
                            xmlns:soap=""http://schemas.xmlsoap.org/
soap/envelope/"">
                        <soap:Body>
                        <Login xmlns=""http://schemas.microsoft.
com/sharepoint/soap/"">
                            <username>{0}</username>
                            <password>{1}</password>
                        </Login>
                        </soap:Body>
                    </soap:Envelope>", mUsername, mPassword);
    var encoder = new UTF8Encoding();

    using (var reqStream = request.EndGetRequestStream(asyncResult))
    {
        var body = encoder.GetBytes(soapEnvelope);
        reqStream.Write(body, 0, body.Length);
        reqStream.Close();
    }

    request.BeginGetResponse(new AsyncCallback(AuthenticationResponseC
allback), request);
}
```

This isn't as much code as it looks because there's a lot of XML in there. First, we get a reference to the HttpWebRequest from the IAsyncResult that was passed in. Then, we set up the SOAP Envelope. The XML for this SOAP envelope can be found at the following address (modifying the URL for your own SharePoint server):

```
http://ssps20110/_vti_bin/authentication.asmx?op=Login
```

We replaced the username and password with the hardcoded values that we set at the top of the class and then created a new text encoder. We'll see why we did this in a minute, but in order for this to work, we'll have to add a using statement at the top of the file:

```
using System.Text;
```

Next, we open a stream to enter the body of the message. This is where the encoder comes in use. We pass the SOAP envelope string into the UTF-8 encoder and from that encoder we get an array of bytes. This array of bytes then gets sent into the body of the request. Finally, we close the request stream.

The last thing we do in this method is let the system know what to do when the response starts coming back. In this case, we want it to call a method named AuthenticationResponseCallback.

```
private void AuthenticationResponseCallback(IAsyncResult asyncResult)
{
    var request = (HttpWebRequest)asyncResult.AsyncState;
    var response = (HttpWebResponse)request.
    EndGetResponse(asyncResult);
    var errorCode = string.Empty;
    using (var responseStream = new StreamReader(response.
    GetResponseStream()))
    {
        var xResult = XmlReader.Create(responseStream);
        xResult.ReadToDescendant("ErrorCode");
        errorCode = xResult.ReadElementContentAsString();
        xResult.Close();
        responseStream.Close();
    }

    if (!string.IsNullOrEmpty(errorCode) && (errorCode.
    ToLowerInvariant() == "noerror"))
    {
        LoadFeed();
    }

}
```

This is the AuthenticationResponseCallback. It looks a lot like the BlogCallBack function we discussed earlier. We start out by getting a reference to the request object and from the request object we get a reference to the response object. We then initialize a variable that will hold the error code. The error code, as we saw from the SOAP definition page, will have one of following three values:

1. NoError

2. NotInFormsAuthenticationMode

3. PasswordNotMatch

In this example, we are only looking for the successful calls and in a production environment, we should handle the error situations by letting the user know that their password was wrong, the server isn't configured properly, or that there was an internal server error.

> In a production environment, we would also be interested in making sure the HTTP response code we get back is 200 OK. If it is anything else, we would need to handle it appropriately and in my experience the most common error is 500 Internal Server Error as I mentioned briefly earlier. As mentioned earlier, we will only look for the successful case. The error handling should be dealt with in a production environment though.

The way we get the error code is a little different than the way we get the RSS feed items. In this case, we are using a forward moving XML reader. We use it to read to the element containing the error code and then read the contents of that element into our error code variable. To do this, we need to add a using reference to System.Xml at the top of our file.

```
using System.Xml;
```

This is a very convenient way of handling this response because we don't need to create another heavy object in memory that holds all of the values in the XML just to read in one value. The XMLReader and StreamReaders are destroyed almost as soon as they are created and all that is left is a single string.

Finally, once we check that there were no errors we make the call to LoadFeed. We have to modify LoadFeed though to pass our cookie container with its HttpWebRequest as can be seen in the highlighted line of the following code:

```
private void LoadFeed()
{
    webRequest = (HttpWebRequest)HttpWebRequest.Create(new
    Uri(siteUrl));
    webRequest.CookieContainer = cookieJar;
    webRequest.BeginGetResponse(new AsyncCallback(BlogCallBack),
    webRequest);
    feedListBox.SelectionChanged += new SelectionChangedEventHandler(f
    eedListBox_SelectionChanged);
}
```

Compile and run the application and you should see the exact same result as before:

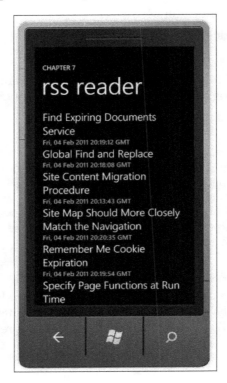

The difference is that now the RSS reader is making a call into an authenticated feed. This can be seen by tapping on an item. We haven't passed the authentication cookie on to the Web browser, so we see the login page as shown in the following screenshot:

We won't continue down the path of how to display the contents of the RSS Item in this book. Instead, now that we are authenticated into the SharePoint site, let's look at getting data from other sources in SharePoint.

 The forms-based authentication discussed here still sends the username and password in clear text over the wire. To be more secure from attacks forms-based authentication should be configured to use SSL.

Managed Client Object Model on the desktop

SharePoint 2010 introduces the managed client object model which allows us to create applications using ECMAScript, .NET managed code, and Silverlight. This new object model is designed around the highly successful server object model and takes a lot of the interfaces directly from the server's API. That means knowing the server object model will provide for an easy transition to the client object model, and vice versa.

 ECMAScript is the scripting language standardized by Ecma International in the ECMA-262 specification and ISO/IEC 16262. For more information, please visit the Wikipedia description at the following URL:

http://en.wikipedia.org/wiki/ECMAScript

The client object model is not a perfect replication of the server object model. The reason for this design was to build an object model that provides for client level development needs. The result of not providing everything in the client object model that exists in the server object model is a smaller footprint on the libraries, and thus a shorter download time.

Because everything in the client object model exists in the server object model, making a call on these interfaces is a simple WCF service call that relays the information to the server in XML. The request is then performed using the server object model and the response is returned using **JavaScript Object Notation (JSON)** or OData. As we'll learn, this is important for writing Windows Phone 7 Applications.

ECMAScript interface

The .js files needed for the ECMAScript interface are automatically included in the standard SharePoint master page. There is nothing that needs to be added to the Web pages to get this interface on the client. We just need to start using it.

Using the ECMAScript interface is relatively easy. We simply need to add a SharePoint Form Digest within the form for the page. These types of pages must run within the context of SharePoint and be deployed to the layouts folder.

The form digest class inserts a security validation into the page. It creates a message digest that helps prevent a specific type of attack where a user is tricked into posting information to the server. Basically, this is analogous to the cookie jar that we created earlier. This security validation has a lifetime and cannot be copied and used on another computer.

The ECMAScript interface into SharePoint demonstrates how SharePoint sites were developed for SharePoint. This type of programming works great when we are concerned with websites. When we create our custom mobile home page, the next step is to create a custom master page that contained all of the required JavaScript files and go to town implementing the various lists and libraries contained within our SharePoint site.

For Windows Phone 7 application programming, building web pages isn't as exciting as building out full featured Silverlight applications.

Silverlight interface

In Silverlight, on the desktop we can reference the Client Object Model's DLL from the SharePoint SDK and build our applications against them. This makes for a very satisfying development environment.

The DLL's are registered into the **Global Assembly Cache (GAC)** on the developer's machine. To reference them in a project, carry out the following steps:

1. Right click on **References** in **Solution Explorer**.
2. Click on **Add Reference**.
3. On the .**NET** tab of the **Add References** dialog box, select the following two DLL's
    ◦ **Microsoft.SharePoint.Client**
    ◦ **Microsoft.SharePoint.Client.Runtime**
4. Finally, click on **OK**.

When the Silverlight application is deployed, the required DLL's are bundled inside the XAP. No additional download or installation is required on the client machine.

Windows Phone 7 applications, although written in Silverlight, only support a subset of Silverlight features. What this means for a developer trying to write Windows Phone 7 applications that take advantage of SharePoint features is that DLL's like those found in the client object model from the SharePoint SDK depend on DLL's that aren't available on Windows Phone 7. Specifically, System.Windows.Browser is missing from the phone. What are we to do in this situation? Enter WCF Data Services.

In addition to ECMAScript and Silverlight, there are .NET managed code libraries that can be used to create WinForms or WPF applications that run on Windows. This is beyond the scope of this book, but for the most part the interfaces are the same as the Silverlight API. Their distribution model is slightly different though. One must use the SharePoint Foundation 2010 Client Object Model Redistributable package. Visit the following URL for more information:

`http://msdn.microsoft.com/en-us/library/ee537247.aspx`

WCF Data Services to the rescue

Developing Windows Phone 7 Applications that integrate with SharePoint data have a lot more in common with developing .NET Managed Applications for the desktop than writing SharePoint Pages or writing Silverlight applications that live inside SharePoint. That is to say while developing custom list templates or Silverlight parts inside SharePoint, these applications have direct access to the SharePoint Context. We will not have that ability in Windows Phone 7.

Although we can't use the managed DLL's that were provided for Silverlight applications in Windows Phone 7, we still have access to the same information and functionality. It's just going to be a lot more work to use them.

The client object model communicates to the server using WCF Data Services, formerly known as ADO.NET Data Services. We will use these same services for our Windows Phone dashboard application. As is the case with a lot of programming problems, there are multiple ways of attacking this problem.

REST

Representational State Transfer, or **REST**, is a way of communicating with services across the Internet or intranet using standard HTTP verbs. Specifically, the common verbs used are GET, POST, PUT, and DELETE. Using simple HttpWebRequests, we can call on the WCF Data Services SharePoint exposes to perform most of the actions that the client object model would have made simple for us.

REST is a fairly generic term for accessing data across a network using a less stuffy format than SOAP. Responses from a REST call are usually either Plain Old XML (POX) or a fairly clean JavaScript Object Notation (JSON). The calls into SharePoint can return XML or JSON, but their output format is a predefined data structure that we'll discuss next.

WCF Data Services and OData

In SharePoint, we can make calls to web services using simple HttpWebRequests. These calls use traditional REST semantics and return data sets either in JSON or in an open data format that Microsoft created named OData. In addition to the traditional REST semantics of using the HTTP protocols and URI strings to tell the server what our intent is with the call, OData defines a QueryString structure for refining our requests.

We make all these calls to the same URL `http://<yourserver>/_vti_bin/ listdata.svc/` and from this location we can gain access to all of the data in SharePoint. For example, to get all of the calendar items we can make a call to this URL `http://<yourserver>/_vti_bin/listdata.svc/Calendar`.

Now with the addition of the OData semantics, we can get just the top five calendar events: `http://<yourserver>/_vti_bin/listdata.svc/Calendar/?$top=5` or even order the items by start date as follows:

```
http://<yourserver>/_vti_bin/listdata.svc/Calendar/?$orderby=StartTim
e&$top=5
```

 To get more information on OData, the best place to start is the official OData website located at the following URL:
`http://www.odata.org/`

In SharePoint, making these calls directly will probably result in a 403 Authentication required error. We'll use the authentication token from earlier in this chapter to make these calls. Also, even with the authentication token, we'll end up with an ATOM response.

ATOM is a data format that uses XML to deliver data. As it is XML based, it is fairly bulky across the wire. It is better than POX though because there is a well-defined schema for passing data through ATOM. That means that for clients accepting ATOM they don't need to know anything about the incoming data in order to deserialize it. Plain old XML requires a lot of knowledge ahead of time for the incoming data.

However, deserialization is a fairly expensive operation. To deserialize ATOM with no prior knowledge of the contents means a lot of reflection and creation of very heavy anonymous objects. Deserialization can come in the form of using the OData tools for Windows Phone 7 from Microsoft. The problem with these tools is they don't support authentication today. On a mobile device, we may be better advised to use alternative methods of getting information.

When making the call to the SharePoint server, we can specify that we accept JSON as a response. This will cause SharePoint to return a JSON string. This string is usually half the size of the ATOM string coming across the network. That's a good thing for mobile devices. Deserializing JSON has some of the same problems as ATOM though in creating heavy objects through reflection. There's a built-in JSON deserializer in the `System.Runtime.Serialization.Json` namespace, but an alternative open source tool named `Json.NET` is smaller, faster, and easier to use.

In the examples provided in this chapter, we will use LINQ to XML to get just the data we need from an ATOM feed, but when building larger applications you may need a more robust toolset and it is important to know that they are out there. My personal recommendation is to use JSON and the Json.NET deserializer. Since Windows Phone 7 development is still young, other tools will come along to make all of this easier. However, this all depends on the application being built. Sometimes, we just need something that works.

ASP.NET Web Services

ASP.NET Web Services should be considered deprecated. In SharePoint 2007, this was an excellent way to communicate with the server. With SharePoint 2010 though, the Web services have been pushed aside for the newer WCF Data Services. The ASP.NET Web Services used SOAP to securely communicate with the server and get responses back. This made the requests and the responses really heavy, which would not be good for employees on a small data plan with their phone. By using more modern techniques, such as REST with JSON, it is very common to see a decrease in network traffic by up to 10x. JSON may be a little slower to deserialize on the phone, but it is much faster than waiting for a large XML package to come across the network.

Creating a dashboard application

Let's get started on a simple dashboard application for the Windows Phone 7. For this application, we are going to write a simple panorama application in Windows Phone 7. This panorama application will have two sections named Panorama Items. We'll read data from a shared calendar containing days off for employees and display them on the screen. We'll then add another panel that will display a pie chart showing the overall status of all projects currently being worked on. This data will come from a project task status site in our SharePoint site.

Creating the calendar

Before we create the calendar, let's create a new site for this chapter. Carry out the following steps to create a new site:

1. Open your SharePoint site.
2. From the **Site Actions** menu, select the **New Site** option.
3. In the **Create** dialog that appears, select **Team Site**.
4. Give the new site a name of **Chapter 7**
5. Give the new site a URL of **Chapter07**.
6. Click on the **Create** button and SharePoint will create our new site.

The Team Site template includes a calendar that we'll use for this example. Go ahead and enter a few appointments on the calendar, so that we have some data to play with. Your calendar will look similar to the one shown in the following screenshot:

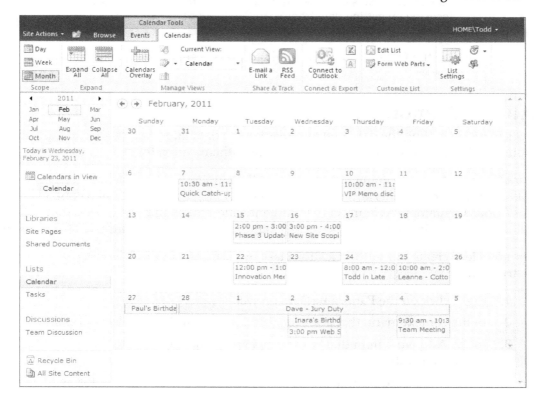

Reading the calendar data

Now that we have a calendar to read data from let's read the data into an application for Windows Phone 7. We need a project before we can read the data from this calendar. To create the project, carry out the following steps:

1. Re-open the Chapter 7 solution we created at the beginning of this chapter.

2. Right click on the solution **Chapter07**.

3. From the context menu, select **Add...** and then select **New Project**.

4. From the **Add New Project** dialog, select **Windows Phone Application**.

5. Give this new project a name such as **PanoramaData**.

> There is a project template for **Windows Phone Panorama Application**. We are not using that template here because it is wired up for an MVVM pattern. MVVM is an excellent pattern, but in this chapter we are focusing on getting data from SharePoint, not MVVM.

6. Click on the **OK** button and Visual Studio will create the new project and open the `MainPage.xaml` file.

Authentication

Let's work on getting the data first and display the data later. Before we can get data from our SharePoint server, we need to get an authentication token.

For this project, we are going to separate out the authentication code into its own class and call it once. This authentication object will have a property that contains our CookieContainer. We'll inject that authentication token into the classes that will get the calendar data here and the project status data later in the chapter.

For now, let's create our authentication class by carrying out the following instructions:

1. Right click on the **PanoramaData** project.

2. In the context menu that appears, select **Add...** and then select **Class...**.

3. In the **Add New Item** dialog that appears, name the class **SPAuthentication.cs**.

4. Click on the **Add** button and Visual Studio will create the class for us.

Now the fun part, let's write some code. First thing is that Visual Studio thinks we are going to be writing a lot of Windows Phone 7 specific code in this file and has helped us out by adding a lot of `using` statements that we really don't need. Remove all of them and replace them with the following:

```
using System;
using System.IO;
using System.Net;
using System.Text;
using System.Xml;
```

Next, add the following two member variables that we'll use:

```
private readonly string mUsername = "JQP";
private readonly string mPassword = "P@ssw0rd";
```

These are the username and password for a user that has read rights to the calendar.

The next line of code we'll add is for the `CookieContainer`:

```
public CookieContainer AuthenticationToken { get; private set; }
```

The final piece of setup code is the class constructor. This initializes the `CookieContainer` as follows:

```
public SPAuthentication()
{
    AuthenticationToken = new CookieContainer();
}
```

The rest of this class will take the code that we wrote previously in this chapter to authenticate. Specifically, we'll take the following methods:

- Authenticate(): change this to a public method!
- AuthenticationRequestCallback(IAsyncResult asyncResult)
- AuthenticationResponseCallback(IAsyncResult asyncResult)

There are a few changes we need to make. First, change Authenticate to be a public method. Second, because the name of the CookieContainer is different, replace the instance of `cookieJar` with `AuthenticationToken` in the `Authenticate` method. The third change we need to make is in the `AuthenticationResponseCallback` method. We no longer need to call `LoadFeed()` because that method doesn't exist here. Instead, we should let somebody know that we've authenticated. This is where we'll enter the wonderful world of eventing. For this class we'll use the `delegate` method of eventing that's been around since .NET 1.0 (we'll get fancier later). Outside the class declaration, but within the namespace, add the following line of code:

```
public delegate void Authenticated();
```

Then after the `AuthenticationResponseCallback` method, add the following code:

```
public event Authenticated AuthenticationTokenSet;
private void OnAuthenticationTokenSet()
{
    if (AuthenticationTokenSet != null)
        AuthenticationTokenSet();
}
```

This allows us to register an event handler to listen for when the authentication cookie has been set and then do whatever work needs to be done at that time. How does this code get called though? In the `AuthenticationResponseCallback` method, replace the `LoadFeed();` call with a call to `OnAuthenticationTokenSet();` as follows:

```
private void AuthenticationResponseCallback(IAsyncResult asyncResult)
{
    var request = (HttpWebRequest)asyncResult.AsyncState;
    var response = (HttpWebResponse)request.
    EndGetResponse(asyncResult);
    var errorCode = string.Empty;
    using (var responseStream = new StreamReader(response.
    GetResponseStream()))
    {
        var xResult = XmlReader.Create(responseStream);
        xResult.ReadToDescendant("ErrorCode");
        errorCode = xResult.ReadElementContentAsString();
        xResult.Close();
        responseStream.Close();
    }

    if (!string.IsNullOrEmpty(errorCode) && (errorCode.
    ToLowerInvariant() == "noerror"))
    {
```

```
    OnAuthenticationTokenSet();
    }
}
```

Now that we can authenticate against SharePoint, open the `MainPage.xaml.cs` file. We want to make sure all the controls have been loaded into the page and then we can start making connections to the server. Modify the Main Page constructor as follows:

```
public MainPage()
{
    InitializeComponents();
    this.Loaded += new RoutedEventHandler(MainPage_Loaded);
}
```

This is where we should authenticate against the SharePoint server. First create a member variable inside `MainPage.xaml.cs` to hold this authentication object as follows:

```
private SPAuthentication auth;
```

Next, add code to the `MainPage_Loaded` event to initialize this variable, set up the event handler, and make the call to authenticate:

```
void MainPage_Loaded(object sender, RoutedEventArgs e)
{
    auth = new SPAuthentication();
    auth.AuthenticationTokenSet += new Authenticated(auth_
    AuthenticationTokenSet);
    auth.Authenticate();
}
```

When the application has successfully authenticated against SharePoint, the event handler named `auth_AuthenticationTokenSet` will be called. It is in this next event handler where we will call the calendar data service to get the data that we will display.

Calendar data service

The calendar data service will pass back a lot of information about each event in the SharePoint calendar. We aren't going to display a lot of information in this application; in fact, we are only going to display the title of the event and the start date. Let's create a simple model to hold this data:

1. Right click on the **PanoramaData** project.
2. In the context menu that appears, select **Add** and then the **Class...** option.

3. Name the class **CalendarItem.cs** and click on the **Add** button.
4. Visual Studio will create a blank class for us to use.

Add the following two properties and save the class:

```
public string Title { get; set; }
public DateTime StartDate { get; set; }
```

What we'll do next is create a class that will call SharePoint to get the data, parse the data into a collection of CalendarItem objects, and expose an IEnumerable of CalendarItems property that we can use to bind to our UI. We will also use an event to alert us when that property changes, so that we know when to bind the data to the UI.

Create a new class in our project named **CalendarOfEvents.cs** and add the following using statements:

```
using System.Collections.Generic;
using System.ComponentModel;
```

Add a custom initializer that takes a single parameter as follows:

```
public CalenderOfEvents(CookieContainer authToken)
{
    mAuthToken = authToken;
}
```

We'll also have to create a member variable to contain the authentication token:

```
private CookieContainer mAuthToken;
```

In addition to this member variable, we will need four others:

```
private readonly string mDataServiceUrl = "http://ssps2010/Chapter07/_
vti_bin/listdata.svc";
private readonly string mCalendarUri = "/Calendar/";
private HttpWebRequest mWebRequest;
private IEnumerable<CalendarItem> mEventList;
```

The first one here will have the URL to the SharePoint data service. The second is the URI to the calendar that we need to get data from. As we are using the default calendar, it should be named "Calendar," but it will be different if it is a custom list. We will be modifying this URI shortly to customize the data that is returned from SharePoint.

The third variable is for our web request, and finally the last one will hold the private event list. Why is this private? Well, we are going to modify the class to implement the `INotifyPropertyChanged` interface:

```
public class CalendarOfEvents : INotifyPropertyChanged
```

Then we are going to implement the following interface:

```
public event PropertyChangedEventHandler PropertyChanged;
public void NotifyPropertyChanged(string propertyName)
{
    if (PropertyChanged != null)
        PropertyChanged(this, new PropertyChangedEventArgs(propertyNa
        me));
}
```

Finally, we will add a property that will set the event list and raise the following event:

```
public IEnumerable<CalendarItem> EventList
{
    get { return mEventList; }
    private set
    {
        mEventList = value;
        NotifyPropertyChanged("EventList");
    }
}
```

Now that all the setup is complete, we can write the action part of this object. This is similar to what we wrote for the RSS feed and the authentication. First, we initialize the request, wait for a callback with the response, and then parse the response.

First up is the `LoadEvents` method. We will call this method to get the data from SharePoint:

```
public void LoadEvents()
{
    mWebRequest = (HttpWebRequest)HttpWebRequest.Create(new
    Uri(mDataServiceUrl + mCalendarUri));
    mWebRequest.CookieContainer = mAuthToken;
    mWebRequest.Accept = "application/atom+xml";
    mWebRequest.BeginGetResponse(new AsyncCallback(EventsCallback),
    mWebRequest);
}
```

There are a couple of differences to what we saw earlier in this chapter with the RSS feed. The first is that we need to concatenate the data service URL with the calendar URI to build up the full URI for the Web request. The second change is that we are specifying the HTTP header for accept. Here we are telling SharePoint explicitly that we want the response stream to be an ATOM feed. The other choice here would be `application/json`, but we will just parse the ATOM XML in this example.

When the response comes back, a callback method named `EventsCallback` is called. This method is almost identical to the one we wrote for the RSS feed earlier. Only the name of the method has changed and instead of binding to a listbox, we are calling a parse method here. Add the following code to the class:

```
private void EventsCallback(IAsyncResult asyncResult)
{
    var request = (HttpWebRequest)asyncResult.AsyncState;
    var response = (HttpWebResponse)request.
    EndGetResponse(asyncResult);
    using (var sr = new StreamReader(response.GetResponseStream()))
    {
        var result = sr.ReadToEnd();
        ParseResults(result);
    }
}
```

Finally, we need to parse the results. This is similar to parsing the RSS feed earlier except this ATOM feed has some XML namespaces that we need to be mindful of. The following is the code for ParseResults:

```
private void ParseResults(string result)
{
    var atomElement = XElement.Parse(result);
    XNamespace atom = "http://www.w3.org/2005/Atom";
    XNamespace dataServices = "http://schemas.microsoft.com/
    ado/2007/08/dataservices";
    XNamespace metaData = "http://schemas.microsoft.com/ado/2007/08/
    dataservices/metadata";
    var entries = from entry in atomElement.Descendants(atom +
    "entry")
                    let startDate = DateTime.Parse(entry.Element(atom
                    + "content").Element(metaData + "properties").
                    Element(dataServices + "StartTime").Value)
                    select new CalendarItem
                    {
                        Title = entry.Element(atom + "title").Value,
                        StartDate = startDate
                    };
```

```
        EventList = entries;
}
```

As we use LINQ to XML in here, we need to add a reference to the System.Xml. Linq.dll assembly:

1. Right click on the project **PanoramaData** in **Solution Explorer**
2. From the context menu that appears, select **Add Reference...**.
3. Find **System.Xml.Linq** and click on **Add**.

Also, we will need to add using statements for both System.Linq and System.Xml. Linq. The code for this method is a little complex. Basically, you need to know the format of the ATOM entries that are coming back from SharePoint. The following is an example of a single calendar event in SharePoint:

```xml
<?xml version="1.0" encoding="utf-8" standalone="yes"?>
<feed xml:base="http://ssps2010/Chapter07/_vti_bin/listdata.svc/"
xmlns:d="http://schemas.microsoft.com/ado/2007/08/dataservices"
xmlns:m="http://schemas.microsoft.com/ado/2007/08/dataservices/
metadata" xmlns="http://www.w3.org/2005/Atom">
  <title type="text">Calendar</title>
  <id>http://ssps2010/Chapter07/_vti_bin/listdata.svc/Calendar/</id>
  <updated>2011-02-24T08:57:44Z</updated>
  <link rel="self" title="Calendar" href="Calendar" />
  <entry m:etag="W/&quot;1&quot;">
    <id>http://ssps2010/Chapter07/_vti_bin/listdata.svc/Calendar(1)</
    id>
    <title type="text">Paul's Birthday</title>
    <updated>2011-02-23T21:55:19-08:00</updated>
    <author>
      <name />
    </author>
    <link rel="edit" title="CalendarItem" href="Calendar(1)" />
    <link rel="http://schemas.microsoft.com/ado/2007/08/dataservices/
    related/CreatedBy" type="application/atom+xml;type=entry"
    title="CreatedBy" href="Calendar(1)/CreatedBy" />
    <link rel="http://schemas.microsoft.com/ado/2007/08/dataservices/
    related/ModifiedBy" type="application/atom+xml;type=entry"
    title="ModifiedBy" href="Calendar(1)/ModifiedBy" />
    <link rel="http://schemas.microsoft.com/ado/2007/08/dataservices/
    related/Attachments" type="application/atom+xml;type=feed"
    title="Attachments" href="Calendar(1)/Attachments" />
    <link rel="http://schemas.microsoft.com/ado/2007/08/dataservices/
    related/Attendees" type="application/atom+xml;type=feed"
    title="Attendees" href="Calendar(1)/Attendees" />
```

```
<link rel="http://schemas.microsoft.com/ado/2007/08/dataservices/
related/Category" type="application/atom+xml;type=entry"
title="Category" href="Calendar(1)/Category" />
<category term="Microsoft.SharePoint.DataService.CalendarItem"
scheme="http://schemas.microsoft.com/ado/2007/08/dataservices/
scheme" />
<content type="application/xml">
  <m:properties>
    <d:Id m:type="Edm.Int32">1</d:Id>
    <d:ContentTypeID>0x010200CF3281A43289874FB1F3B18B10D52A5D
    </d:ContentTypeID>
    <d:ContentType>Event</d:ContentType>
    <d:Title>Paul's Birthday</d:Title>
    <d:Modified m:type="Edm.DateTime">2011-02-23T21:55:19
    </d:Modified>
    <d:Created m:type="Edm.DateTime">2011-02-23T21:55:19
    </d:Created>
    <d:CreatedById m:type="Edm.Int32">11</d:CreatedById>
    <d:ModifiedById m:type="Edm.Int32">11</d:ModifiedById>
    <d:Owshiddenversion m:type="Edm.Int32">1</d:Owshiddenversion>
    <d:Version>1.0</d:Version>
    <d:Path>/Chapter07/Lists/Calendar</d:Path>
    <d:Location m:null="true" />
    <d:StartTime m:type="Edm.DateTime">2011-02-27T00:00:00
    </d:StartTime>
    <d:EndTime m:type="Edm.DateTime">2011-02-27T23:59:00
    </d:EndTime>
    <d:Description>&lt;div&gt;&lt;/div&gt;</d:Description>
    <d:AllDayEvent m:type=»Edm.Boolean»>true</d:AllDayEvent>
    <d:Recurrence m:type=»Edm.Boolean»>false</d:Recurrence>
    <d:Workspace m:type=»Edm.Boolean»>false</d:Workspace>
    <d:CategoryValue m:null=»true» />
  </m:properties>
</content>
</entry>
</feed>
```

As you can see, there is a lot of information here. The actual StartTime for the event is buried inside a properties element that is inside the content element that is inside the entry element. The `d:` and the `m:` are the dataServices and metadata namespaces that we created in the 3rd and 4th lines of the method.

Finally, in this method, we take the entries we get and stuff them into the `EventList` parameter. The `EventList` parameter is wired to fire the `NotifyPropertyChanged` event when it is changed, so we just need to hook up the code in the Main Page.

Go back to the `MainPage.xaml.cs` file and add a new member variable to hold the calendar of events:

```
private CalendarOfEvents calendar;
```

Then either find the event handler `auth_AuthenticationTokenSet()` and add the following code or write one as follows:

```
void auth_AuthenticationTokenSet()
{
    calendar = new CalendarOfEvents(auth.AuthenticationToken);
    calendar.PropertyChanged += new PropertyChangedEventHandler
    (propertyChanged);
    calendar.LoadEvents();
}
```

Here we initialize the calendar object by passing in the authentication token. Then we hook up an event handler to listen for a property change event. Finally, we call `LoadEvents` to kick off the action.

The event handler we will reuse when we are also calling for a project list, so we need to be sure which property was updated. This is a simple process. For now, this is what our event handler code will look like:

```
void propertyChanged(object sender, PropertyChangedEventArgs e)

{
    if (e.PropertyName.ToLowerInvariant() == "eventlist")
        Dispatcher.BeginInvoke(() => { /* code to update our UI */
        });
}
```

As we can see from the comment inside the code, we have reached the end of what we can do without a UI. We will implement that now.

Displaying the calendar data

The first thing we need to do is fix the display to show a panorama instead of the default single page application. The panorama controls are in an assembly that isn't included by default in this template. To add these controls, we need to first reference the assembly that contains them. Carry out the following instructions for adding the reference:

1. Right click on the project **PanoramaData** in **Solution Explorer**.

2. From the context menu that appears, select **Add Reference...**.

3. Select **Browse…** and navigate to `C:\Program Files (x86)\Microsoft SDKs\ Windows Phone\v7.0\Libraries\Silverlight\`.

 The actual location of the Windows Phone SDK depends on your system and your installation options. This is the default location for a computer running 64-bit Windows.

4. Select the **Microsoft.Phone.Controls.dll** assembly and click on **Open**.

5. Finally, click on the **Add** button in the **Add Reference** dialog.

At the top of the `MainPage.xaml` file, there are a series of XML namespace definitions like the following:

```
xmlns:x="http://schemas.microsoft.com/winfx/2006/xaml"
```

Add the following line specifying that the namespace `controls` comes from the `Microsoft.Phone.Controls` assembly:

```
xmlns:controls="clr-namespace:Microsoft.Phone.
Controls;assembly=Microsoft.Phone.Controls"
```

Now that we have the namespace that contains the panorama controls, we can replace the `LayoutRoot` grid with the following code:

```
<Grid x:Name="LayoutRoot" Background="Transparent">
    <controls:Panorama Title="panorama example">
        <controls:PanoramaItem Header="calendar">
            <Grid>
            </Grid>
        </controls:PanoramaItem>
    </controls:Panorama>
</Grid>
```

This recreated the LayoutRoot with a panorama control on the inside. We only have on PanoramaItem for now, but we'll add another in the next section. Inside the PanoramaItem is an empty grid that we will use to populate our calendar information.

To populate that calendar information, let's put a ListBox inside the grid element. Add the following code after the <Grid> and before the </Grid>:

```
<ListBox x:Name="calendarListBox" HorizontalAlignment="Left">
    <ListBox.ItemTemplate>
        <DataTemplate>
        </DataTemplate>
```

```
        </ListBox.ItemTemplate>
    </ListBox>
```

This is the typical boilerplate for a listbox. Next, we'll populate the `DataTemplate` element with a StackPanel containing two TextBlocks. Add the following code after <DataTemplate> but before </DataTemplate>:

```
<StackPanel Orientation="Horizontal" Width="396">
    <TextBlock Text="{Binding StartDate}"
               VerticalAlignment="Top"
               HorizontalAlignment="Center" />
    <TextBlock Text="{Binding Title}"
               TextWrapping="Wrap"
               Width="282"/>
</StackPanel>
```

The StackPanel allows us to place the two text blocks right next to each other and let the title wrap in its area.

Now, let's bind the data to the UI. Reopen the `MainPage.xaml.cs` file and look for the method propertyChanged. Replace the comment `/* code to update our UI */` with the following code:

```
calendarListBox.ItemsSource = calendar.EventList;
```

Now save the all files, compile, and run the application. It should look something like this:

There's a bit of cleanup we should do to make it more readable. First, let's put the whole list in a box. Surround the ListBox with the following code in the MainPage.xaml:

```
<Border BorderBrush="{StaticResource PhoneForegroundBrush}"
        BorderThickness="{StaticResource PhoneBorderThickness}"
        Background="#80808080">
ListBox code...
</Border>
```

This will put a border around our listbox. The border uses the foreground brush. That means if we are in the dark theme, it will be white and if we are in the light theme it'll be black. Also, we use the phone border thickness static resource because this has been optimized to look best on our phone. Finally, we set the background color to a light gray with partial alpha transparency. If we had an image in the background, it would shine through.

Next, let's look at the start date. For this application, we only want to show the month and day of the event. We could then extend the application to allow the user to tap on an event to see full details. To change the output of the DateTime to a formatted string, we will use a value converter.

Create a new class named DateTimeValueConverter and have it implement the IValueConverter interface. Create the class file by carrying out the following steps:

1. Right click on the **PanoramaData** project.
2. In the context menu that appears, select **Add** and then the **Class...** option.
3. Name the class **DateTimeValueConverter.cs** and click on the **Add** button.
4. Visual Studio will create a blank class for us to use.

In the class that is created, add the following using statement:

```
using System.Windows.Data;
```

Then add the following code to the class:

```
public class DateTimeValueConverter : IValueConverter
{
    public object Convert(object value, Type targetType, object
    parameter, System.Globalization.CultureInfo culture)
    {
        throw new NotImplementedException();
    }

    public object ConvertBack(object value, Type targetType, object
    parameter, System.Globalization.CultureInfo culture)
```

```
    {
        throw new NotImplementedException();
    }
}
```

The `IValueConverter` interface defines two methods for converting and converting back. The second method is useful for TwoWay binding, but we are only using OneTime binding in this book. We will only modify the `Convert` method.

 The Value Converter we are writing here is incredibly specific for our situation. Ideally, we'd write a more generic value converter that we could pass any value in and a format string. This would lead to more reusable code.

The following is the code we'll use for the `Convert` method:

```
public object Convert(object value, Type targetType, object parameter,
System.Globalization.CultureInfo culture)
{
    if (value.GetType() == typeof(DateTime))
    {
        var dt = (DateTime)value;
        return string.Format("{0}/{1}", dt.Month.ToString(), dt.Day.
        ToString());
    }
    else
        return string.Empty;
}
```

This first ensures that what was sent in is a DateTime. It then formats the string and returns it. Now let's attach it to the UI.

First, we need to add another XML namespace to our XAML. At the top where we added the controls namespace earlier, add the following line:

```
xmlns:converter="clr-namespace:PanoramaData"
```

Next, we have to tell our application about the converter. Add the following code before the opening `LayoutRoot` grid element:

```
<UserControl.Resources>
    <converter:DateTimeValueConverter x:Key="DateFormatConverter" />
</UserControl.Resources>
```

This lets the app know that when we call for a static resource named `DateFormatConverter` that what we mean is our new DateTime Value Converter. Now, let's modify the `StartTime` binding:

```
<TextBlock Text="{Binding StartDate,
Converter={StaticResource DateFormatConverter}}"
           VerticalAlignment="Top"
           HorizontalAlignment="Center"
           Style="{StaticResource PhoneTextLargeStyle}"/>
```

Let's do a little more design on this before moving on. In the preceding code, we also added a style to make this text much larger. Let's also change the style of the title text block:

```
<TextBlock Text="{Binding Title}"
           TextWrapping="Wrap"
           Width="282"
           Style="{StaticResource PhoneTextTitle2Style}"/>
```

Finally, let's surround the start time text block with a border much like we did for the whole calendar:

```
<Border CornerRadius="10"
        Background="{StaticResource PhoneAccentBrush}"
        Height="45" Width="100"
        Margin="7,7,7,7" VerticalAlignment="Top">
StartTime TextBlock...
</Border>
```

This gives us a box under the start time that has the phone accent color. Saving all these changes and running the app will yield this:

Organizing the calendar data

The problem here is that the full day events are listed first and the appointments are listed second. Also, we should probably only show the first six events and we only want events either today or in the future. We can do this very easily by modifying the URI that we pass to the list data service.

Reopen the `CalendarOfEvents` class file. Modify the member variable `mCalendarUri` as follows:

```
private readonly string mCalendarUri = "/Calendar/?$orderby=StartTime&
$filter=StartTime%20ge%20DateTime'{0}'&$top=6";
```

This orders by the `StartTime`, then gets only items in the future, and finally it only grabs the first six items. The filter for grabbing items greater than or equal to today needs to be formatted when we actually use it. Find the `LoadEvents` method and change the first line to this:

```
mWebRequest = (HttpWebRequest)HttpWebRequest.Create(new
Uri(mDataServiceUrl + string.Format(mCalendarUri, DateTime.Now.
ToString("yyyy-MM-dd"))));
```

This replaces the {0} with the current date. Save everything, compile, and run. The output should look similar to the one shown in the following screenshot:

In this demo, we saw how to get information from a SharePoint calendar using OData. We then bound it to a ListBox, creating a value converter to display the start time in a specific format, and we updated the UI. A panorama with only one panel isn't very interesting though. In the next demo, we'll add a task status site.

Creating the task status site

For this example, we are going to take a task status site, count all of the projects in each status and use that information to populate a pie chart which we will put on the first pane of our panorama control from the previous example. As we should be old pros now at doing many of the common tasks, we'll go faster in this section.

The first thing we need is a new task status site, so carry out the following steps:

1. Open our Chapter 7 SharePoint site.

2. From the quick links menu on the left, select **Lists**

3. At the top, click on the **Create** link to create a new list.

4. This will open the **Create** dialog.

5. Find the **Project Tasks** template and give it the name **ProjectTaskStatus**.

6. This will create a blank task list. Populate it with some data. Make sure to give tasks status of **In Progress**, **Completed**, or **Not Started** for each task.

Once finished, the task status site should look like the one shown in the following screenshot:

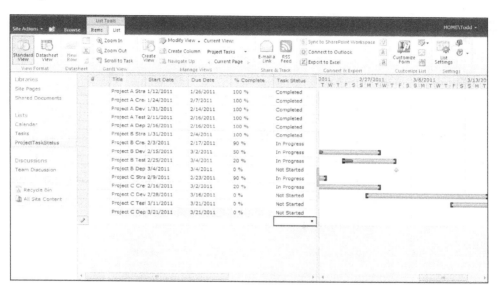

This really is an idealized example, but the point still is valid.

Reading the task status site data

We are only interested in the following three statuses from the task status site:

1. In Progress
2. Complete
3. Not Started

For each of these, we'll need to know how many tasks are in that state. We'll write a really simple class to hold that data.

Carry out the following instructions to create the class:

1. Right click on the **PanoramaData** project.
2. In the context menu that appears, select **Add** and then the **Class...** option.
3. Name the class **ProjectStatus.cs** and click on the **Add** button.
4. Visual Studio will create a blank class for us to use.

Now enter the following code:

```
public class ProjectStatus
{
    public string Status { get; set; }
    public int Count { get; set; }
}
```

Then we'll create another new class named `ProjectTaskStatus`.

Carry out the following instructions to create the class:

1. Right click on the **PanoramaData** project.
2. In the context menu that appears, select **Add** and then the **Class...** option.
3. Name the class **ProjectTaskStatus.cs** and click on the **Add** button.
4. Visual Studio will create a blank class for us to use.

In the class which is created, add the following `using` statement:

```
using System.ComponentModel
```

This will be where we call SharePoint to get the data. Add the following code to this new class:

```
public class ProjectTaskStatus : INotifyPropertyChanged
{
    private CookieContainer mAuthToken;
    private HttpWebRequest mWebRequest;

    public ProjectTaskStatus(CookieContainer authToken)
    {
        mAuthToken = authToken;
    }

    public event PropertyChangedEventHandler PropertyChanged;
    private void NotifyPropertyChanged(string propertyName)
    {
        if (PropertyChanged != null)
```

```
PropertyChanged(this, new PropertyChangedEventArgs
(propertyName));
    }
}
```

Like the `CalendarOfEvents` class, the `ProjectTaskStatus` class will implement the `INotifyPropertyChanged` event, which will let us know when all of the data has been downloaded. We will have a member variable to hold the authentication token that is passed in to the constructor, and we'll have a member variable for the HttpWebRequest.

Next, let's add a variable for the project URL and one for the query URI:

```
private readonly string mProjectUrl = "http://ssps2010/Chapter07/_vti_
bin/listdata.svc";
private readonly string mQueryUri = "/ProjectTaskStatus/?$filter=TaskS
tatusValue%20eq%20'{0}'&$top=0&$inlinecount=allpages";
```

The first one is the same as we had in the calendar example. The `mQueryUri` is a little different. Not only is it looking for data in the `ProjectTaskStatus` site, but we are looking for specific TaskStatusValues, which we'll cycle through in a minute to get each one.

We don't actually want any of the tasks, so we ask for the system to return the top 0 items. This may sound strange, but if all we want is the number of records then it doesn't make sense to send all the records down to the phone just to count them. We should have SharePoint count them for us. That's exactly what the last part `$inlinecount=allpages` does for us.

Finally, we'll add a property for our data:

```
public List<ProjectStatus> Projects { get; set; }
```

This is a simple generic list of ProjectStatus, but we'll need to initialize it. Add the following line of code to the class constructor:

```
Projects = new List<ProjectStatus>();
```

Now we are ready to query the server for data. Let's create a method named `LoadData` that will call a method named `GetCount` and pass in the status we are looking for:

```
public void LoadData()
{
    GetCount("In Progress");
    GetCount("Completed");
    GetCount("Not Started");
}
```

GetCount will start the actual request to the server with the now familiar three pronged attack:

1. Initialize the Web request
2. Get the request callback
3. Parse the results

Here's the code for GetCount:

```
private void GetCount(string status)
{
    var uri = new Uri(mProjectUrl + string.Format(mQueryUri, status));
    mWebRequest = (HttpWebRequest)HttpWebRequest.Create(uri);
    mWebRequest.CookieContainer = mAuthToken;
    mWebRequest.Accept = "application/atom+xml";
    mWebRequest.Headers["TaskStatusValue"] = status;
    mWebRequest.BeginGetResponse(new AsyncCallback(asyncCallback),
    mWebRequest);
}
```

This code includes the first of two hacks that I've put in here. We've added a TaskStatusValue header to the request. As we aren't getting any tasks back from the SharePoint server when we are parsing the data, we won't know which of the three statuses we are getting data for. By passing the status in the header, we can just look at the header at the time of parsing and we'll have all the information we need.

The rest of this method is the same as we've used a couple of times in this chapter. Next, let's look at the asyncCallback method.

```
private void asyncCallback(IAsyncResult asyncResult)
{
    var request = (HttpWebRequest)asyncResult.AsyncState;
    var response = (HttpWebResponse)request.
    EndGetResponse(asyncResult);
    using (var sr = new StreamReader(response.GetResponseStream()))
    {
        var result = sr.ReadToEnd();
        ParseResults(result, request.Headers["TaskStatusValue"]);
    }
}
```

You can see here where we pulled the TaskStatusValue out of the request headers, so we can pass it into the `ParseResults` method. The rest of this is exactly the same as we had in the calendar example. This is a common theme. We are now running into code we've written before several times and it should trigger an indication that we should refactor out the common patterns into their own classes. This three-pronged attack to get data is a prime example of that. We won't do that here, but as we go on, you should see similar patterns.

Finally, let's look at the `ParseResults` method.

```
private void ParseResults(string result, string status)
{
    var atomElement = XElement.Parse(result);
    XNamespace atom = "http://www.w3.org/2005/Atom";
    XNamespace dataServices = "http://schemas.microsoft.com/
    ado/2007/08/dataservices";
    XNamespace metaData = "http://schemas.microsoft.com/ado/2007/08/
    dataservices/metadata";
    var countString = atomElement.Descendants(metaData + "count").
    FirstOrDefault().Value;
    int count = 0;
    if (!int.TryParse(countString, out count))
        count = 0;
    Projects.Add(new ProjectStatus { Status = status, Count = count
    });
    if (Projects.Count > 2)
        NotifyPropertyChanged("Projects");
}
```

This is boilerplate parsing. We initialize the namespaces and then use LINQ to get the value of the count. This value comes out as a string, so we parse it into an integer. Finally, we add a new Project Status to our Projects property and if we have all three ProjectStatus populated, we call `NotifyPropertyChanged`.

Let's move back to the `MainPage.xaml.cs` file and hook up this class. Add a member variable to hold our new ProjectTaskStatus object. Then in the `auth_AuthenticationTokenSet` method, we previously initialized the calendar object. Add in the following lines to initialize, hook up the `propertyChanged` event, and start the data load after the lines initializing the calendar:

```
tasks = new ProjectTaskStatus(auth.AuthenticationToken);
tasks.PropertyChanged += new PropertyChangedEventHandler(propertyChan
ged);
tasks.LoadData();
```

Now, we are calling the same event handler when the task list is filled as we did for the calendar event. We already have a conditional in the `propertyChanged` event handler for calendar events; let's add in a new conditional to listen for the tasks:

```
void propertyChanged(object sender, PropertyChangedEventArgs e)
{
  if (e.PropertyName.ToLowerInvariant() == "eventlist")
    Dispatcher.BeginInvoke(() => { calendarListBox.ItemsSource =
      calendar.EventList; });
  else if(e.PropertyName.ToLowerInvariant() == "projects")
    Dispatcher.BeginInvoke(() => { /* code to update our UI */ });
}
```

The highlighted code shows the new path and this is as far as we can go without our UI.

Displaying the task status overview chart

Not too long ago, Microsoft bought a charting company and integrated their components into .NET. Those controls have found their way into the Silverlight Toolkit, which is freely distributed at the following URL:

`http://silverlight.codeplex.com`

In August of 2010, a Microsoft developer named David Anson took those charts and figured out how to make them work in Windows Phone 7. It isn't hard, you just use the two assemblies and go, but the UI was designed for Silverlight on the Web not Silverlight on the phone. David wrote a Resource Dictionary for use with these charts and Windows Phone 7. The following is the URL to the post:

`http://blogs.msdn.com/b/delay/archive/2010/08/04/why-didn-t-i-think-of-that-in-the-first-place-windows-phone-7-charting-example-updated-to-include-reusable-platform-consistent-style-and-templates.aspx`

It is worth a read, and his blog is a great resource in general.

For displaying the chart, we are going to follow his instructions. First, download his Windows Phone 7 Data Visualization sample linked to from the preceding blog post. Then unblock it and unzip the package. This is a full solution that will demonstrate his example. We only need the two DLL's that are from the Silverlight Toolkit and the `PhoneDataVisualizationResource.xaml`. Carry out the following directions to add them to our project:

1. Right click on the **PanoramaData** project and select **Add Reference...**

2. In the **Add Reference** dialog box, select **Browse** and navigate to where you unzipped the Windows Phone 7 Data Visualization project.

3. Select the following two DLL's:

   ° `System.Windows.Controls.DataVisualization.Toolkit.dll`

   ° `System.Windows.Controls.dll`

4. Click on the **Add** button and Visual Studio will add them to our project.

5. Right click on the **PanoramaData** project.

6. Select **Add** and then **Existing Item...**

7. Once again navigate to where you unzipped the Windows Phone 7 Data Visualization project.

8. Select the resource file **PhoneDataVisualizationResources.xaml**

9. Click on the **Add** button and Visual Studio will add it to our project.

Next, we have to tell our application to use these tools. To tell the application about the phone data visualization resources, open up `App.xaml`. This file we haven't touched yet, but when dealing with larger scale applications and different design patterns, we would be in here all the time. Right now it's fairly empty. Locate the `Application.Resources` section and add the highlighted code:

```
<Application.Resources>
    <ResourceDictionary>
        <ResourceDictionary.MergedDictionaries>
            <ResourceDictionary Source="/PanoramaData;component/
            PhoneDataVisualizationResources.xaml" />
        </ResourceDictionary.MergedDictionaries>
    </ResourceDictionary>
</Application.Resources>
```

This will merge the resources we just added to the system, so that we can call them using the same familiar syntax we're used to.

Next, let's add the namespace attribute to our `MainPage.xaml`. We've done this twice before. At the top, there are a series of XML namespaces. Add this one to the list:

```
xmlns:charting="clr-namespace:System.Windows.Controls.
DataVisualization.Charting;assembly=System.Windows.Controls.
DataVisualization.Toolkit"
```

Next, we'll need a place to put our chart. Let's make the pie chart the first thing that appears in the application. Find the opening `controls:Panorama` element and add this on the very next line:

```
<controls:PanoramaItem Header="status chart">
    <Grid>

    </Grid>
</controls:PanoramaItem>
```

This creates another PanoramaItem with a title of "status chart". Next, we'll put the chart inside the grid with the following code:

```
<charting:Chart Name="ProjectStatusChart"
                LegendTitle="legend"
                Style="{StaticResource PhoneChartStyle}"
                Template="{StaticResource
PhoneChartPortraitTemplate}">

</charting:Chart>
```

This sets up the basic chart with a legend title, a style that is from the PhoneDataVisualizationResource and based on a template from the same resource file. Inside this chart, we'll add a pie chart series:

```
<charting:PieSeries ItemsSource="{Binding}"
                    DependentValuePath="Count"
                    IndependentValuePath="Status">
    <charting:PieSeries.LegendItemStyle>
        <Style TargetType="charting:LegendItem">
            <Setter Property="Margin" Value="5 0 5 0" />
        </Style>
    </charting:PieSeries.LegendItemStyle>
</charting:PieSeries>
```

There is a lot going on here. First, we create the pie series and tell it that we will bind to the ItemsSource. The dependent value path is the count or the number of items in each status. The independent value path is the status name. Finally, we add in some style for the legend to supply the margin values.

All of the XAML work is done, now we can hook up the binding. Go back to `MainPage.xaml.cs` and find the comment `/* code to update our UI */` and replace it with the following:

```
ProjectStatusChart.DataContext = tasks.Projects;
```

We are giving the chart itself a data context here and the pie series will bind off this data context. Once we've finished doing that save, compile, and run. We should see something like this:

This is just the start of what could be a really useful little application. We could have data flowing in from various metrics such as bug tracking systems, backlog reports, burn down charts, employee productivity, sales quota metrics, and so on. Realistically any data that we have in SharePoint could be pulled out and displayed on the Windows Phone 7 app. Also, a pie chart is only one chart that can be displayed here. We could also use bar charts and line charts. Experiment with each of these different types.

Summary

We started this chapter with a discussion of forms-based authentication. We demonstrated how to enable it and how to modify the RSS reader application to use forms authentication to get the same data from a protected feed. Next, we were presented with a high level overview of the client object model for programming against SharePoint in the Web, Silverlight, and managed .NET applications. We saw that these tools aren't ready yet for Windows Phone 7 and instead turned our attention to using the WCF Data Services to get data from SharePoint from our Windows phones. Finally, we demonstrated this technique by writing a dashboard application that showed a pie chart of the status of projects on one pane and a calendar of events on another.

In the sample code included with this chapter, the RSS reader has also been added to this panorama application.

Index

Symbols

$inlinecount=allpages 355
.rules extension 220
.xap file 103

A

Access denied by Business Data
Connectivity error 206
activity
  about 220
  types 220
activity, types
  container 220
  control flow 220
  standard 220
AddBackgroundMusic method 163
AddFieldAsXml method 178
AddImage method 152
ADO.Net Entity Designer 205
AllowDeletion attribute 217
announcement list
  hyperlink column, adding 296, 298
anonymous access
  customizing 268
  enabling, steps 268
anonymous access, FBA
  Authenticate method 324
  AuthenticationResponseCallback method
    326
  BeginGetRequestStream method 324
  BlogCallBack function 326
  ContentType header, setting to text/xml;
    charset=utf-8 324
  LoadFeed 327

  MainPage_Loaded event handler 323
  removing 321, 323
  StreamReaders 327
  XMLReader 327
application lifecycle management 20
Application Page termplate 15
Approval Workflow 195
ASP.NET web services 334
aspx files 299
asset library, SharePoint 2010
  content, adding to 114-117
  creating 112
  creating, steps 112, 113
  structures, browsing 118, 119
AssetsBrowserWebPart class 125
AssignedTo property 262
association data 198
Association Form 221
asyncCallback method 356
ATOM 333
auth_AuthenticationTokenSet() 345
Authenticate() method 337
authentication.asmx web service request 321
authentication, dashboard application
  about 336
  AuthenticationResponseCallback
    method 338
  class, creating 336
  CookieContainer 337
  MainPage_Loaded event 339
  OnAuthenticationTokenSet() 338
AuthenticationRequestCallback
  (IAsyncResult asyncResult) 337
AuthenticationRequestCallback method 325
AuthenticationResponseCallback(IAsync
  Result asyncResult) method 337

T

Tagged Image File Format (TIFF) files 292
Tagging and Tag Cloud
  about 34
  adding, to community site 34
TargetName property 153
task
  about **220**
  creating, from workflow 249-255
Task Delete 263
Task Forms 222
task status overview chart, dashboard application
  displaying 358-361
task status site, dashboard application
  creating 352, 353
task status site data, dashboard application
  auth_AuthenticationTokenSet method 357
  ParseResults method 357
  propertyChanged event 357
  reading 353-357
TechNet website
  URL 317
template
  customizing 306-308
templates 170
templates, Visual Studio 2010
  Application Page 15
  Basic Site Page 16
  Blank Site Definition 16
  Branding 16
  Event Receiver 15
  Fluent UI Visual Web Part 16
  Full Trust Proxy Operation 16
  Module 15
  Sequential Workflow 15
  SPMetal Definition 16
  Starter Master Page 16
  State Machine Workflow 15
  Visual Web Part 15
  WCF Service 16
  Web Part 15
text block
  adding, to display WebClient results 271
  display, replacing with list box 277

Three-State workflow 222
Throw activity 256
TransactionScope activity 256
Type attribute 217

U

URI, simple page navigation
  building 284, 285
URN (Uniform Resource Name) 246
using statement 340, 348, 354

V

videos
  adding 159-162
  controlling 159-162
  formats, in Silverlight 4 163
viewport 151
Virtual Machine
  setting up 50
  test script, running 51
  working 52
Visual Studio 205
Visual Studio 2010
  about 15
  templates 15
Visual Studio CmdLet 72, 74
Visual Web Part
  about 120
  adding, in Web page 144-150
  controls, organizing 150, 151
  creating 120-126
  files, reading from assets library 151, 152
  linking to Silverlight RIA 141-144
Visual Web Part termplate 15

W

WCF
  about 219
  URL 219
WCF based services 11
WCF data services
  about 332
  and OData 333, 334
  ASP.NET web services 334
  REST 332

Thank you for buying
Microsoft SharePoint 2010 Developer's Compendium:
The Best of Packt for Extending SharePoint

About Packt Publishing

Packt, pronounced 'packed', published its first book "*Mastering phpMyAdmin for Effective MySQL Management*" in April 2004 and subsequently continued to specialize in publishing highly focused books on specific technologies and solutions.

Our books and publications share the experiences of your fellow IT professionals in adapting and customizing today's systems, applications, and frameworks. Our solution-based books give you the knowledge and power to customize the software and technologies you're using to get the job done. Packt books are more specific and less general than the IT books you have seen in the past. Our unique business model allows us to bring you more focused information, giving you more of what you need to know, and less of what you don't.

Packt is a modern, yet unique publishing company, which focuses on producing quality, cutting-edge books for communities of developers, administrators, and newbies alike. For more information, please visit our website: www.PacktPub.com.

About Packt Enterprise

In 2010, Packt launched two new brands, Packt Enterprise and Packt Open Source, in order to continue its focus on specialization. This book is part of the Packt Enterprise brand, home to books published on enterprise software – software created by major vendors, including (but not limited to) IBM, Microsoft and Oracle, often for use in other corporations. Its titles will offer information relevant to a range of users of this software, including administrators, developers, architects, and end users.

Writing for Packt

We welcome all inquiries from people who are interested in authoring. Book proposals should be sent to author@packtpub.com. If your book idea is still at an early stage and you would like to discuss it first before writing a formal book proposal, contact us; one of our commissioning editors will get in touch with you.

We're not just looking for published authors; if you have strong technical skills but no writing experience, our experienced editors can help you develop a writing career, or simply get some additional reward for your expertise.

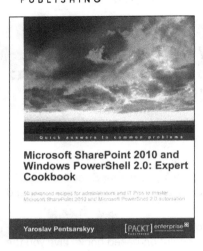
Microsoft SharePoint 2010 and Windows PowerShell 2.0: Expert Cookbook

ISBN: 978-1-84968-410-1   Paperback: 310 pages

50 Advanced recipes for administrators and IT Pros
to master Microsoft SharePoint 2010 and Microsoft
PowerShell 2.0 automation

1. Dive straight into expert recipes for SharePoint
    and PowerShell administration without dwelling
    on the basics

2. Master how to administer BCS in SharePoint,
    automate the configuration of records
    management features, create custom PowerShell
    cmdlets, and much more in this book and e-book

3. A hands-on cookbook focusing on only the most
    high level tips and tricks for mastering SharePoint
    and PowerShell administration

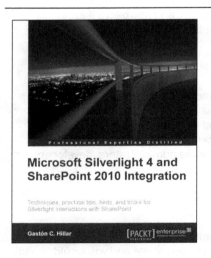
Microsoft Silverlight 4 and SharePoint 2010 Integration

ISBN: 978-1-849680-06-6   Paperback: 336 pages

Techniques, practical tips, hints, and tricks for Silverlight
interactions with SharePoint

1. Develop Silverlight RIAs that interact with
    SharePoint 2010 data and services

2. Explore the diverse alternatives for hosting a
    Silverlight RIA in a SharePoint 2010 Page

3. Work with the new SharePoint Silverlight Client
    Object Model to interact with elements in a
    SharePoint Site

4. Use Visual Studio 2010's new features to debug
    Silverlight RIAs that interact with SharePoint 2010

Please check **www.PacktPub.com** for information on our titles

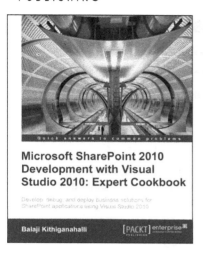

Microsoft SharePoint 2010
Development with Visual
Studio 2010: Expert Cookbook

Develop, debug, and deploy business solutions for
SharePoint applications using Visual Studio 2010

Balaji Kithiganahalli   [PACKT] enterprise ⌗

Microsoft SharePoint 2010 Development with Visual Studio 2010 Expert Cookbook

ISBN: 978-1-84968-458-3   Paperback: 296 pages

Develop, debug, and deploy business solutions for
SharePoint applications using Visual Studio 2010

1. Create applications using the latest client object
   model and create custom web services for your
   SharePoint environment with this book and ebook

2. Full of illustrations, diagrams and key points for
   debugging and deploying your solutions securely
   to the SharePoint environment.

3. Recipes with step-by-step instructions with
   detailed explanation on how each recipe works
   and working code examples.

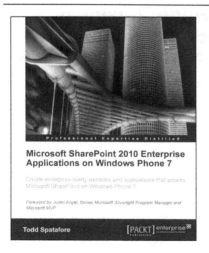

Microsoft SharePoint 2010 Enterprise
Applications on Windows Phone 7

Create enterprise-ready websites and applications that access
Microsoft SharePoint on Windows Phone 7

Foreword by Justin Angel, former Microsoft Silverlight Program Manager and
Microsoft MVP

Todd Spatafore   [PACKT] enterprise ⌗

Microsoft SharePoint 2010 Enterprise Applications on Windows Phone 7

ISBN: 978-1-84968-258-9   Paperback: 252 pages

Create enterprise-ready websites and applications that
access Microsoft SharePoint on Windows Phone 7

1. Provides step-by-step instructions for integrating
   Windows Phone 7-capable web pages into
   SharePoint websites

2. Provides an overview of creating Windows Phone
   7 applications that integrate with SharePoint
   services

3. Examines Windows Phone 7's enterprise
   capabilities

4. Highlights SharePoint communities and their use
   in a Windows Phone 7-connected enterprise.

Please check **www.PacktPub.com** for information on our titles

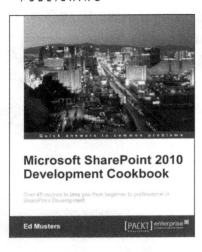

Microsoft SharePoint 2010 development cookbook

ISBN: 978-1-84968-150-6   Paperback: 276 pages

Over 45 recipes to take you from beginner to professional in SharePoint Development

1. Learn the most important SharePoint 2010 development skills quickly

2. Progress through a carefully thought out selection of topics that build upon each other as you move through the book

3. Build "schema" for SharePoint data and leverage that schema appropriately in your application

4. Understand the important role SharePoint Designer 2010 can play alongside Visual Studio 2010.

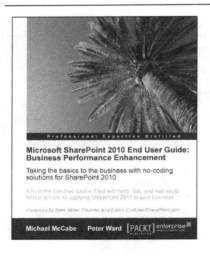

Microsoft SharePoint 2010 End User Guide: Business Performance Enhancement

ISBN: 978-1-84968-066-0   Paperback: 424 pages

A from-the-trenches tutorial filled with hints, tips, and real world best practices for applying SharePoint 2010 to your business

1. Designed to offer applicable, no-coding solutions to dramatically enhance the performance of your business

2. Excel at SharePoint intranet functionality to have the most impact on you and your team

3. Drastically enhance your End user SharePoint functionality experience

4. Gain real value from applying out of the box SharePoint collaboration tools

Please check **www.PacktPub.com** for information on our titles

SharePoint Designer Tutorial

ISBN: 978-1-847194-42-8   Paperback: 188 pages

Get started with SharePoint Designer to put together a business site with SharePoint

1. Become comfortable in the SharePoint Designer environment

2. Learn about SharePoint Designer features as you create a SharePoint website

3. Step-by-step instructions and careful explanations

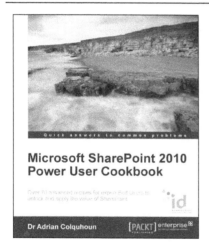

Microsoft SharePoint 2010 Power User Cookbook

ISBN: 978-1-84968-288-6   Paperback: 344 pages

Over 70 advanced recipes for expert End Users to unlock and apply the value of SharePoint

1. Discover how to apply SharePoint far beyond basic functionality.

2. Explore the Business Intelligence capabilities of SharePoint with KPIs and custom dashboards

3. Take a deep dive into document management, data integration, electronic forms, and workflow scenarios

4. Join the dots by building three composite "no code" applications

Please check **www.PacktPub.com** for information on our titles

www.ingramcontent.com/pod-product-compliance
Lightning Source LLC
Chambersburg PA
CBHW060922060326
40690CB00041B/2974